African Dress

Dress, Body, Culture

Series Editor: Joanne B. Eicher, Regents' Professor, University of Minnesota

Books in this provocative series seek to articulate the connections between culture and dress which is defined here in its broadest possible sense as any modification or supplement to the body. Interdisciplinary in approach, the series highlights the dialogue between identity and dress, cosmetics, coiffure, and body alternations as manifested in practices as varied as plastic surgery, tattooing, and ritual scarification. The series aims, in particular, to analyze the meaning of dress in relation to popular culture and gender issues and will include works grounded in anthropology, sociology, history, art history, literature, and folklore.

ISSN: 1360–466X

Previously Published in the Series

Helen Bradley Foster, *"New Raiments of Self": African American Clothing in the Antebellum South*
Claudine Griggs, *S/he: Changing Sex and Changing Clothes*
Michaele Thurgood Haynes, *Dressing Up Debutantes: Pageantry and Glitz in Texas*
Anne Brydon and Sandra Niessen, *Consuming Fashion: Adorning the Transnational Body*
Dani Cavallaro and Alexandra Warwick, *Fashioning the Frame: Boundaries, Dress and the Body*
Judith Perani and Norma H. Wolff, *Cloth, Dress and Art Patronage in Africa*
Linda B. Arthur, *Religion, Dress and the Body*
Paul Jobling, *Fashion Spreads: Word and Image in Fashion Photography*
Fadwa El Guindi, *Veil: Modesty, Privacy and Resistance*
Thomas S. Abler, *Hinterland Warriors and Military Dress: European Empires and Exotic Uniforms*
Linda Welters, *Folk Dress in Europe and Anatolia: Beliefs about Protection and Fertility*
Kim K. P. Johnson and Sharron J. Lennon, *Appearance and Power*
Barbara Burman, *The Culture of Sewing*
Annette Lynch, *Dress, Gender and Cultural Change*
Antonia Young, *Women Who Become Men*
David Muggleton, *Inside Subculture: The Postmodern Meaning of Style*
Nicola White, *Reconstructing Italian Fashion: America and the Development of the Italian Fashion Industry*
Brian J. McVeigh, *Wearing Ideology: The Uniformity of Self-Presentation in Japan*
Shaun Cole, *Don We Now Our Gay Apparel: Gay Men's Dress in the Twentieth Century*
Kate Ince, *Orlan: Millennial Female*
Nicola White and Ian Griffiths, *The Fashion Business: Theory, Practice, Image*
Ali Guy, Eileen Green and Maura Banim, *Through the Wardrobe: Women's Relationships with their Clothes*
Linda B. Arthur, *Undressing Religion: Commitment and Conversion from a Cross-Cultural Perspective*
William J. F. Keenan, *Dressed to Impress: Looking the Part*
Joanne Entwistle and Elizabeth Wilson, *Body Dressing*
Leigh Summers, *Bound to Please: A History of the Victorian Corset*
Paul Hodkinson, *Goth: Identity, Style and Subculture*
Leslie W. Rabine, *The Global Circulation of African Fashion*
Michael Carter, *Fashion Classics from Carlyle to Barthes*
Sandra Niessen, Ann Marie Leshkowich and Carla Jones, *Re-Orienting Fashion: The Globalization of Asian Dress*
Kim K. P. Johnson, Susan J. Torntore and Joanne B. Eicher, *Fashion Foundations: Early Writings on Fashion and Dress*
Helen Bradley Foster and Donald Clay Johnson, *Wedding Dress Across Cultures*
Eugenia Paulicelli, *Fashion under Fascism: Beyond the Black Shirt*
Charlotte Suthrell, *Unzipping Gender: Sex, Cross-Dressing and Culture*
Irene Guenther, *Nazi Chic? Fashioning Women in the Third Reich*
Yuniya Kawamura, *The Japanese Revolution in Paris Fashion*
Patricia Calefato, *The Clothed Body*
Ruth Barcan, *Nudity: A Cultural Anatomy*
Samantha Holland, *Alternative Femininities: Body, Age and Identity*
Alexandra Palmer and Hazel Clark, *Old Clothes, New Looks: Second Hand Fashion*
Yuniya Kawamura, *Fashion-ology: An Introduction to Fashion Studies*
Regina A. Root, *The Latin American Fashion Reader*
Linda Welters and Patricia A. Cunningham, *Twentieth-Century American Fashion*
Jennifer Craik, *Uniforms Exposed: From Conformity to Transgression*
Alison L. Goodrum, *The National Fabric: Fashion, Britishness, Globalization*
Annette Lynch and Mitchell D. Strauss, *Changing Fashion: A Critical Introduction to Trend Analysis and Meaning*
Catherine M. Roach, *Stripping, Sex and Popular Culture*
Marybeth C. Stalp, *Quilting: The Fabric of Everyday Life*
Jonathan S. Marion, *Ballroom: Culture and Costume in Competitive Dance*
Dunja Brill, *Goth Culture: Gender, Sexuality and Style*
Joanne Entwistle, *The Aesthetic Economy of Fashion: Markets and Value in Clothing and Modelling*
Juanjuan Wu, *Chinese Fashion: From Mao to Now*
Brent Luvaas, *DIY Style: Fashion, Music and Global Cultures*
Jianhua Zhao, *The Chinese Fashion Industry*
Eric Silverman, *A Cultural History of Jewish Dress*

African Dress

Fashion, Agency, Performance

Edited by Karen Tranberg Hansen and D. Soyini Madison

B L O O M S B U R Y
LONDON • NEW DELHI • NEW YORK • SYDNEY

Bloomsbury Academic
An imprint of Bloomsbury Publishing Plc

50 Bedford Square
London
WC1B 3DP
UK

175 Fifth Avenue
New York
NY 10010
USA

www.bloomsbury.com

First published 2013

British Library Cataloguing-in-Publication Data

A catalogue record for this book is available from the British Library.

ISBN: HB: 978 0 85785 380 6
PB: 978 0 85785 381 3
ePDF: 978 0 85785 820 7
epub: 978 0 85785 418 6

Library of Congress Cataloging-in-Publication Data

A catalog record for this book is available from the Library of Congress.

Typeset by Apex CoVantage, LLC

For Joanne B. Eicher, our *Dress Mother,* with admiration and gratitude for inspiring an interdisciplinary research agenda on dress practices

Contents

List of Illustrations

PLATES

FIGURES

List of Contributors

Lauren Adrover is a PhD candidate in the anthropology department at Northwestern University. Her research examines the relationship between cultural spectacle, global capital, and the bodily production of social value in the context of corporate-sponsored festivals in West Africa. She is the recipient of the Association for Africanist Anthropology Graduate Student Paper Award (2009), the Society for Economic Anthropology Harold K. Schneider Prize (2010), and the Fulbright-Hays doctoral dissertation fellowship (2011).

Misty D. Bastian is professor and chair in the department of anthropology at Franklin & Marshall College. She has published widely on gender, popular media, and religious practice in southwestern Nigeria and is coeditor with Jane L. Parpart of *Great Ideas on Teaching about Africa* (Lynne Rienner Publishers 1999).

Karen Tranberg Hansen is professor emerita of anthropology at Northwestern University. As an urban and economic anthropologist, she has conducted extensive research in Zambia. She has published widely on urban life in Zambia—gender, housing, the informal economy, and work and consumption—including *Salaula: The World of Secondhand Clothing and Zambia* (University of Chicago Press 2000), as well as many essays on secondhand clothing, dress practices, fashion, and consumption.

Bennetta Jules-Rosette is distinguished professor of sociology and director of the African and African American Research Center at the University of California, San Diego. She has conducted extensive research on religion, culture, art, and film in Africa and France and is the author of several books including *African Apostles: Ritual and Conversion in the Church of John Maranke* (Cornell 1975), *Messages of Tourist Art: An African Semiotic System in Comparative Perspective* (Plenum 1984), *Black Paris: The African Writers' Landscape* (Urbana 1998), and *Josephine Baker in Art and Life: An Icon and the Image* (Urbana 2007).

Candace M. Keller is assistant professor of African Art in the department of art, art history and design and the Residential College in the arts and humanities at Michigan State University. Her research centers on the histories of photography in Mali and studies of art and culture through the lens of Mande social theories and aesthetic values. Her work has been published in *African Arts* and, most recently, she contributed an essay to the edited volume *Portrait Photography in African Worlds* (Indiana University Press, 2013).

Kelly Kirby is a PhD candidate in the department of anthropology at the University of Michigan. Her dissertation research examines the social interconnections between aesthetics, value, and commodity politics in the production and consumption of cloth and fashion in Senegal and in the Senegalese diaspora.

D. Soyini Madison is professor of performance studies with affiliate appointments in the department of anthropology and African American studies at Northwestern University. She has published widely on the interconnections between human rights, local activism, and indigenous performance tactics in Ghana. She staged her research in two productions, *Water Rites* and *Is It a Human Being or a Girl?* in Ghana and the United States. Her most recent books include *Critical Ethnography: Methods, Ethics, and Performance* (Sage 2012) and *Acts of Activism: Human Rights as Radical Performance* (Cambridge 2010).

Tina Mangieri is academic dean for Africa south of the Sahara at SIT Study Abroad in Battleboro, Vermont, and a member of the graduate faculty of the College of Geosciences at Texas A&M University. A cultural and economic geographer (PhD, University of North Carolina at Chapel Hill), she has conducted research and published on globalization, transnationalism, development, and identity, with a focus on the production of South-South spatialities. She is currently pursuing these interests through a study of consumption spaces in Africa and Arabia, and an interrogation of (export) commodity fetishisms.

Adeline Masquelier is professor of anthropology at Tulane University. She is the editor of the *Journal of Religion in Africa*. She has conducted extensive research on spirit possession, gender and Muslim identity, and youth culture. She is author of *Prayer Has Spoiled Everything: Possession, Power and Identity in an Islamic Town of Niger* (Duke University Press 2001) and *Women and Islamic Revival in a West African Town* (Indiana University Press 2009), and is editor of *Dirt, Undress, and Difference: Critical Perspectives on the Body's Surface* (Indiana University Press 2005).

Leslie W. Rabine is professor emerita of women and gender studies and French at the University of California, Davis. She is author of *The Global Circulation of African Fashion* (Berg 2002), as well as books on French literature and several essays on African fashion and photography.

Keith Rathbone is a PhD candidate in the department of history at Northwestern University. His current research interests include the German occupation of France during World War II, Vichy sports policy, and the intersection of conceptions of the state, the body, gender, race, resistance, collaboration, and leisure under occupation.

Elisha P. Renne is professor in the department of anthropology and the department of Afroamerican and African studies at the University of Michigan, Ann Arbor. Her research focuses on religion and textiles, reproductive health, gender relations, and the anthropology of development, specifically in Nigeria. Recent publications include *Yoruba Religious Textiles,* coedited with Babatunde Agbaje-Williams (BookBuilders Publishers,

2005), and articles in the *American Anthropologist, Journal of the Royal Anthropological Institute, Material Religion,* and *Textile History.*

Victoria L. Rovine is an associate professor in art history and the Center for African Studies at the University of Florida. Her book on the contemporary manifestations of a traditional Malian textile, *Bogolan: Shaping Culture through Cloth in Contemporary Mali,* first published by Smithsonian Institution Press (2001), was republished in an updated edition by Indiana University Press in 2008. Her current research concerns African fashion design in global markets. She has published numerous articles and book chapters on African fashion designers, on Africa's presence in Western fashion, and on innovation in longstanding African dress practices.

Nina Sylvanus is an assistant professor of anthropology at Northeastern University in Boston. During 2011–12, she held a Mellon Fellowship at the Center for the Humanities at University of the Western Cape to complete a book manuscript provisionally entitled *Print Value: The Dressed Body and its Economies in West Africa.* Her work is concerned with the materiality of social regimes of value and political economies in Togo. She has published several articles and book chapters, among others in *Anthropological Theory, les Temps Modernes,* and *Politique Africaine* and shorter pieces on African dress and fashion in the *Berg Encyclopedia of Dress, Africultures,* and *Africa e Mediterraneo.*

Katherine Wiley is a PhD candidate in sociocultural anthropology at Indiana University. Her research interests include the anthropology of exchange and value, market work, dress, and Islam. She focuses on the Islamic Republic of Mauritania where she taught high school English from 2001 to 2003 as a Peace Corps volunteer.

Acknowledgments

This book is the result of conversations in anthropology and performance studies at Northwestern University that prompted us to launch two events focusing on dressed body politics in Africa and the diaspora. In 2008, we organized a panel at the annual meeting of the American Anthropological Association on Dress, Performance, and Social Action in Africa. The success of this panel clearly demonstrated that dressed bodies comprise a rich topic for interdisciplinary research. Subsequently, we used the sixty-year celebration in 2009 of the Program of African Studies at Northwestern University for, among many other events, a conference on Dress, Popular Culture, and Social Action in Africa. Most of the chapters in this volume were presented at one of these events.

Launching the dress conference at Northwestern University, we benefitted from the opportunity provided by the graduate school to fund a conference to showcase the work of graduate students. We wish to acknowledge the encouragement of Dean Andrew Wachtel whose support made the event possible. We also give special thanks to the staff of the program of African studies, Kristine Barker and Kate Dargis, for handling the logistics of the conference.

Because the conference aimed to promote an interdisciplinary collaboration between graduate students and faculty members, the call for papers invited graduate students and faculty from several disciplines to present papers. Graduate students from Northwestern University participated at all stages of the organization, providing logistics, working as rapporteurs, presenting papers, and serving as discussants, as did several colleagues at Northwestern University including Caroline Bledsoe (anthropology), Jonathon Glassman (history), and Sandra Richards (theater). We wish in particular to thank Andrea Felber Seligman who worked as our assistant throughout the process as well as the graduate students involved in a variety of tasks: Lauren Adrover, Ariel Bookman, Bethlehem Dejene, Alana Glaser, Valerie Freeland, Jimmy Piertse, and Kimberly Seibel. Many thanks also to Hilary Cooperman, Soo Ryon Yoon, who helped prepare the final version of the manuscript prior to its publication.

Most of the photographs in this book were taken by the authors unless a specific source is recognized. Some individuals supplied images from their private collections for which we are very grateful.

Above all, we want to recognize the stimulating role of Joanne B. Eicher, who served as discussant on the anthropology panel in 2008 and as a special observer at the conference at Northwestern University in 2009. Throughout her academic career, she has worked actively and creatively to promote scholarship on dress practice, bringing it from home economics departments into the mainstream social sciences and humanities as a legitimate scholarly domain. She is our *Dress Mother,* and we dedicate this volume to her. This volume would never have been possible without her enthusiastic encouragement. Thanks are also due to our editor, Anna Wright, at Berg and her helpful staff for their support during all the stages of preparing the manuscript. And we thank all the contributors for sharing their creative work with us in this volume and for their patience during the long process leading to its publication.

Karen Tranberg Hansen
D. Soyini Madison

Introduction

Karen Tranberg Hansen

In more ways than one, this book is about arrivals and departures. It is about global encounters and local reinventions. The contributors demonstrate vividly that what we see, regarding dress, depends on what else we have seen (Hollander 1980). As a busy crossroads of change throughout history, Africa has had a long experience of lively interactions between local dress practices and other people's clothes. Well before the twentieth century, regional, long-distance, and external trade triggered contact and exchange, and, along with that, the circulation of people, practices, ideas, and material goods. Among the most popular imported goods were textiles and apparel (Alpern 1995; Johnson 1974; Kriger 2006). The long-term effects of these engagements on the development of dress and fashion and their relationship to different cultural, economic, and political forces across much of Africa still invite research.

We are more confident in the shorter term because recent interdisciplinary scholarship is providing compelling insights into the importance of production, exchange, and consumption and their active roles in changing patterns of life from the colonial period and on. New dress conventions and fashion styles developed in dialogue with local and external influences (Allman 2004; Hansen 2000; Hendrickson 1996; Martin 1994; Perani and Wolff 1999; Rabine 2002). Today in most African societies, on an everyday basis people wear the same garments as in the rest of the world, namely dresses, suits, jeans, and sneakers, along with special occasion wear such as colorful tailored dresses and loose flowing gowns, richly embroidered and of fabrics that often originate elsewhere.

This passion and cultivation of fashionable body display in Africa draw on a variety of apparel from numerous sources, depending of course on people's means. But when it comes to the study of dress practice in Africa, we are confronted by a widespread scholarly tendency that privileges Western exceptionalism and denies any non-Western agency in the development of fashion. When we approach fashion as a one-way process that merely responds reactively to external exposures, we effectively hide what is at the heart of African dress encounters. For clearly, some external influences in lifestyle, material culture, and dress conventions have become part of what people across Africa consider to be their own. The creative tensions that result from these processes are key to vibrant fashion encounters. We insist on calling such encounters African because, as the contributors to this book vividly demonstrate, in many different ways the local takes over.

The beauty about dress as a research topic is that it has so many meanings, pertaining to identity, status and rank, protest, power, and much more. Above all, dress practices have an incomparably rich research potential because of their malleability. One reason for this has to do with the dressed body itself and the way the body surface intimately mediates between the self and society. A second reason arises from the inclusive notion of dress which comprises both body modifications and/or supplements (Eicher and Roach-Higgins 1992). A third reason why dress practices have many meanings concerns context and the ways that dressed bodies are situated and change across space and time. Because of the contingent and emergent characteristics of embodied performance, dress practices always differ by context. With Africa in the heart of such general observations about dress, enormously productive research vistas open up due to the continent's position as a cultural crossroads, historically and today. When it comes to dress practice, regionally changing contacts within and across the continent interact creatively with influences from the West and the worlds beyond the Indian Ocean. There are diasporas as well. This is the rich and diverse world of African dress practices which localizes this book's focus on fashion, agency, and power.

FRAMING DRESS PRACTICE

What is it about the dressed body that has prompted so much recent interdisciplinary scholarship to approach it as a site of convergence for local, urban, regional, global, and transnational forces (Bruzzi and Gibson 2000; Breward and Gilbert 2006; Riello and McNeil 2010)? Because it both touches the body and faces outward toward others, dress has a dual quality, as Terence Turner noted (1993 [1980]) when he coined the notion of the social skin. This two-sided quality invites us to explore both the individual and collective identities that the dressed body enables. Yet the subjective and social experiences of dress are not always mutually supportive but may contradict one another or collide. As the contributors to this book demonstrate, tensions between these two experiences of dress give rise to considerable ambiguity, ambivalence, and, therefore, uncertainty and debate over dress. As a result, dress readily becomes a flash point of conflicting values, fueling contests in historical encounters, in interactions across class, between gender and generation, and in recent global cultural and economic exchanges.

Dress is embodied practice (Entwistle 2000). Erasmus of Rotterdam recognized this a long time ago when he likened dress to "the body of the body" (Elias 1978: 78), in this way capturing how bodies are worn through the attributes of the person. Jennifer Craik caught this well when she noted that "clothes are activated by the wearing of them just as bodies are actualized by the clothes they wear" (1994: 16). Yet while "dress cannot be understood without reference to the body and while the body has always and everywhere to be dressed," according to Joanne Entwistle, "there has been a surprising lack of concrete analysis of the relationship between them." Theories of the body, she goes on, often overlook dress, while theories of fashion and dress often leave out the body entirely (2001: 34).

MATERIALITY

Showcasing dressed bodies, most chapters in this book combine an analysis of the materiality of dress with a focus on dress as embodied practice. Adopting the term dress in the inclusive sense defined above allows us to reckon with the strategic effects that arise from the material properties of dress and their expressive abilities. Because clothes are so eminently malleable, we shape them to construct our appearance. As the contributors to this book demonstrate, there is an experiential and physical dimension to the power of clothing, both in its wearing and its viewing. Our lived experience with clothes, how we feel about them, hinges on how others evaluate our crafted appearance, and this experience in turn is influenced by the situation and the structure of the wider context. Turning attention to materiality as surface that helps to constitute states of being and social relations enables us to explore how material properties affect what people do with fabric and dress (Kuchler and Miller 2005). In this view, dress, body, and performance come together as dress as embodied practice.

Body and dress are intimately entangled. Their entanglements in turn are deeply entwined with the biographies of their wearers and particularities of time, space, location, site, and context. While efficacy is a property of materiality, it works out in context. Its translation hinges both on wearer and viewer, which is why the meaning of dress does not inhere in the garments themselves but is attributed to them in ongoing social interaction. Materiality is a key to much of what precedes the success or failure of the demonstrative moment of display. Materiality is important in the scrutiny of fabric, quality, durability, and utility of garments and their assembly into "the latest." It entails immaculate care for clothing. Materiality is a key property of being "clothing savvy," the critical skill that I have called "clothing competence." This skill is displayed in the presentation and comportment of the dressed body to produce a "total look" that may succeed or fail, depending on context (Hansen 2003). In short, materiality is an active force involved in constituting and imagining states of being and drawing connections between persons and relationships (Miller 2005).

BODY WORKS: AGENCY AND POWER

Clothes are not worn passively; they require people's active involvement. Demanding the skills and comportment that constitute "clothing competence," dress performance takes place in interaction with many diverse inspirations to produce fashion. Likening the learning process to a technique of acculturation, Jennifer Craik describes it as a means by which "individuals and groups learn to be visually at home with themselves in their culture" (1994: 10). She argues that fashion comprises technologies of the body, encompassing both everyday and more exclusive practices (1994: 30). Invoking Pierre Bourdieu, we may consider *clothing habitus* as the way we learn to dress our bodies and how our bodies are structured not only by our social situation but also by our own embodied activities (1994). This habitus predisposes us to specific types of dress practice and demeanor. That is, our dress choices in particular situations are oriented by categories and norms we acquire through socialization, given our specific social backgrounds. Deeply gendered, clothing habitus serves to reproduce society. But dress choices also change. In effect, the notion of an acquired clothing habitus also entails scope for agency as is evident, for example, in Elisha Renne's analysis of Muslim women's changing veiling practices in northern Nigeria.

FASHION

When we approach dress in Africa as fashion, we have to come to terms with some long-standing scholarly concerns that have obstructed research on dress practices in general. One is the trivialization of consumers' interests in clothes, an antifashion tendency that devalues the significance of dress as a cultural and economic phenomenon. Today this tendency is less of an issue as dress practice has become a part of new and compelling research agendas, connecting with important questions about identity, performance, and power in a rapidly changing world.

The second concern is the distinction between fashion in the West and the "traditional" clothing of much of the rest of the world, unchanged for generations, drawn by scholars who attribute fashion's origins to the development of the capitalist production system in the West. In Africa, "traditional" dress was always a changing practice, remaking itself in interaction with other dress styles, with garments of Western commercial manufacture and the West's fashion system. But in today's era of high velocity communication, globalization is creating a new "world in dress" and in the process breaking down conventional fashion boundaries (Hansen 2004; Maynard 2004; Niessen et al. 2003). Understanding fashion as a global phenomenon is further supported by shifts in the location and organization of textile and garment production (Bhachu 2003; Collins 2003; Lynch 2007). The worldwide production, export, and import circuits of textiles and garments have altered their availability both on high streets in the West and in open-air markets and tailors' ateliers in Africa, as Nina Sylvanus demonstrates in her account of the Chinese involvement in the manufacture of printed textiles and subsequent changes in trade and consumption of wax prints in Togo. Today's hugely expanded availability of textiles and apparel not only facilitates individualism but also pushes the diversification of tastes in numerous directions, turning African consumers into arbiters of stylistic innovations that are contributing to offset fashion's Western hegemony. In short, contemporary technology has helped push the emergence of new fashion systems, including in Africa, with many diverse points of departure that are modeled on different cultural principles than those animating Western fashion.

A third concern arises from the lingering effects of trickle-down theories that have restrained our understanding of the sources and currents of dress inspirations. We have to battle with Thorstein Veblen (1953 [1899]) and Georg Simmel (1957 [1904]), who, writing at the beginning of the twentieth century, regarded fashion as a specifically modern phenomenon of class, a means of differentiation between social groups. The fashion dynamics they identified invoked imitation in a causal dynamic that saw the upper strata turn away from a fashion to adopt a new one as soon as the lower strata of society began to appropriate their style. When it comes to Africa, Veblen's notion of conspicuous consumption explains away what is at the center of dress practice regardless of class, namely the individual and social delight in adornment and spectacular display. Toward the end of the twentieth century, Pierre Bourdieu invoked much the same dynamic as Veblen and Simmel in his work on judgment and taste (1984), in a class-based explanatory model of differentiation that accentuated distinctions between French mass and high culture. But Bourdieu's concept of distinction does not translate straightforwardly in cross-cultural terms nor does it travel well across time. For the cultural dispositions that prompt consumers to purchase particular garments do not everywhere work in twentieth-century French class terms. What is more, they may differ even regarding the same object, depending on where and between whom these objects circulate.

In today's globalized world, style inspirations travel in all directions, across class lines, between urban and rural areas, and around the globe as we see in this book—for instance, in Adeline Masquelier's lively discussion of young Muslim men's engagement in Niger with dress styles emanating from the West. There is also "Islamic" or "Muslim fashion" of truly transnational influences traveling across the world, aided by the Internet, that appeal to Muslim women who wish to signal modesty and to Muslim men, signaling their faith (Tarlo 2010). Islamic fashion is always reworked locally (Moors and Tarlo 2007) as the chapters by Wiley, Renne, and Mangieri vividly demonstrate.

The hallmark of fashion everywhere is change. Fashion in Africa, notes Victoria Rovine, "appears in the global, Western-dominated realm as *haute couture* as well as in indigenous fashion economies, where designers may draw from international styles yet remain distinctly local" (2009: 134). In her chapter in this book, Rovine describes fashion as changing styles of dress and body adornment that are motivated by the social value placed on innovation. Recognizing the complex nature of African fashion systems, Suzanne Gott and Kristyne Loughran (2010) draw our attention to how localized notions of modernity—fueled by accelerating access to electronic mass media, international travel, and transnational migration—are influencing the globalization of fashion and instantaneous dialogues between different peoples, nations, and continents. The presence of African designers on the world's fashion scene and the wave of new African designers whose styles are on view at fashion weeks and events across the continent provide creative evidence of ongoing local-global interactions (Jennings 2011). Detaching fashion from its conventional association with the Western-dominated international fashion industry, this book showcases an additional dimension of fashion, namely its individuality and experiential efficacy. When understood in this way, fashion helps constitute the person. I have suggested using the terms *fashioning* and *fashionability* to capture the performative quality of dress practice. To speak of fashionability entails shifting the focus from the garments onto the practices and situations of which they are part (Hansen 2007: 18–19). For clothes are not worn passively; they require people's active participation. There is an experiential dimension to dress, both in the wearing and viewing. Thus fashionability refers to "an aesthetic sensibility involving discerning skills from a variety of sources in creating an overall look that results in pride, pleasure, and experiences of feeling good" (Hansen 2003: 303). The presentational form—the "total look"—that results from this process has reference to a spectrum of desirable ways of looking that are tied up with global fashion trends and local notions of aesthetics and of what constitutes acceptable dress.

THE BOOK

Focusing on dressed bodies and questions of agency and power, this book draws on recent interdisciplinary scholarship in African Studies undertaken by an exciting group of young scholars on the make and more seasoned professionals who all present new research. The book's canvas is unique because it not only features scholars who enjoy exceptional access to sources close to public persona like Josephine Baker, Léopold Sédar Senghor, and Malick Sidibé but also contributors who have experienced the trials and tribulations as well as the joys of conducting research on clothing in the context of everyday life in some of Africa's most bustling cities.

The three parts of the book concern specific dimensions of the issues we have set out in the introduction, developing them from several angles. Part One, "Dressed Bodies and Power," showcases the richness of dress practice as a research topic in chapters deliberately chosen for their diversity. Misty Bastian introduces us to Nwanneka, an Igbo woman from Nigeria whose manner of dress announced her ambition for social mobility in her local society. Bastian approaches beauty as a form of productive labor whose potentially performative role scholars have not adequately acknowledged. Hairstyle, head ties, jewelry, purses, and fashionable fabrics all were part of creating Nwanneka's dressed body, announcing both her ambition and arrival at a change of status. Ultimately, Nwanneka's ambitions were not realized; her hopes were dashed when her house was burglarized and her clothing collection and jewelry stolen. That dressing for success is not always a guarantee is also an issue in Nina Sylvanus's chapter, which focuses on factory-printed textiles, counterfeiting, and fashion in Togo. Sylvanus argues that counterfeiting has brought about a crisis of representation. Dutch wax *pagnes* tailored into three-piece outfits once were an index of status and rank. But as Chinese textiles have flooded newly liberalized markets, notions of authenticity become questioned. The conventional signifiers are breaking down, values and signs redefined, in a process in which counterfeiting almost can be read as democratization.

The importance of the visual impression is central to the chapter by Lauren Adrover on dressed body presentations at annual chiefly festivals in Ghana. Such festivals are increasingly underwritten by corporate sponsors such as Nestle, Unilever, and Guinness. Adrover explores the effects of corporate sponsorship on festive dress in the use of T-shirts that display corporate logos alongside local colors, symbols, and vernaculars. As multinational corporations struggle to fashion their products in locally identifiable ways, the body is also refashioned. Adrover offers an insightful analysis of how dressed bodies become vehicles of value production in the creation of a festive habitus in a process in which culture and economics converge.

Part Two, "Material Culture, Visual Recognition, and Display," continues these themes, developing them further. The chapter by Kelly Kirby takes us to the clothing scene of Dakar, Senegal, for a discussion of fashion and social display. Her focus is on dressing up and the desire to appear beautiful, *sañse,* which she demonstrates with reference to *bazin,* an imported damask fabric that is dyed and then sewn by local tailors. Bazin is produced in several qualities in Austria, Germany, and China, especially for West African markets. Brilliantly dyed, starched, and embroidered garments of *bazin riche* are in fashion in Senegal and many other cities in West Africa. Each step of the finishing process of the fabric's transnational journey augments the value of bazin. The pressure to look stylish and to display social wealth at special events make people tap into kin networks in order to afford garments tailored from bazin riche. Kirby's chapter pays loving attention to the materiality of clothing and the close relationship between body and fabric in dress embodiment and the presentation of self.

Katherine Wiley discusses the popularity of a particular veil in Mauritania, the handsewn and dyed *malaḥfas.* Although more and more clothing styles and apparel are available from all over the world in Nouakchott, the capital, women still like to buy and wear locally produced melahfas. She explains the garment's links with Islam and ideas about the nation. She also discusses the veil's aesthetics, the individualized design, and the creation process, which resonate with the production process and the many diverse actors who take part in it. The general public, at least in the West, often views veiling as evidence of women's subordination. Yet as Wiley demonstrates in her chapter, and Elisha Renne elaborates from Zaria City in northern Nigeria, veiled women do not loose their identity; the adoption, adaptation, and rejection of veiling practices depends on context. The public space is a moral space, Renne explains in her discussion of changes of women's use of veiling. With attention both to history and materiality, she demonstrates how women belong both to the world of religion and that of fashionable dress.

The themes of local, national, and global interactions are worked through in Part Three, "Connecting Worlds through Dress." All four chapters focus on men, and they all query the meaning of "the local" against the backdrop of much broader processes. Keith Rathbone discusses how two Senegalese World War I veterans mobilized their military uniforms to reshape moral imagination and alter colonial discourse, ultimately contributing to reshaping the relationship between Africans and Europeans. Their military garb, including red fezzes, once were coveted pieces of clothing. Victoria Rovine's discussion of the Ghana Boy tunic, made by young male migrants from Mali and brought home when they returned from Ghana, offers a lively account of migration, exploration, and adventure. The young men wear these tunics proudly to display their status as returning migrants who have acquired new consumer knowledge. The tunics are embroidered with scenes that allude to their experiences, revealing several cultural influences: to Ghana, Great Britain, and to Bollywood movies. Rovine also offers an interesting stylistic analysis of the connection of embroidery to Islamic scholarship. Inspired by a world outside Mali, the Ghana Boys tunics illustrate compellingly that the "exotic" from the Mali perspective has few direct links to global fashion markets or industries. In effect, as fashion innovations, these tunics draw from but do not replicate global sources of inspiration.

The next two chapters have Islamic backdrops, and they both address questions about dress choice. In her discussion of young men and consumption in a small town in Niger, Adeline Masquelier talks of their desire to be *branché,* plugged in, connected to the wider world through dress such as jeans and T-shirts and accessories such as sunglasses and cell phones. Niger is one of the poorest countries in the world with an economy that has unsettled many conventional expectations of development, yet young men forge global/transnational connections through consumption. Such connections operate in many directions as Tina Mangieri reminds us with a South-South exposure in her chapter on Swahili men's dress choices in coastal East Africa. Attending both to commodity flows and consumption, her chapter identifies Swahili men's normative dress practices which are inspired by their Muslim faith; these practices highlight an element of choice of dress innovations that stem from exposure to garments and styles from Oman and the United Arab Emirates. Clothing identities are never fixed, she argues, but are perceived differently in East Africa, the Near East, and elsewhere in the world.

In "Transculturated Bodies," Part Four of this book, the contributors trace linkages and draw connections beyond Africa to Europe and North America. The chapters demonstrate richly how the power of the dressed body can be studied from several disciplinary perspectives and from very different approaches, using highly diverse sources. In Leslie Rabine's chapter, the sources are poetry and photography, which she creatively bridges in an innovative analysis of the place of the dressed body in Léopold Sédar Senghor's poetry and in images of him from political reportage. The photo archive she uses, with images of Senghor, who always wore Western suits, is stunning in itself. But in his poetry, the place of the differently dressed body changes, especially after Senghor's wartime experience of internment in France. The red fez, introduced earlier by Rathbone, reappears in this chapter as an icon of racial subordination. Rabine raises issues about poetry and photography as sign media and suggests that dress may serve as a third sign image to bridge the two.

Photographs take center stage in Candace Keller's chapter, showcasing an extraordinary fashion shoot featured in the *New York Times Magazine* in 2009. The photos were taken in the Bamako studio of Malick Sidibé, a Malian photographer who has caught the attention of Western audiences because of his striking portraiture, compositions, and props. In this shoot, several of Sidibe's relatives appeared as models displaying the latest high-end fashion from Milan and beyond. Keller describes these displays as transculturated because the occasion of the photo shoot gave agency to all participants, photographer as well as models. Bennetta Jules-Rosette also explores links between images and agency in her chapter on the place of Africa in Josephine Baker's dressed body presentations and its "exotic" inspirations. Her central theme is Baker's "self-fashioning" as a form of activism. Baker's costumes and personas both shocked and compelled her audiences, challenging notions of race and gender, reversing dress codes by cross-dressing, playing black-and-white-faced clowns, and appearing nearly nude.

In the last chapter, D. Soyini Madison connects Africa and the United States through bodies and dress. What happens, she asks, to the meanings and power of the dressed body, what does it actually do in and to the world, when it travels across space and enters different domains, or when it is strategically (dis)placed from its expected social context to an unexpected, perhaps, contentious one? Madison explores the dressed body's transformation from a sign into a symbol of both racial pride and economic injustice when an Obama commemorative cloth, from Ghana, was worn at the 2009 Emmy Awards ceremony. Her examination of dress as a "matter out of place" invokes prior conceptualizations of dress as a sign that ties our understanding of dress to theories of performance and performative practices.

CONCLUSION: DRESS ENCOUNTERS

Dress inspirations travel in many directions, as we noted at the outset. This book's chapters illustrate their recent arrivals and departures in conflict with, or accommodation to, local dress norms. Diverse in its interdisciplinary contents and rich in its attention to detail, this book draws us both intimately and publicly into an African world of dress that is visibly global and resolutely local at the same time. There is everywhere a "wow" factor at work, turning heads in admiration or opprobrium of the way bodies are dressed, depending on context. There is a cultural performance economy at play throughout the book, involving a creative preoccupation with fashioning, a delight in presentations of dressed bodies in "the latest"—such as young men's hip-hop-styled outfits in Niger, mature matrons' three-piece printed cloth ensembles in Lome, the *nikab* among Muslim women in northern Nigeria, along with the hand-sewn and hand-dyed veil, melahfa, among Muslim women in Mauritania. There are hand-sewn and imported veils, Chinese printed fabric wrappers, and mass produced apparel keeping local tailors, aspiring designers, owners, and workers in small market stalls, boutiques, and stores busy, dressing bodies.

Most of the countries that are the backdrops for the individual chapters in this book are among the world's least developed in formal United Nations terms. They have large populations of the really poor, meaning people who subsist on less than one

United States dollar per day. What is more, they have vast and growing income disparities. But poverty does not preclude desire; rather, needs and wants often go together. Desire and the efficacy of surfaces as a communicative practice and as social agency often preclude dress as an economic issue. Despite decades of economic decline, many people in Africa invest a great deal of time, energy, and resources into looking stylish. The opening up of markets in many liberalizing countries in Africa toward the end of the previous millennium has expanded the scope and nature of the pursuit of clothing desires through consumption. In this way, dress has important bearings on grand questions about people's place in society. As this book demonstrates, dress and fashion constitute an incredibly rich research topic that enables us to identify and examine how people in Africa engage with the world, actively and creatively, and are deeply implicated in reconfiguring their place within it.

ACKNOWLEDGMENTS

This introduction is inspired by several dress-related comments I have written following the publication of my book on secondhand clothing in Zambia (Hansen 2000), and it draws specific insights from several other publications as well (e.g., Hansen 2003, 2004). I thank D. Soyini Madison for her very constructive feedback while I drafted this introduction.

REFERENCES

Allman, Jean, ed. 2004. *Fashioning Africa: Power and the Politics of Dress.* Bloomington: Indiana University Press.

Alpern, Stanley B. 1995. "What Africans Got for Their Slaves: A Master List of European Trade Goods." *History in Africa* 22: 5–43.

Bhachu, Parmindar. 2003. *Dangerous Designs: Asian Women Fashion the Diaspora Economies.* London: Routledge.

Bourdieu, Pierre. 1984. *Distinction: A Social Critique of the Judgment of Taste.* Cambridge MA: Harvard University Press.

Bourdieu, Pierre. 1994."The Field of Cultural Production." In P. Press, ed., *The Polity Reader in Cultural Theory,* 50–65. Cambridge: Polity Press.

Breward, Christopher, and David Gilbert, eds. 2006. *Fashion's World Cities.* Oxford: Berg.

Bruzzi, Stella, and Pamela Church Gibson. eds. 2000. *Fashion Cultures: Theories, Explorations and Analysis.* London: Routledge.

Collins, Jane L. 2003. *Threads: Gender, Labor, and Power in the Global Apparel Industry.* Chicago: University of Chicago Press.

Craik, Jennifer. 1994. *The Face of Fashion: Cultural Studies in Fashion.* London: Routledge.

Eicher, Joanne B., and Mary E. Roach-Higgins. 1992. "Definition and Classification of Dress: Implications for Analysis of Gender Roles." In Ruth Barnes and J. B. Eicher, eds., *Dress and Gender: Making and Meaning,* 8–28. Oxford: Berg.

Elias, Norbert. 1978. *The Civilizing Process: The History of Manners.* New York: Urizen Books.

Entwistle, Joanne. 2000. *The Fashioned Body: Fashion, Dress and Modern Social Theory.* London: Polity Press.

Entwistle, Joanne. 2001. "The Dressed Body." In Joanne Entwistle and Elizabeth Wilson, eds., *Body Dressing,* 33–58. Oxford: Berg.

Gott, Suzanne, and Kristyne Loughran, eds. 2010. *Contemporary African Fashion.* Bloomington: Indiana University Press.

Hansen, Karen Tranberg. 2000. *Salaula: The World of Secondhand Clothing and Zambia.* Chicago: University of Chicago Press.

Hansen, Karen Tranberg. 2003. "Fashioning: Zambian Moments." *Journal of Material Culture* 8(3): 301–309.

Hansen, Karen Tranberg. 2004. "The World in Dress: Anthropological Perspectives on Clothing, Fashion, and Culture." *Annual Review of Anthropology* 33: 369–392.

Hansen, Karen Tranberg. 2007. "From Grandmother's Dress to Runway Fashion: *Chitenge* Styles in Zambia." Unpublished paper presented at the Annual Meeting of the African Studies Association, New York, October 18.

Hendrickson, Hildi, ed. 1996. *Clothing and Difference: Embodied Identities in Colonial and Post-Colonial Africa.* Durham: Duke University Press.

Hollander, Anne. 1980. *Seeing through Clothes.* New York: Knopf.

Jennings, Helen. 2011. *New African Fashion.* London: Prestel.

Johnson, Marion. 1974. "Cotton Imperialism in West Africa." *African Affairs* 73(291): 178–187.

Kriger, Colleen. 2006. *Cloth in West African History.* Lanham: AltaMira Press.

Kuchler, Susanne, and Daniel Miller, eds. 2005. *Clothing as Material Culture.* Oxford: Berg.

Lynch, Caitrin. 2007. *Juki Girls, Good Girls: Gender and the Cultural Politics in Sri Lanka's Global Garment Industry.* Ithaca: Cornell University Press.

Martin, Phyllis. 1994. "Contesting Clothes in Colonial Brazzaville." *Journal of African History* 35(3): 401–426.

Maynard, Margaret. 2004. *Dress and Globalisation.* Manchester: Manchester University Press.

Miller, Daniel, ed. 2005. *Materiality.* Durham: Duke University Press.

Moors, Annelies, and Emma Tarlo, eds. 2007. "Muslim Fashions." *Fashion Theory* 11(2/3).

Niessen, Sandra, Ann Marie Leshkowich, and Carla Jones, eds. 2003. *Re-Orienting Fashion: The Globalization of Asian Dress.* Oxford: Berg.

Perani, Judith, and Norma H. Wolff. 1999. *Cloth, Dress and Art Patronage in Africa.* Oxford: Berg.

Rabine, Leslie W. 2002. *The Global Circulation of African Fashion.* Oxford: Berg.

Riello, Georgio, and Peter McNeil, eds. 2010. *The Fashion History Reader: Global Perspectives.* London: Routledge.

Rovine, Victoria L. 2009. "Viewing Africa through Fashion." *Fashion Theory* 13(2): 133–140.

Simmel, Georg. 1957 [1904]. "Fashion." *Journal of American Sociology* LXII(6): 541–558.

Tarlo, Emma. 2010. *Visibly Muslim: Fashion, Politics, Faith.* Oxford: Berg.

Turner, Terence. 1993 [1980]. "The Social Skin." In C. B. Burroughs and J. Ehrenreich, eds., *Reading the Social Body,* 15–39. Iowa City: University of Iowa Press.

Veblen, Thorstein. 1953 [1899]. *The Theory of the Leisure Class: An Economic Study of Institutions.* New York: Mentor Books.

PART I

Dressed Bodies and Power

–1–

Dressing for Success: The Politically Performative Quality of an Igbo Woman's Attire

Misty L. Bastian

When I first went to the field in southeastern Nigeria in the late 1980s, I was privileged to live with a woman I will call Nwanneka, who was a veritable artist of dress. West African dress practice has been well-described by anthropologists, historians, and art historians as a potent form of wealth (Heath 1992; Daly et al. 1995; Galletti et al. 1995; Bastian 1996; Masquelier 1996; Mustafa 1998; Rabine 2002; Allman 2004a; Byfield 2004; Renne 2004; Kriger 2006). However, the performative and political quality of that dress is less well-explored, with some exceptions (Hendrickson 1996; Allman 2004b).

Women's wealth in Igbo-speaking areas has historically been encoded in lavish displays of cloth and jewelry. Clean, rich, and eye-catching dress helped prove a woman's worth. If a woman emerged unkempt from her house, she was likely to be treated with disdain. People would inquire about her health, and she might be offered a better wrapper and hairdressing services. A woman hoping to demonstrate her mastery of feminine skills would never be caught in anything but a contained and controlled state of dress. Her control of dress practice must appear effortless, a part of everyday routine. Away from home, a woman pursuing public stature must wear striking clothing while observing local norms of modesty and restraint.

This chapter explores how one highly respected and deeply political woman used her wardrobe strategically to negotiate her social status, as well as that of her lineage and household, including the anthropologist living in her house. Thanks to her beauty, charisma, and wealth-in-cloth, and to the select clients and kin who borrowed from her wardrobe, Nwanneka's politically charged fashions circulated in public clothing spectacles. Such spectacular use of dress constituted a particular political performance with ramifications for larger questions of how politics around the globe are encoded.

FIRST IMPRESSIONS: NWANNEKA AT HOME

I first met Nwanneka in February 1987. She had heard about my interest in working in the city's Main Market through one of her daughters, an undergraduate at a university in the United States. As Nwanneka later told me, she was intrigued to meet an American who wanted to learn about Onitsha, the city containing what Nwanneka called her home village. When I was ushered into her bungalow, my first impression was that I had stumbled into a female aristocratic salon.

Nwanneka was dressed in one of her favorite outfits: a dark red *agbada* (Dutch wax cotton print) wrapper with matching, low-cut blouse. Everything was crisply starched and pressed. Her hair was braided with attachments and pulled back into a large bun. Her Western-style jewelry was gold, set with small diamonds: earrings, necklace, and bangles. Placed by her armchair, her soft, black leather sandals with small heels exposed her feet and red toenails. Whenever Nwanneka moved, there was a strong and pleasing fragrance from her perfume.

Several gentlemen wearing stylish long shirts and trousers were in attendance. My arrival had interrupted the presentation of kola: a small table with a plate containing kola nuts and a kitchen knife was placed in front of a high-ranking male guest wearing an embroidered, red velvet cap. One of the younger men vacated his chair for me, and I was invited to draw closer to Nwanneka and tell her about my journey. Nwanneka and her friend "the Chief" then plied me with kola, beer, Fanta and *chin-chin,* a fried dough snack. The Chief and his younger male friends stayed for dinner.

I was too much of a greenhorn to know, but everything that occurred during this first meeting had been carefully choreographed, including Nwanneka's clothing, the guests who were present when the *nwa bekee* (white person) arrived, what people ate and drank, and who had dinner with Nwanneka and her unusual visitor. The Chief was Nwanneka's friend, age-mate, and would-be business partner, who loved to demonstrate his fluent English and sophisticated ways. Nwanneka cooked the dinner earlier, demonstrating gendered competence to the Chief, graciousness to the bekee, and disdain of the Chief's junior clients, who served themselves only after the Chief and I had taken the choice pieces of meat from the communal pot. Those who were not invited to dinner received a political message: They were not of the proper status to eat with such select company. Still, they could tell all of Onitsha about Nwanneka's sartorial tastes, her local and bekee guests, and how the new bekee was feasted along with the Chief. This telling and retelling of my arrival in Onitsha launched Nwanneka's campaign to establish herself as one of the town's leading female citizens.

BURYING CHARLIE PARKER: PERFORMING FASHION, PERFORMING POLITICS

In addition to instructing me about the arts of politics and life, Nwanneka taught me how to dress for success, Onitsha-style. Soon after my arrival, Nwanneka announced that we would attend a funeral for an uncle (FB), who was popularly called "Charlie Parker." She took an exceedingly long time to dress, finally appearing in a lace blouse, George wrapper, and shiny scarlet-and-gold headdress.[1] She wore a coral necklace with gold pendant, earrings, and a purse and shoes that matched the headdress. On this initial night of "wake keeping," no funeral events began until after 9:30 P.M., so Nwanneka told me to attend Saturday's events. In the interim, I should go find "traditional wears." On Saturday morning, she would assess whether my dress and I reflected well on her household and "the late."

Opening my suitcases, I looked for anything that might pass for "traditional wears." Fortunately, I had been to the Port Harcourt market to practice my fledgling Igbo and purchased a double wrapper of *akwete,* a strip-woven cotton fabric that many Igbo-speakers consider the true indigenous style of weaving. The akwete wrapper was bright red with black, white, and yellow stripes. Since I did not have a suitable blouse, I selected a long, white linen shirt that reminded me of the shirts worn by men in southeastern Nigeria. Although I did not possess any matching accessories, I had some imitation coral ceramic beads.

Around dawn, Nwanneka returned for a nap. Too nervous to go back to sleep, I ironed the shirt and wrapper. Even at this early stage in my acquaintanceship with Nwanneka, I understood that how I appeared in her company was important. This funeral would also be, as I wrote in my field journal, "my first real anthropological experience in Onitsha," so I felt a sense of occasion. But tying the wrapper around my waist seemed impossible. No matter how much I pulled the thick akwete cloth, it began to unravel as soon as I moved. Just as I was contemplating sneaking back to Lagos to catch a flight to the United States, Nwanneka emerged from her bedroom, took one look at the mess, burst out laughing, and sent me back to my room to put on something else. I was instructed to iron the akwete again, this time to make sure that it was stiffly starched. I was also told to put on a slip before attempting the all-important wrap.

Returning from her bedroom, Nwanneka brought a handkerchief, which she tore into strips and tied firmly to the knotted ends of the bottom wrapper. She wrestled the cloth around my waist, tied it at the back with the handkerchief strips, and covered the fix with the top of the cloth. Bundled into seven yards of fabric, I could hardly breathe, but I could move and sit down comfortably. She thought the linen shirt hilarious: "Grandmother on the bottom; man on the top!" Nonetheless, she allowed me to wear it, calling it "*oyibo* [white person, slightly derogatory] style," noting that white women rarely have the shoulders or back to carry off the revealing lace blouses worn by Igbo fashion experts. When I brought out my imitation coral necklace, Nwanneka surprised me, approving it as modest and age-appropriate.

Even though I had "no hair, no earrings," she explained that a head tie was too advanced at this stage, which was a relief after the fiasco of tying the akwete on my own. I later learned that the head tie was the part of the Igbo high fashion display that Nwanneka farmed out to others, notably a younger half-sister who was renowned for her skill at "tying head." In return, the sister often borrowed pieces of Nwanneka's gold jewelry or wrappers for her own displays.

My part of the day's fashion performance was to pay respect to Charlie Parker, honor Nwanneka, and complement her elaborate presentation. The nwa bekee in akwete and imitation corals, "oyibo style," was sensational enough to cause the attention and talk she was looking for. I was only going to be on view briefly, to excite interest; then she would take over adding glamour and generosity.

When we arrived at the funeral compound, the reception was what Nwanneka had hoped for. Everyone murmured her name or called out a praise name for the most lovely or well-dressed women: "*Ezenwaanyi* [Queen of Women]!" One brash, younger woman even yelled an English praise to me, "Our clothes fit you, *onye ocha* [white person, polite form]!" Nwanneka's outfit was worthy of the praise; it was discreetly sumptuous: an ivory lace blouse with traces of gold thread, another George wrapper in dark green with golden palm trees woven into the fabric, gold and diamond jewelry, golden slipper sandals, and a beautiful, dark green head tie that matched her wrapper.

This entrance was sealed in the crowd's mind as a favorite when Nwanneka's driver, Linus, ostentatiously opened the trunk of the Mercedes, unloading cases of soft drinks and beer, along with jerry cans of palm wine. This sparked applause and praise, since the expectation of food and drink drew people to funerals. The chief mourners were pleased, as close relatives share the burden of providing for funeral attendees. Charlie Parker's eldest son fanned Nwanneka to "cool her down" after the demonstration of beauty, wealth, and respect for the dead. In the main house, Nwanneka held a brief conference with the youthful mourners, signaled to Linus to bring her a bottle of Johnny Walker Black from the car, patted me on the shoulder, and told me to join "my friends."

"My friends," the grandchildren of Charlie Parker, took me and the whiskey to a back area where about twenty men and women were drinking and sharing kola. One of the grandsons announced, in English, that Nwanneka "sent" me and handed one of the men the whiskey bottle. A woman close to my hostess' age enfolded me in an embrace. "*Nno,* you are welcome here!" she said and introduced herself as Felicia, Nwanneka's age-mate in the Ezedimpke age-grade. Felicia was nicely but inexpensively dressed in a Nigerian lace outfit in the Yoruba style of "up and down." Most of the others wore good but less-spectacular garments. The women had small, gold earrings and, like me, wristwatches instead of bangles, while the men wore the "traditional" male attire, the long-shirt-and-pants combination still common today throughout southeastern Nigeria.

Felicia introduced me to the group and explained that they were age-mates of Nwanneka and of Nwanneka's cousin (FBS), Charlie Parker's eldest son. As the age-mates of these important mourners, they could not take part in the funeral dances and were not even supposed to look at "the late's" corpse, so they were holding their own wake. If Nwanneka sent me to stay with them, then I was the responsibility of the Ezedimpke age-grade as a whole.

As I subsequently learned, Onitsha politicians seek to consolidate their power and prestige by sponsoring age-mates at events like large funerals. This, in turn, obligates the age-grade to support their colleague in other, public forums. In this instance, placing the bekee with Ezedimpke honored the age-grade and meant that one of their wealthiest mates, Nwanneka, would take care of their needs during this time. The whiskey bottle was a token of that promise, as was the presence of their age-mate's unusual guest.

This move also limited the bekee's interaction in public, making her more scarce, of greater intrigue among the crowd, and a source of pride for Ezedimpke.[2]

When Nwanneka visited Ezedimpke's space a few hours later with helpers carrying basins of jollof rice and cases of drinks, she was greeted with acclaim. Everyone commented on her beauty, praised her for *omenani* (respecting tradition), and demonstrated their ties with her through shared stories. I was called up to take *mai oku* and kola to demonstrate how the age-grade had successfully schooled me in civilized behavior, and the senior man of the age-grade made a speech complimenting both to Nwanneka and Ezedimpke as a whole.

Some news of the funeral was shared with the Ezedimpke. Mostly this was a moment to enjoy the company of age-grade members and boast about its significance in Onitsha. Gauging the depletion of her Johnny Walker gift, Nwanneka sent helpers for more. She also touched the first dishes of rice and meat, demonstrating her responsibility and wishes for those about to eat from her hands, but mostly she abstained from eating as a mark of mourning. After about two hours of visitation and commensality, she sent me home for a break from the long day.

NNEMMUO: DRESSING FOR THE ELDERS AND THE SPIRITS

Throughout the following months, Nwanneka's political ambitions within Onitsha became clearer to her anthropological guest. Since the early twentieth century, Onitsha women had watched and struggled for the return of their greatest office: *Omu Onicha* (market queen, or simply queen, of Onitsha; H. K. Henderson 1969), abolished by an Obi (king of Onitsha) during the 1900s. Since then, various kings had promised to reinstate the title, should the "right woman" be found. Such promises were mostly given during moments of crisis, when the support of the daughters of Onitsha could help the Obi. The Obi during my fieldwork had also made vague promises about returning the queenship. Nwanneka was one of the women who actively contested the office at the king's court and in the powerful, informal court of Onitsha public opinion. She carried out her campaign on several fronts: developing a reputation for the feminine arts, gaining a publicly recognized and celebrated persona, and demonstrating an ability to work with and through powerful male elders. Dress was part of each of these strands of political contestation (see Plate 1).

But during 1987, Nwanneka was walking a very fine fashion line, and not only because of the difficult standards of the world in which she lived or the position to which she aspired. Although her businesses had been successful, she was beginning to feel the pinch of the structural adjustment program imposed upon Nigeria by the World Bank in 1987. She had been married several times and was the mother of several children but lived in her own compound without a spouse. My presence, albeit clearly marked as "other" by my stranger status, reminded Onitsha of Nwanneka's success as a mother.

The fact that I lived with her also justified Nwanneka's entertainment of male elders, as I could attest that nothing untoward was taking place. A woman entertaining *ndichie ume* (senior, titled men) is required to be impeccable in her choice of dress and to demonstrate knowledge of the intricacies of court protocol. These elders were drawn to Nwanneka's house, and possibly to her cause, by her reputation as a beautiful, wealthy woman who enjoyed talking about omenani, as an excellent cook and generous hostess, and as a mediator among men and women.

Besides enjoying the company of *ndichie ume,* Nwanneka gained entrée into the Onitsha world of powerful spiritual forces through her visitors. Senior, titled men were the patrons of Onitsha's most prestigious masquerade societies, the holders of important ritual offices, and, ultimately, the kingmakers behind every Obi (Henderson 1972). Since Onitsha women lacked access to the Omu's court, their main avenue to ritual authority depended on the good graces of such men. Their ceremonial regalia were saturated with dangerous, spiritual potency—from their red felt caps to their snowy *agbada* (robes worn over tunics and trousers) to the magically enhanced leather fans that rarely left their hands. Any woman who spent time with them had to have her own power garments and talismans.

Nwanneka's upcoming fiftieth birthday helped her campaign to become the first Omu since the beginning of the century. This birthday was considered the moment for an Onitsha woman to take on new roles not associated with physical reproduction but with enabling the reproduction of the community and its institutions. Such senior women could dress for the enjoyment of all, not just their husbands or even their lineages' honor. In Nwanneka's case, her lineage had declared it would no longer accept bridewealth on her behalf. That is, she could no longer be married but would remain a "daughter of the lineage," never again required to move to a husband's town or allowed, at death, to be buried anywhere but her natal village within Onitsha. She could engage in liaisons with Onitsha men (outside several degrees of prohibited kindred), but there was an underlying sense that her interactions with the male elders who were her coevals in status ought to be limited to exclude sex. This negation of an Onitsha female elder's sexuality was a prerequisite for taking the highest women's titles and an absolute requirement for the queenship.

Nwanneka's circumspection in dress and demeanor paid dividends as one of the *ndichie ume* invited her to be a patron of a youthful age-grade's masquerade society. Officially, Onitsha women are not allowed to know the secrets of men's societies. However, some senior women past the age of child bearing and rearing with resources to help fund the masquerades may be initiated into the societies' secrets. I first had an intimation that something was going on between Nwanneka, her chiefly friend, and a masquerade group when Nwanneka announced that we would soon host an age-grade and that she would need a special George wrapper for the event. I was dispatched to retrieve this wrapper from the half-sister who had borrowed it. The sister hesitated to return it until she heard that Nwanneka was planning a "special party" for a younger age-grade. Learning this, she gave me the cloth and also two lace blouses to "fit" the wrapper. These garments of very expensive and highly prized fabric were embroidered with gold and small, glittering paste gems. Seeing the blouses, Nwanneka told me that her half-sister meant to be part of the event and that she would honor her by wearing one of the blouses, along with the George, when the age-grade came to visit.

The age-grade's "special party" consisted of squeezing as many young men into the sitting room as possible and feeding them generously with meat, fish, pounded yam, and plentiful kola and drinks. Nwanneka presided over the feast, along with her chiefly colleague, wearing the beautiful George and one of her sister's blouses. The chief offered blessings, and the age-grade leaders made speeches. They described Nwanneka's person, house, and hospitality in glowing terms, and she and the patron received a counter-invitation to visit the age-grade. I was surprised by not being included in the age-grade's reciprocal entertainment, since I was routinely invited to many major Onitsha events.

Asked about this later, Nwanneka said that they were planning a "business meeting" and that the age-grade wanted me to participate in the masquerade outing. So I was surprised when I saw Nwanneka's dress for the business meeting. She was wearing one of her most precious wrappers—a George again, which was once worn by her mother and rarely taken out of its box—and the second lace blouse from her half-sister. She summoned her head-tying sister, Chinyelu, to create a lofty headdress, and she wore her coral and gold necklace, matching earrings, bangles, and ring.

Chinyelu and I were barely able to help Nwanneka into the "owner's corner" of the car without squashing her head tie and wrinkling her outfit. I wondered if the attire was too elaborate for conducting business with the age-grade. Chinyelu laughed and told me this was the "business" of initiation and that Nwanneka's handbag was stuffed with naira notes to help compensate for her new title. The notes would serve as seed money for the outing, including payments to the artists who carved and constructed masks for the masquerades. When Nwanneka returned, she would be a *Nnemmuo* (mother of the masquerade), an Onitsha woman treated like a man with respect by junior men and most women. At the masquerade group's outing in October, this new status would be publicly confirmed.

The lead-up to the masquerade would find Nwanneka everywhere in the town, dressed in exquisite outfits as she invited everyone to attend. Although some had hoped that the new Nnemmuo would purchase expensive cloth to construct a "uniform" for the lineage, Nwanneka's kin had to settle for borrowing wrappers, blouses, and head ties. Their "uniform" would be to wear Nwanneka's recognizable clothing, demonstrating their support for her achievement and allegiance to her in the most personal way possible. There would not be just one Nwanneka circulating but a whole variety of what we might call her sartorial clones, an illusion strengthened because the members of her father's lineage bore a strong family resemblance. Everyone within her close kin would share in the honor of being Nnemmuo for the first time. And no one in the audience could ignore Nwanneka's wealth and generosity.

The one exception to kin wearing Nwanneka's clothing was her son, Chijoke, who was allowed to choose his own expensive attire (Bastian 1996). Looking like no one else at the outing, Chijoke augmented Nwanneka's reputation for being "fashion forward."

As Nwanneka's son, he was an attractive person with an expensive, foreign education. And his mother had wealth, her kin group had status, and he was the "child of a daughter," one of the most auspicious marriage partners in preferentially endogamous Onitsha. Chijoke's presence ensured participation from some of Onitsha's best-known lineages, hinting at future alliances.

The only kin missing were Nwanneka's daughters, who were abroad on business. This meant that I played the role of junior female supporter, and I dressed accordingly. My wardrobe, which had expanded under Nwanneka's tutelage, was not sufficient for this challenge. Instead, she chose a lavish outfit for me from her boxes: thick, white lace with glittering beads. She opened her jewelry case and put gold and diamonds around my neck and in my ears. I was also loaned a red-and-gold head tie, which Chinyelu folded for me.

Nwanneka was more splendidly attired in rich colors of turquoise and green and literally hung with gold. Her new blouse, purchased from an exclusive importer in Lagos, blazed with paste gems. Her head tie, another of Chinyelu's astonishing efforts, extended the new Nnemmuo's presence spatially, in height and in breadth. Her leather handbag and shoes matched the extraordinary colors of her wrapper. In short, she was as eye-catching as the masquerades we were going to watch.

My white lace outfit made a good foil for Nwanneka's colorfulness. Holding Nwanneka's purse, I carried a part of her current attire, wore her clothing and jewelry, and served as her fashion accessory rather than being well-dressed in my own right. When we danced into the outing grounds, I knew how and where to move. This was a moment of political triumph for my hostess. At a young age, she had reached the highest levels of Onitsha women's title-taking, was recognized as a colleague by the *ndichie ume,* and was able to dance with the masquerades. Besides the elusive queenship, there was only one more step she could take in the town's female hierarchy. Vibrant with color, she was a Mother of the Masquerades surrounded by her luxuriously dressed kin, her age-mates, and most of the aristocrats of Onitsha. Nwanneka used her first masquerade outing to announce her intentions to "take *odu* title." She desired to become an Elephant of Onitsha and that meant a special dress strategy.

ENYI ONICHA! BECOMING A MOTHER OF THE TOWN

Taking odu title—being recognized as a Mother of the Town, given special title names by the society, and wearing the ruinously expensive elephant ivory regalia (odu)—involved more than declaring intentions and a stupendous fee. Both were required, but neither was a guarantee for acceptance. To take odu, a candidate must first make public her desire to be part of this exclusive women's society and then endure the agony of the group's decision-making process. The result is announced, in a subtle and potentially devastating fashion, through individual odu title-holders' verbal approbation or shrugs and pronouncements that the candidate is "not mature enough." Such a failure was discussed widely in late 1987 for the case of a powerful, wealthy woman, Dibueze, who was seeking the odu title.

Dibueze was a long-term Onitsha resident and was successful in a local economy not always generous to women. She came from an important patriclan and had married wealthily. She had impeccable connections to the town's male and female powerbrokers, was the mother of a small household (maternity is a requirement for induction into the odu society), and ran a successful set of businesses. Dibueze seemed a surer bet than Nwanneka, whose credentials were slightly more suspect.

Nwanneka also came from a prominent patriclan, albeit one tarnished by accusations of sorcery, but she had lived most of her life away from the town. She had married outside Onitsha and more frequently than was considered respectable. Her connections to local powerbrokers were good, although she had experienced a break with one of the oldest and richest lineages. Nwanneka was the mother of attractive children, including a daughter secretly courted by the son of a powerful man. Yet it was the virtuous Dibueze who was the embarrassed recipient of the Mothers' verdict that she was not yet "mature" enough to take odu title, while the more edgy Nwanneka learned that she might seriously approach the society. Yet my hostess did not rush. Instead, she suddenly left Onitsha for Lagos and London, deserting her household and participation in town events.

Her eldest daughter, Adaeze, was home. Neither of us understood why Nwanneka left without finalizing her admission into the odu society. We were even more puzzled when an odu elder arrived demanding to know when the group might schedule the initiation ceremony. Wearing an imposing George wrapper and an aggressively tied headdress resting low and tight on her forehead, she meant business. Fortunately, one of Nwanneka's friends arrived at that moment. Auntie Justine was a formidable person, dressed for negotiation. Although not an Onitsha woman and therefore technically ineligible to arrange Onitsha ritual events, Auntie Justine moved her elaborate head tie further down her forehead, tightened her top wrapper, and announced herself as Nwanneka's surrogate. In the ironic exchange between female elders, Adaeze and I were referred to as "small girls."

In the negotiation, the titled woman suggested dates for the ceremony, including Christmas day, which Auntie Justine dismissed. Dutifully serving our elders, Adaeze and I took up positions beside Justine, expressing agreement and encouragement to the visible annoyance of the odu representative, who perhaps timed her visit to catch the household in disarray. Finally, Justine offered December 27, a Sunday, as the best possible date. Responding that she had a church event that morning, the elder suggested that the society would accept the date if the ceremonies began after noon. We knew she was beaten because just then she pushed back her head tie and smiled. Auntie Justine also relaxed her head tie, and the two knocked elbows in agreement.

When Nwanneka returned, she professed herself satisfied with the date. She also revealed why she had disappeared: to collect spectacularly lavish cloth and have it made into outfits for the ceremony. She complained that every cloth trader in Onitsha's enormous market sold "rubbish" and that no "rubbish cloth" would be allowed to touch her during the initiation. She would make this an "odu with a difference" by wearing not one magnificent lace wrapper but three, and her children would be attired in imported lace uniforms to match her first change of dress. Even I was included among the children and was to have a Yoruba wrapper, my favorite style.

Such a gift came with expectations of reciprocity. We were not only to look good during the ceremony, we would also have to demonstrate our ties to Nwanneka. The day we received news of our new wrappers, Adaeze and I were assigned several tasks for the initiation. Wearing her mother's clothing and jewelry, Adaeze was to make important visits, inviting the parents of her friends and age-mates to Nwanneka's compound on the 27th. I was sent to the Main Market, a site of much of my fieldwork, with a shopping list drawn from the handbook of the odu society, the admonition to pay the lowest possible price, and a lot of naira. Although Onitsha women of Nwanneka's stature rarely ventured into the markets, they liked to be known there. Part of my job was to announce the purpose of the enamel basins, imported soap, white towels, scented powders, and exotic foodstuffs I was procuring.[3]

Mobilizing her kin and dependents to take part in the odu preparations, Nwanneka was not idle. Her wealthiest brother with many titles had to offer cash, since he refused to come to Onitsha for the event. Nwanneka's younger brother became involved in bringing important *ndichie* to the event, which meant sending liquor to his house for the entertainment of titled men. He also borrowed George wrappers to make his own "traditional" sartorial statement. Female kin and dependents set up kitchens all over the compound, converting one large room into a locked storehouse for food and drink. Nwanneka's sisters and sisters-in-law were promised access to her wardrobe, while others hoped to receive gifts of cloth, food, and other objects associated with the ceremony. Even her son, Chijoke, agreed to stay in Onitsha through the end of December, although he vetoed the turquoise lace for his ceremonial attire, demanding a costly black velvet chieftancy shirt decorated with crowns.[4] Nwanneka's other "children," the age-grade masquerade society, who were to perform, were disappointed that their Nnemmuo did not purchase them uniform cloth for their outing.

While we were busy, Nwanneka also engaged in trade. Although she owned a set of odu ivories—enormous pieces of elephant tusk, hollowed out and worn as anklets and bracelets—that had belonged to her mother, the "odu with a difference" planned a great gesture. Taking the title herself, she would fund a sister-in-law's title-taking, giving her mother's ivories to her favorite brother's wife. On top of other expenses associated with the initiation, Nwanneka had to find money to purchase a brand-new set of odu for herself. Because trading in ivory was prohibited, finding what amounted to two elephant tusks meant going onto the black market and spending the equivalent of thousands of dollars. And the only way to raise the cash was to do something that few Onitsha people relished: selling landed property.

Alienating land was discouraged and few patriclans owned enough property in the highly commercial Waterside area to sell land. But during the 1970s, when her lineage was politically connected, Nwanneka obtained the deed to prime real estate within the market district. The house on this land was the source of rents and a regular income. However, such was the importance of "traditional" status for Nwanneka that she sold it. Buying a new set of odu would not only "wash away poverty," according to an initiation ritual, but it might also wash away the taint of "fast money" or "wealth for nothing" (Apter 2005) associated with persons gaining from the oil boom politics and the culture of official corruption.

The new odu regalia were brought to the house, wrapped in cotton, and placed in a locked box in Nwanneka's bedroom. They could not be tried on until the morning of December 27th, when they would be washed by an odu-titled woman and placed on Nwanneka's legs and wrists. The older set of odu was polished, rewrapped, and taken to Nwanneka's sister-in-law. According to Chinyelu, this was like sending their mother to stay with her son and his wife, an emotional moment. The removal of the old odu opened the way for a new titled woman in the lineage, who would be famous in her own right. The new odu also marked a radical break with the practice that a woman's husband or brothers purchase odu for her. The mother's odu was the regalia of a wife of the lineage, and Nwanneka ensured the continuity by giving it, an heirloom, left specifically to her, to her brother's wife. As an "odu with a difference," she intended to demonstrate that this was a title of an honored daughter of the lineage who would never again leave Onitsha for marriage and was committed to her patriclan and own. This was to be the odu ceremony of a candidate for the Omu-ship, a woman who could put the welfare of clan, village-group, and town ahead of any other tie.

It is not possible to do justice to the complexity of Nwanneka's odu ceremony here, but something can be said about the garments that she wore and distributed. Unlike most odu initiates, who wear one beautiful white outfit, Nwanneka's three different attires marked particular moments in the ceremony: a turquoise and off-white lace with a pattern like ocean waves capped with foam (see Figure 1.1), a white lace with tiny blue sequins that cost at least £50 a yard, and a delicate, lavender-and-pearl lace that cost almost as much.

Nwanneka wore the turquoise lace right after she put on her ivories. Its color and pattern perfectly matched the turquoise lace uniform cloth she purchased for her children. The uniform wearers appeared visually as a bloc, with Nwanneka standing out in the phalanx of bluish green. This gorgeous cloth was wrapped in the oldest Onitsha style, with one length across the breasts, then another length wrapped tightly around the hips, leaving the shoulders and lower extremities bare. The style enabled everyone to see the new odu and hinted at Nwanneka's respect for "tradition." It also kept the ivories from being entangled in cloth and maximized Nwanneka's mobility, otherwise severely limited by the odu.[5]

All members of the kin group were encouraged to wear jewelry, and several had raided Nwanneka's jewelry boxes. Nwanneka herself purchased barrel-shaped coral beads of extraordinary size and color that were strung into two enormous necklaces. These corals, along with her gold, set her apart from the crowd while also tying her to Onitsha

Figure 1.1 Nwanneka, prepared for her odu outing. Photo by Misty Bastian.

ideals of feminine beauty and masculine power displays, since chiefs and the Obi were most often seen wearing such valuable jewelry. Parading with Nwanneka at our head, proclaiming her imminent induction into the title society, her physical instantiation of personal and communal *mma* (wealth/beauty/health) was striking.

Nwanneka's first change of dress took place after this outing and a private, family ceremony. The second garment was the lavish white lace sprinkled with blue spangles. Chinyelu folded a large white head tie, extending her height significantly. Again, the lace was tied in the antique style to showcase the odu. As part of her "odu with a difference," Nwanneka purchased white leather shoes with a lacy design and a small handbag matching the shoes. Clearly, Nwanneka meant to (and did) upstage the other odu-titled women in richness of fabric and accessories.

Finally, when the initiation proper was finished and Onitsha could start the party, Nwanneka retired again and emerged in the lavender-and-pearl lace. She still tied it in the old style and kept on her odu, but she draped a gold necklace around her head as a tiara and removed the corals (see Figure 1.2). This outfit enabled her to take part in the dancing. As the evening wore on and most *ndi odu* returned to their homes,

Figure 1.2 Nwanneka on the morning of the odu ceremony. Photo by Misty Bastian.

she removed the awkward anklets to move with more ease, celebrating her personal achievement late into the evening.

FINAL THOUGHTS ON SUCCESS DRESSING IN ONITSHA

The "odu with a difference" marked a high point in Onitsha's historical memory. Over the next two decades, structural adjustment and corruption made it nearly impossible for the town's elites to put on the politicized displays marshaled by Nwanneka and her kin in 1987. Even Nwanneka could not keep up this level of dressing in the 1990s as large business deals began to elude her and the culture of violence intensified. Widespread anxiety about wealth displays was brought home in a series of coordinated armed robberies, one of which targeted Nwanneka's compound. She escaped, although her jewelry was stolen, including the large coral and gold necklaces that featured prominently in her initiation. The robbers also defiled her less fungible wealth-in-cloth. This robbery turned out to be an inside job, masterminded by a former servant who had been fired.

This changing Nigerian society was particularly brutal toward women with political ties to older regimes of power. Nigerian women were barely tolerated in any powerful role in the 1990s except as wives, lovers, and mothers of male officials and billionaires. Even in Onitsha, where women's wealth was part of town culture, wealthy women provoked suspicion, and there were many men who were not sorry to see autonomous women like Nwanneka taken down a few pegs. Talk of the Omu-ship dissipated as local men, including the Obi, struggled to maintain control over their positions. There is no *Omu Onicha* as I write this in 2011 and little possibility of one.

Women still dress beautifully in Onitsha—but especially in Onitsha's diaspora, where displays of cloth wealth can be safely made in the confines of a Chicagoland Marriott, swanky London party, or suburban Atlanta home. These contemporary displays among the diaspora community, however, rarely showcase powerful, heavyset women in ritually sanctioned dress, wearing regalia that proclaim them part of an Onitsha system of title taking and reciprocity. Twenty-first-century diasporic celebrations like birthday parties, weddings, and outings to honor guests from the homeland include private, fashionable women rather than public persons engaged in community fashioning. Something has been lost, along with the generation of women like Nwanneka, who consumed conspicuously but with purpose beyond individual aggrandizement.

ACKNOWLEDGEMENTS

I would like to thank the editors and other contributors of this volume, all of whom gave me helpful advice at a 2009 conference sponsored by Northwestern's Program of African Studies. Particular thanks go to the surviving family of the woman I call Nwanneka in this chapter. The child of the king is golden!

NOTES

1. George was considered a "traditional" fabric at the time. A heavily patterned cotton fabric, it is often double woven and usually manufactured in South Asia.
2. I was tested during my seclusion with Ezedimpke by being blessed with drinks, kola nuts, and "garden eggs," a local eggplant. They taught me the proper way to respond to a chiefly summons, how to receive food gifts politely, and when to engage in repartee with my age-mates.
3. In the earlier twentieth century, when odu-titled women ruled Onitsha's markets, a newly initiated woman was expected to parade through the marketplace after taking her ivories, giving gifts to everyone. By the late 1980s, this practice had ceased, although it was still considered important for the traders to hear about initiations.
4. Chijoke wanted to wear black velvet, but he agreed to compromise because his mother considered solid black to be fit for mourning, not for a celebratory event like the odu-taking.
5. Nwanneka's center of gravity was compromised by the ivories when she first donned them. The titled woman from her father's patrilineage who helped her put them on also tutored her in the dignified-but-rolling gait she needed to perform to keep the anklets from clashing as she moved.

REFERENCES

Allman, Jean, ed. 2004a. *Fashioning Africa: Power and the Politics of Dress*. Bloomington: Indiana University Press, 31–49.

Allman, Jean. 2004b. "'Let Your Fashion Be in Line with Our Ghanaian Costume': Nation, Gender, and the Politics of Cloth-ing in Nkrumah's Ghana." Jean Allman, ed., *In Fashioning Africa: Power and the Politics of Dress*, 144–165. Bloomington: Indiana University Press.

Apter, Andrew. 2005. *The Pan-African Nation: Oil and the Spectacle of Culture in Nigeria.* Chicago: University of Chicago Press.

Bastian, Misty L. 1996. "Female 'Alhajis' and Entrepreneurial Fashions: Flexible Identities in Southeastern Nigerian Clothing Practice." In Hildi Hendrickson, ed., *Clothing and Difference: Embodied Identities in Colonial and Post-Colonial Africa,* 97–132. Durham, NC: Duke University Press.

Byfield, Judith. 2004. "Dress and Politics in Post-World War II Abeokuta (Western Nigeria)." In Jean Allman, ed., *Fashioning Africa: Power and the Politics of Dress,* 31–49. Bloomington: Indiana University Press.

Daly, M. Catherine, Joanne B. Eicher, and Tonye V. Erekosima. 1995. "Male and Female Artistry in Kalabari Dress." In Mary Ellen Roach-Higgins, Joanne B. Eicher and Kim K. P. Johnson, eds., *Dress and Identity,* 343–348. New York: Fairchild Publications.

Galletti, R., K. Baldwin and I. O. Dina. 1995. "Clothing of Nigerian Cocoa Farmers' Families." In Mary Ellen Roach-Higgins, Joanne B. Eicher and Kim K. P. Johnson, eds., *Dress and Identity,* 179–184. New York: Fairchild Publications.

Heath, Deborah. 1992. "Fashion, Anti-Fashion and Heteroglossia in Urban Senegal." *American Ethnologist* 19(2): 19–33.

Henderson, Helen K. 1969. "Ritual Roles of Women in Onitsha Ibo Society." PhD diss., University of California, Berkeley.

Henderson, Richard N. 1972. *The King in Every Man: Evolutionary Trends in Onitsha Ibo Society and Culture.* New Haven, CT: Yale University Press.

Hendrickson, Hildi, ed. 1996. *Clothing and Difference: Embodied Identities in Colonial and Post-Colonial Africa.* Durham, NC: Duke University Press.

Kriger, Colleen E. 2006. *Cloth in West African History.* New York: Altamira Press.

Masquelier, Adeline. 1996. "Mediating Threads: Clothing and the Texture of Spirit/Medium Relations in *Bori.*" In Hildi Hendrickson, ed., *Clothing and Difference: Embodied Identities in Colonial and Post-Colonial Africa,* 66–94. Durham, NC: Duke University Press.

Mustafa, Haditha Nura. 1998. "Sartorial Ecumenes, African Styles in a Social and Economic Context." In Els van der Plas and Marlous Willemsen, eds., *The Art of African Fashion,* 13–48. Trenton, NJ: Africa World Press.

Rabine, Leslie W. 2002. *The Global Circulation of African Fashion.* Oxford: Berg.

Renne, Elisha. 2004. "From Khaki to Agbada: Dress and Political Transition in Nigeria." In Jean Allman, ed., *Fashioning Africa: Power and the Politics of Dress,* 125–143. Bloomington: Indiana University Press.

–2–

Fashionability in Colonial and Postcolonial Togo

Nina Sylvanus

Lomé's buzzing semicircular boulevard portrays a decaying cityscape of dilapidated hotels, restaurants, government offices, and vacant buildings alongside street eateries, cybercafés, and stalls with pirated DVDs. Large-scale billboard advertisements decorate the boulevard: Air France promotes distant Parisian dreams and Western Union promises money transfers around the world, while Moov, a Dubai cell phone provider, promotes its latest prepaid plan. In December 2010, a series of glamorous fashion billboards by the Dutch textile brand Vlisco dominated the visual landscape of the *boulevard circulaire,* which connects the Atlantic Ocean near the Ghanaian border on the west and the free-trade zone and the port on the east. Vlisco's advertising campaign staged its new wax-print cloth collection in the style of Marie-Antoinette (see Plate 2).

The model's theatrical, bold posture—her high coif, powdered face, and lavish gown tailored in beautiful Vlisco wax-cloth—plays with the appeal of fashion. Signaling fashionable excess, à la Marie-Antoinette, the ad campaign's eye-catching mise-en-scène plays with the desires for fashionability in a time of financial hardship and economic volatility. Few consumers, of course, are able to afford Vlisco fashions, not to mention extravagant haute couture designs. Yet wax-print cloths, *and* copies thereof, constitute an essential ingredient in women's clothing practices in large parts of West Africa. In Togo, they are called *pagnes* from the Portuguese word *pano.* Pagnes are wrappers that are draped and tailored in a great variety of styles and used both as a basic wardrobe of the everyday and for special events. In the aftermath of currency devaluation and economic liberalizations during the 1990s, the value of Dutch pagne cloth has skyrocketed, such that a piece of the Dutch fabric costs as much as the average monthly income of many Togolese. And so one wonders, what is at stake in Vlisco's glamorous ad campaign if so few consumers can actually afford to buy the Dutch fabrics?

Since 2008, when Chinese brands began advertising wax-prints throughout Lomé that were counterfeits of Dutch designs, the Dutch manufacturer repositioned its marketing strategy. Vlisco began launching four collections a year to reduce the production time necessary for Chinese counterfeits to arrive on the market. With the launching of its new fabric designs, Vlisco not only shifted its image from manufacturer to fashion house, but it also instantiated the brand's image as the superior "true original." The company has subsequently spent a great deal of money to protect its brand and image culture and, in the process, has repeatedly used the appeal of "authenticity" as its chief marketing strategy.[1] In this chapter, I explore how the social construction of authenticity, or "realness," has factored into the sartorial practices of Togolese consumers from the colonial period to the present by tracing the changing use of printed cloth. Concerned with the constitution of *fashionability,* this chapter discusses the shifting notions of what constitutes style and fashion in Togo. I argue, along with Karen Tranberg Hansen (2003), that we speak of fashionability instead of searching for a fashion aesthetic, or a readable "fashion system" in Roland Barthes's terms, because Togolese fashion practices are essentially performative. The chapter chronicles how the dressed body emerged as a central mediator of changing gender roles and aspirations of upward social mobility in the colonial cityscape—where leisure time and work time redefined claims to individuality and community—while suggesting that the body surface has reemerged as a crucial mediator in neoliberal times, when work itself has become elusive and where reinventions of old and new styles mark aspirations for a better life.

I begin with a brief discussion of the historical trajectory of wax-cloth, namely its hybrid character from earlier Dutch colonial influences in West Africa, to lay out its long-held popularity. The attractiveness of the Dutch wax-print, I suggest, is linked to the pivotal role it played in the social construction of "authenticity," which constituted an essential ingredient in status performances in Togo and other parts of West Africa until currency devaluations of the 1990s made the Dutch textile a luxury available only to the elite. Following a discussion of the constitution of fashionability among Togolese urbanites during the late colonial and early postcolonial period, a final section discusses how status performances of the past have shifted with the emergence of superior Chinese copies, on the one hand, while young women have reinvented their mothers' dresses to generate social capital in a context of economic instability and despair, on the other hand.

CIRCULATION

Nicholas Thomas (1991) has suggested that the social significance of objects in colonial systems of exchange is not inherent in the objects themselves, but rather derives from culturally established models and practices though which the objects acquire meaning and value over space and time. In a similar vein, Christopher Steiner (1985) and Sidney Mintz (1986) have suggested that the invention of national practices and traditions has often been based on imported objects. Steiner suggests that East Indian calicoes and China ware had become so integral to English taste during the nineteenth century that they indeed came to represent "Englishness"; similarly, Mintz discusses the centrality of Caribbean sugar in the British afternoon tea ritual. Arjun Appadurai (1986) has offered productive insights by pointing to the constructed nature of objects whose value and meanings change as they move through time and space. Karen Tranberg Hansen complicates this perspective by adding an important dimension to Appadurai's theory of materiality by suggesting that objects in fact require people's active participation, taking on the critique formulated by Jonathan Friedman: "Objects don't have social lives, social lives have objects" (cited in Hansen 2003: 301).

When industrialized reproductions of Javanese batik cloth, a failed attempt of the Dutch to conquer the Netherlands' Indies markets, were first introduced to West Africa in the late nineteenth century, they faced competition with an array of already well-established European and Indian cottons on the coast. But the batik replications offered something new, albeit unforeseen. They appealed to local aesthetics, not only because of the advantages associated with the lightness of their cotton and the new and unprecedented choice for color possibilities offered, but most importantly because of their unique potential for distinction. The industrial imitation process of batik cloth produced the differentiation of each yard of cotton, an unintended technical fault that made the designs unacceptable to the Javanese. The mechanical reproduction process replicated the Javanese wax-reserve technique. Its duplex roller-printer imprinted hot resin on both faces of the cloth with the result that the subsequent indigo dying procedures reversed the designs much like the original, hand-made, batik. But the replication process had one major shortcoming: as the resin dried up, it cracked and inadvertently "imprinted" small veins and spots on the cloth. The small imperfections appeared when the cloth was rinsed out and additional colors were hand-blocked onto it. And although the mechanical reproduction process allowed for precise measurements, it could not manage the unpredictability of the cracking effects—traces of which we can see in the 1956 Vlisco design "Gilette" (Figure 2.1).[2] Javanese considered these imperfections "faulty workmanship" (Robinson 1969: 73) and snubbed the Dutch productions, which they considered suitable only for subaltern groups.[3]

The same imperfections that imparted to the designs a variegated quality appealed to West African taste sensibilities (Kroese 1976; Picton 1995; Sylvanus 2007). Each yard of cloth, by virtue of its marks of imperfections, was unique, situating the batik copy, now renamed *wax-print,* with a special potential for distinction and as a pivotal ingredient for upholding and reproducing identity.[4] As scholars of dress have noticed, cloth and dress constitute central vehicles through which social relations are produced and reproduced (Schneider and Weiner 1989; Eicher 2000; Hansen 2004a). The power of the dressed body to mediate notions both of self and society is significant, and when the wax-print was introduced to West Africa, it assumed this special power through its materiality.

By the late nineteenth century, European manufacturers had established special Africa departments dedicated to the design, manufacture, and marketing of these new fabrics (Steiner 1985). In a lengthy "trial and error" process, European manufacturers attempted to capture African taste and began studying indigenous styles (Nielsen 1979; Steiner 1985). The Dutch firms Vlisco and Ankersmit as well as a Manchester manufacturer soon got ahead and came to dominate this market during the 1930s with an

Figure 2.1 Vlisco design #H905. The design called "Gilette," produced by Vlisco since 1956, has been used in earlier motifs by Vlisco since 1912. © Vlisco Helmond B.V.

iconographic repertoire and quality that by far exceeded their numerous European competitors. Eventually, the Dutch product outsold its Manchester competitor and dominated the market by responding to changing local tastes and demand. Vlisco's success built on a particular relationship with a group of Togolese textile merchants, the famous Nana Benzes, who had made Lomé's Grand Marché home to the largest textile market in West Africa market and who distributed (and marketed) the Dutch cloth from Vlisco as *le wax hollandaise*.[5]

DRESSMAKING AND CLASS IN COLONIAL LOMÉ

Under the French colonial system, Togo's emerging administrative, educational, and commercial elites readily took wax-prints as their preferred means through which to display and embody social status and economic wealth. Expressing their ability to participate in new consumption possibilities and the project of modernity, the use of wax-print fashions provided a space for identity claims for the emerging middle class, while simultaneously building on the vertical disposition of social status and rank of the precolonial era. Operating as powerful symbols of modernity, indexing class and status, as well as matrimonial rank, the urban elite readily appropriated wax fabrics to the social practice of dressing-up. Togolese men dressed in European attire to index their educational, financial, and cosmopolitan status; particularly well-dressed clerks were called Togolese dandies, reflecting the uneasy perception of African colonial subjects whose sartorial arrangements were more "modern" than those of Europeans. Togolese women, by contrast, adopted European fashions while also developing a hybrid form of dress based on the light, color-intense cottons from Holland and England that came to reflect changing gender roles in the public spaces of urban society. Female consumers used the wax-print as a special material vehicle to map distinction, discernment, and class onto the dressed body, forming an "invented tradition" (Hobsbawn and Ranger 1983). This project of invented "African" tradition and modernity is nicely reflected in a conversation I had in 2000 with a ninety-year-old Togolese woman, a former schoolteacher in the French colonial education system:

> The Dutch made the cloth only for us. It was different from those other European goods like bikes, or radios, or hats and other fashion accessories . . . they produced *le pagne* [the print material or wrapper to be tailored] exclusively for us, Africans. Seamstresses were making beautiful garments that were different from European styles . . . of course we were also reading French fashion magazines and would use them as a source of inspiration, especially the *taille-basse* [a tight-fitting bodice with a flounce around the waste that enveloped the body, loosely derivative of Dior's postwar New Look].

The making of a modern "African look," which my informant described as a form of cosmopolitan self-fashioning, became a currency to Lomé's colonial elite. The display of fashionable pagne outfits was carefully scrutinized during ceremonial and public events when a person's fashionability, which involved financial and aesthetic capability, was carefully evaluated. Both the efforts that went into conceiving the garment's style and the choice of the fabric, its color and design as well as its quality, attested to a woman's taste and social location. During such embodied dress performances, the social value or status of a person was assessed and attached (fixed) to the material value of the fabric itself. The Dutch fabric ranked highest in a fabric hierarchy which was organized by origin and quality, followed by English wax-cloth.

The development of dressmaking was linked to the import of sewing machines, which took off during the 1930s and 1940s when urbanites increasingly ordered tailored outfits from Lomé's many emerging couture ateliers. During the colonial period, male tailors were commonly trained in various colonial institutions where they were employed to make uniforms (see Marguerat and Peleï 1993). When tailors began to set up their own ateliers and took apprentices, women entered the field of dressmaking. In responding to the increasing demand for tailored outfits, women began to specialize in women's

Figure 2.2 Couturiere sewing and selling Dutch and English wax-cloth. Lomé, 1936. © Fondation Pierre Verger

couture, which required different techniques than men's tailoring, while men catered to men's tailoring.

Soon, couturieres began setting up their sewing machines in the market before forming their own ateliers. In the image in Figure 2.2, which was taken by Pierre Verger in 1936 in the Lomé market, we can see such an early market atelier. Here the couturiere sews while also selling both Dutch and English wax-cloth. In Lomé, women's couture was drawing from diverse, hybrid sources such as French and colonial women's magazines and photographs, as well as local garments, which competed, if not outperformed, the fashion practices of the colonizer. Women's dressmaking consisted of both Western-style dresses and skirts and *taille-basse* fashions such as the *complet trois-pièces* (or simply, *complet*).

The first complet outfits, or at least their predecessors, are likely to have appeared in Lomé during the early 1930s, if not earlier.[6] When I interviewed Adèle, the daughter of an influential cloth trader in the Lomé market during the 1940s, she recalled how her mother used to take newly arrived wax-prints from Unilever's United Africa Company (UAC) warehouse to her tailor to design pagne outfits. Adèle recounts that her mother worked closely with the tailor to whom she brought European fashion magazines she recuperated from her European UAC suppliers. She would dress up in new wax-print fashions as a way to promote her business as well as affirm her economic power among Lomé's cosmopolitan elite, explains her daughter.

THE STYLE OF RESPECTABILITY

During the early postcolonial period, the complet outfit developed into the preferred style for urbanites in Togo. The style of respectability was based on dress competence and sartorial elegance, which became a crucial element of urban lifestyle expression, providing the elites with a new set of affirmation and differentiation possibilities. The complet is composed of three elements: a bodice, a skirt, and a wrapper, which can be used in various ways. The bodice can be worn in two different styles: *manières* and *taille basse* (Sylvanus 2010). The manières style refers to a shorter blouse with a simpler and widening base; this creates a fuller shape that conceals the body. The manières evokes a level of maturity associated with elder women, while the taille basse style, a tight-fitting bodice with a flounce at the waist, is the preferred choice for younger, urban, and upwardly mobile women.

Building on longstanding local textile hierarchies, the complet reflects the historical concern with body decoration as a sign of status, as scholars of African dress have suggested (on the latter aspect, see Eicher 1995, 2000; Weiner and Schneider 1989; Hansen 2004a,b). For example the third wrapper, which is worn over the shoulder, often serves as a versatile accessory and is used in highly performative ways which Mustafa (1998) has described as self-mastery or self-presentation in Senegal. Indeed, a woman with dress competence would change the position of the third wrapper several times during a soirée. But more than just displaying her knowledge of how to command and combine the different elements of this fashion, her choice in how to wear the wrapper also attests to the historical constitution of respectability and social hierarchy in southern Togo. Records of royal ceremonies and fashions describe how chiefs and their entourage displayed wrappers over their left shoulder to indicate political power. The re-appropriation of male authority into a distinctly female sartorial regime underscores the flexible assemblage of fashion in Togo.

As an ensemble, the complet operates as a shared, readable outfit that simultaneously indicates taste and financial capacity as well as notions of respectable femininity. Unlike the Victorian ideals of idealized femininity and middle-class domesticity that became a symbol of national culture, respectable femininity in Togo was less concerned with modesty and discretion than it was with dress competence, power, and taste. Respectable femininity was evaluated by means of a woman's fashionability. During the early postcolonial period, the ability to enact dress knowledge and competence with style and skill and the dynamic field of complet fashion required harmonizing colors with body shape as well competence in how effectively to accessorize the outfit with the appropriate purse, shoes, jewelry, hair, and makeup.

The elegant dress styles of Lomé's female population are renowned throughout the coast of Guinea and beyond.[7] The sense of style that is attributed to Lomeans is closely linked to the capital's status as the main textile market in this area of West Africa long fed by the Dutch and British, and today by Chinese counterfeits. Lomé's economic elite, along with public figures and couturières such as Bamondi, Timothé, and Annick, has long been seen as setting pagne fashion trends. Pagne knowledge is indeed closely intertwined with the place of Lomé's textile market in the region. Because of the strategic proximity to access the latest Vlisco designs (and their counterfeits), elegant Lomeans keep their wardrobes up to date and do not miss the opportunity to dress up in the latest pagne fashion. Indeed, Lomeans have many mocking stories to tell about their neighbors in Benin, who with their "large, unfitted outfits" have no sense for style, according to Yvette, a fashion-savvy customer whom I frequently encountered in the market's textile section. She swiftly elaborates: "These women spend lots of money on fabrics, but instead of making them into a nice complet with a fine taille basse, they wear them in unfitted boubou style and large collars." In Togo, such a fashion crime would be impossible, according to Yvette and many other women, because in Togo, they all agreed, *"Les femmes savent s'habiller!"* That is, Togolese women know how to dress.

Dress knowledge and competence are part of a system of distinction where accumulation capacity, notoriety, and elegance are equally measured and all contribute to the wearer's social and economic status. In Côte d'Ivoire and in the Democratic Republic of Congo, performing pagne fashion and public display operate according to a different strategy because the brand label itself functions as proof of authenticity. In Togo, pagne fashion never focused on the display of the label. Indeed, Togolese like to think of their fashion ability and competence as serious, if not superior. As Chantale, a pharmacist, commented:

> In Abidjan or Kinshasa, people are crazy about clothing and fashion. You could see someone dressed like a millionaire on the street, *flamber,* during the day and return to his shantytown at night where he would sleep on cardboards. They live for dress. Their culture is all about appearance. But in Togo, it's not like that. We are much more traditional. We've been in contact with Europeans for so long, that we are more classic in our dress choices. We have different values. You know, real values. We don't appear to have something we don't. That's just not part of our culture.

It is important to recognize here that the development of couture fashion in Togo emerged by drawing on diverse sources and in close interaction with "international traveling systems," as discussed by Victoria Rovine (2006). It is in this entangled and hybrid environment that pagne fashion appeared and evolved. Within this dynamic dress space, former clothing practices coexist with more modern ones: the skirt element of the complet when not tailored into a *maxi* (an ankle-length skirt) is worn in "traditional"[8] style, wrapped around the waist in precise manner, leaving the lower ends descending symmetrically. The dress competence involved when draping the wrapper and wearing this style demonstrates the clothing knowledge of its wearer. In Lomé, a woman wearing a poorly wrapped fabric that ends in a sloppy asymmetrical arrangement of folds is mockingly compared to a lame duck.

Dress knowledge and competence are part of a system of distinction where accumulation capacity, notoriety, and elegance are equally measured and all contribute to the wearer's social and economic status. The enactment of respectable femininity and middle-class-ness hinge on the material support of the fabric, which makes such performances real. Hence the genuineness of the cloth is an essential element in the upholding and reproduction of women's middle-class values. Embedded in an aesthetic regime of the body, the enactment of such values pushes the boundaries of static ideals of proper femininity. Such performances do not contradict values of propriety and family but they instantiate them as dynamic and "modern." Past and present dress practices in Togo are not static, as captured in the constantly reassembled elements of the complet.

SHIFTS IN FASHION VALUES

The faculty of fashionability operates according to class lines whose boundaries were defined by background and education. During the late 1980s and early 1990s, when the dictatorship was forced to enact structural adjustments policies, Lomé's trade economy began to decline and so did its status as West Africa's "Little Switzerland." As the distribution of wealth became much more unequal and middle-class civil servants began to experience salary shortages while prices for basic necessities began to increase, class disparities spiraled. In the past, it was a standard practice to judge a husband's ability to "evaluate" his future bride by the choice and number of classical designs he provided in the dowry; this also offered and guaranteed married women the possibility to pursue fashionability (if they didn't already). Likewise, civil servants had been able to afford the Dutch cloth as their preferred fabric for special occasions while relying on so-called *fancy-prints*[9] for quotidian events. Initially, wax-prints and fancy-prints had different designs, but during the 1990s, copies of Dutch designs appeared in the market giving momentum to the language of "authenticity." Although the copies prompted embarrassment among consumers, they were quickly resolved, as was noted by Rose, a Togolese pharmacist:

> I came home from church, and I was walking into my kitchen and there I found my domestic worker who was wearing the exact same pagne design! I was shocked and told her to change. You know, it's unacceptable for a woman of my standing to be challenged by a girl like this . . . a couple of weeks later, she wore the *same* pagne again but it was already faded, and ugly . . . the quality really showed and I was happy to wear my *Hollandais* again.

These imitations were not seen as fake; instead they were considered as authorized copies that helped reinforce the value of the original Dutch, highlighting what Simmel called the "attraction of the genuine" (1950: 343). The machine-printed copies were easily identifiable, as the roller-printing technique imprinted the signs of imperfections on the cloth in a manner that could only mimic the characteristics of the original (the subtle lines, cracks, and bubbling effects). As Togolese continued to locate their sense of distinction and fashionability in their ability to discern with precision between different fabric qualities, the language of authenticity became relevant to differentiate between a superior original and an inferior copy. The authorized fakes did not pretend to be the real thing, but instead "underscored the uniqueness of the original, with which it [exists] in a reciprocally reinforcing relationship" (Comaroff and Comaroff 2006: 14).

However, in the mid-2000s, when superior copies of the Dutch cloth entered the Lomé market from China, the rules of fashionability shifted. Prices for the original Dutch textile skyrocketed in the aftermath of the currency devaluation and liberalizations of the 1990s and enduring economic crisis, excluding the majority of Togolese from the purchase of what had become a luxury item, inevitably transforming long-held practices of social reproduction. Vlisco fabric only became available to exceptionally affluent Togolese consumers, who could afford the exclusive cachet of the Dutch original. In the midst of these transformations, Chinese manufacturers began producing high-quality copies of the Dutch designs. In 2010, Chinese-produced copies no longer mimicked the wax-prints' signs of imperfection but actually produced them; this made the cloth, in a sense, equally as "original" as each yard of cotton had an unevenness to it that was akin to and yet distinct from the superior original. Chinese wax-prints, which initially were considered "inauthentic" because they inevitably displaced what previously counted as "authentic," have come to hold *real* standing in the practicalities of the everyday. As Chinese wax-prints blatantly counterfeit Vlisco designs, only the most experienced eye can distinguish between Dutch and Chinese. Middle-class consumers, who had long cherished Vlisco, have switched to Chinese brands, such as Hitarget, Phoenix or Binta Wax, as one of my friends, a lecturer at the University of Lomé, explained:

> You know, even though nobody talks about it, and nobody wants to confess it, this really is what most women of my class do. They switch. You can't spend 70.000 francs [CFA, approximately US$150] to tailor a cutting-edge outfit that has dramatic effect with a provocative neckline et cetera from Vlisco . . . it goes out of fashion too quickly. Who can keep up with that? And *why* keep up with it actually? The popular Dutch designs are copied so quickly that you can't wear them for long anyways; the turnover is too quick . . . the cycle of fashion is much faster than before. It's so much more fashionable to be à la mode in Hitarget these days. And the quality has gotten really good too, the colors resist, the designs are precise, and they don't itch, like they did in the beginning.

My friend's sharp commentary indicates that Chinese brands have come to successfully rival the prestige of the original Dutch such that they are now influencing ideas about fashionability. For her the shift from Dutch to Chinese, which she initially experienced as disenfranchising (as a form of social unranking rather than reranking), allows her to continue to participate in changing fashion styles on her terms, freed from the dictate of originality. But how do Togolese women who do not experience the rare privilege of job security—that is, the majority of the population—experience fashionability at the current moment?

RECONSIDERING FASHIONABILITY

Representations of well-being and extravagant style have gained momentum in neoliberal Togo where young, educated Lomeans are unable to find jobs and only have their bodies and kinship networks to rely on. Middle-aged women, for instance, carefully put themselves together in older, albeit immaculate, complet outfits, which they wear with pride and distinction. Many of the older women I spoke to explained that they simply refused to participate in the dictate of constantly changing styles, claiming that presently neither the Dutch nor the Chinese produce the same quality prints that their mothers had worn. Reviving their mothers' heritage—their "cloth wealth," which is transmitted from mother to daughter—these women sometimes reintroduced long-out-of-print Dutch designs and prompt both the admiration of young fashionistas and the respect of elders.

Like in the fashion centers of the Global North, vintage styles have gained momentum in Lomé, generating a vibrant visual culture in the decaying cityscape where Togo's urban youth struggles to make ends meet. A young university graduate, who, like so many Togolese, has come to rely on the hustle economy instead of a formal job, explained to me that she had reassembled her grandmother's old garment. With the help of a friend, an apprentice tailor, they had modeled the complet into a garment loosely inspired by one of Beyoncé's outfits. Although the skirt was not as provocatively short as Beyoncé's, and they had added large buttons to the top, her outfit provoked ample commentary on the decaying streets of Lomé. She recalls how older women would sometimes stop her asking where she had found the fabric, commenting on its beauty, while others complemented her on the unique style of the outfit.

In the crisis-ridden urban setting of Lomé, novelty and style have emerged at the intersection of the street, popular Nollywood videos, global soap operas, and MTV. Together they form an idiosyncratic image culture that revisits the complet as well as long-held sumptuary modalities. At present, dress patterns and styles are much more eclectic, assembled, and reinvented as they obscure marital status and other conventions of respectability that defined fashionability before economic hardship and social precariousness came to structure a new pragmatics of the everyday. Such a pragmatics, I argue, might be better understood when we read it not as a reaction (or resistance) to the experience of marginalization, but rather as a way of embodying one's own displacement in Togo's urban geographies. I suggest that the body takes on renewed importance that surpasses the body techniques of conventional pagne fashions and fashionabilities, forming an image culture that reflects the unpredictability, limitations, and possibilities of material and social life. On the street, the body's fleshy mise-en-scène gains new momentum, a body that is flush with its own material reality which acts upon society as much as it is enacted upon. When this embodiment is accounted for, I suggest, it has potential to generate social capital at a moment when Togo's urban youth has been forced to enact ever more creative ways to generate incomes.

As young women adorn their bodies, often tailoring the garments themselves from garments they inherited from their mothers, the street becomes the site where a person's social skin is carefully evaluated. The embodied performance of sartorial style builds on the woman's ability to play with dominant fashion conventions through colors, fabric, and lengths, as well as her capacity to mobilize accessories (hair extensions, earrings, sunglasses). But the creation of a dramatic look requires much more than the skillful combination of material artifacts—knowing how to identify what is a primary, secondary, and tertiary quality, what is new and how to wear it. The crafting of a sensuous look involves mastering a set of carefully orchestrated bodily techniques, namely the revolving movement of the buttocks à la Beyoncé, or the positioning of the hands on the hips. The bodily rendering of such a look involves much more than the emulation of global signifiers; a successful performance of a total look establishes a reputation of urban savvy that produces value of a different kind. At a moment when university degrees and other recognized forms of qualifications have lost their value, the body itself becomes a valuable site of production for generating social capital that can potentially lead to unexpected employment opportunities. The fashionableness of the young woman who had reassembled her grandmother's old garment in Beyoncé style, for example, was remarked upon by a hostess agency that recruited her off the street to work at the Lomé trade fair.

CONCLUSION

By way of conclusion, I would like to return to the Vlisco ad campaign with which I began this chapter. I suggested that a shift in Vlisco's brand image, from manufacturer to fashion house, constitutes a reflection of the firm's strategy to reposition itself in light of a market dominated by Chinese copies.[10] Unlike major fashion houses of the *Global North,* which increasingly rely on street-style inspirations for their collections—a trickle-up aesthetic, so to speak—Vlisco has opted to play with the fraught desire for authenticity and a conservative trickle-down fashion aesthetic. In this chapter, I have argued that product authenticity in the context of pagne fashion appears as a highly ambiguous state that is constantly reconfigured, reinterpreted, and interrogated anew in interaction with a whole lot of other processes. While authenticity is the product of social struggles over who controls the production of values, the experience and performance of authenticity at the contemporary moment, I have argued, lies as much with the small Vlisco cloth-purchasing elite as it does with middle-class consumers adopting China prints, and with the reassembled styles of urban youth on the streets of Lomé.

ACKNOWLEDGMENTS

Research for this chapter was primarily conducted in Lomé, Togo, from 2002 to 2004 as part of my PhD dissertation. Follow-up field research was conducted in March and April of 2008 and in December 2010. The paper's argument on the constitution of fashionability draws on semiformal interviews and numerous informal conversations, which took place mostly in the market but also in my interviewees' houses, cafes, maquis-bars, and other public and private spaces. Reconstructions of events and quotes are all based on the collected data. While the interviewees consented that their stories could be made publicly accessible, I have chosen to conceal their identities. My profound gratitude goes out to Karen Tranberg Hansen, who has helped shape this project in numerous ways and whose mentorship for many years has been invaluable. Finally, I wish to thank the Center for the Humanities at the University of the Western Cape (UWC), especially Premesh Lalu, and the Mellon Foundation for a generous fellowship which allowed me to work on revisions of this chapter amongst other things.

NOTES

1. Vlisco, "where authenticity is guaranteed," reads the website.
2. The art historian John Picton describes these technical imperfections in more detail: "Resin cracked to allow an essentially unpredictable veining in the patterned background; there was difficulty in cleaning all the resin off, leaving spots, also extra colours tended not to provide an exact fit, but instead overlapped with adjacent parts of the design" (1995 50).
3. While the copies found a market among the latter, they were increasingly displaced when an Indian printing-block technique was introduced to local workshops, reducing labor time and making the cloth much more affordable. The Dutch imports were competing with local producers, and Javanese consumers soon appeared to prefer the local hand-blocked batiks.
4. As a marker of distinction, wax-cloth was integrated into local forms of discernment, likely to have been built on an earlier model and desire for social differentiation, which Hodder (1980) traces back to court societies of the precolonial period.
5. Several films have focused on the wealthy Togolese cloth merchants who controlled the West African trade of printed cloth from Lomé, Togo (see Katia Pederson's 1993 *God Gave Her a Mercedes Benz* or Karin Junger's 2001 *Mama Benz and the Taste for Money*).
6. With evangelization, the participation in "Sunday clothing" practices (Balandier 1967) added an additional layer to the nexus of the public display of social statuses.
7. The number of couturiers has increased with the crisis. Traditionally, hairdressers and seamstresses (the assumption here being an economic argument: people always need haircuts and clothing) have been the main occupations for young women to explore when leaving school. In light of persisting and aggravating economic crisis, the realm of couture continues to be one of the main ways for Togolese to make a living. With the influx of cheap fabrics, couture remains a vital sector of employment and survival.
8. I am referring here to the local expression used for this style, rather than pointing to a binary between traditional and modern style.
9. Fancy-prints were introduced to West Africa as a result of the popularity of wax-prints and in an attempt by European textile manufacturers to expand their markets by way of creating a cheaper, technologically less sophisticated, lower-quality roller-print. They were drawing on a distinct iconographic repertoire; the variety in color and design appealed particularly to lower-income populations who could not afford wax-prints but nevertheless desired to participate in elegant pagne fashions. As an affordable alternative to wax-prints, fancy-prints became highly popular.

10. It is worth mentioning that as of October 2010, the Dutch group Vlisco is no longer in Dutch hands. Vlisco was sold for US$151 to Actis, an investment firm specializing in emerging markets (see http://www.howwemadeitinafrica.com/interview-actis-acquires-african-fabric-manufacturer/4091/).

REFERENCES

Appadurai, Appadurai, ed. 1986. *The Social Life of Things: Commodities in Cultural Perspective.* Cambridge: Cambridge University Press.

Balandier, Georges. 1967. *Anthropologie Politique.* Paris: Presses Universitaire de France.

Comaroff, Jean, and J. Comaroff. 2006. *Law and Disorder in the Postcolony.* Chicago: University of Chicago Press.

Eicher, Joanne B. 1995. *Dress and Ethnicity: Change Across Space and Time.* Oxford: Berg.

Eicher, Joanne B. 2000. "The Anthropology of Dress." *Dress* 27: 59–70

Hansen, Karen Tranberg. 2003. "Fashioning: Zambian Moments." *Journal of Material Culture* 8(3): 302–309.

Hansen, Karen Tranberg. 2004a. "The World in Dress: Anthropological Perspectives on Clothing, Fashion, and Culture." *Annual Review of Anthropology* 33: 369–392.

Hansen, Karen Tranberg. 2004b. "Dressing Dangerously: Miniskirts, Gender Relations, and Sexuality in Zambia." In Jean Allman, ed., *Fashioning Africa: Power and the Politics of Dress,* 166–188. Bloomington: Indiana University Press.

Hobsbawn, Eric, and Terence Ranger. 1983. *The Invention of Tradition.* Cambridge: Cambridge University Press.

Hodder, B. W. 1980. "Indigenous Cloth Trade and Marketing in Africa." In Dale Idiens and Kenneth Ponting, eds., *Textiles of Africa,* 203–210. Bath: Pasold Research Fund.

Kroese, W. T. 1976. *The Origin of the Wax Block Print on the Coast of West Africa.* Hengelo: Smit van Uitegeverij.

Marguerat, Yyes, and Tichtchekou Peleï. 1993. *Si Lomé m'était contée…Tome II.* Lomé: Presses Universités du Bénin.

Mintz, Sidney. 1986. *Sweetness and Power. The Place of Sugar in Modern History.* New York: Penguin.

Mustafa, Hudita. 1998. "Sartorial Ecumenes: African Styles in a Social and Economic Context." In Els van der Plas and Marlous Willemsen, eds., *The Art of African Fashion,* 13–48. Trenton, NJ: Africa World Press.

Nielsen, Ruth. 1979. "The History and Development of Wax-Printed Textiles Intended for West Africa and Zaire." In Justin Cordwell and Ronald Schwartz, eds., *The Fabrics of Culture: The Anthropology of Clothing and Adornment,* 467–498. The Hague: Mouton.

Picton, John. 1995. *The Art of African Textiles: Technology, Tradition, and Lurex.* London: Lund Humphries Publishers.

Robinson, Stuart. 1969. *A History of Printed Textiles.* Cambridge, MA: MIT Press.

Rovine, Victoria. 2006. "African Fashion Design: Global Networks and Local Styles." *Africultures* 69: 104–109.

Schneider, Jane, and A. Weiner. 1989. *Cloth and the Human Experience.* Washington, DC: Smithsonian Institution Press

Simmel, Georg. 1950. "Adornment." In Kurt Wolff, ed., *The Sociology of Georg Simmel*, 338–345. Glencoe, IL: Free Press.

Steiner, Christopher. 1985. "Another Image of Africa: Toward an Ethnohistory of European Cloth Marketed in West Africa 1873–1960." *Ethnohistory* 32(2): 91–110.

Sylvanus, Nina. 2007. "The Fabric of Africanity. Tracing the Global Threads of Authenticity." *Anthropological Theory* 7(2): 201–216.

Sylvanus, Nina. 2010. "Counterfeited Fashions: The Politics of Dress and Style in Togo." *Africa e Mediterraneo* 69: 26–31.

Thomas, Nicholas. 1991. *Entangled Objects. Exchange, Material Culture and Colonialism in the Pacific.* Cambridge: Harvard University Press.

Weiner, Annette, and Jane Schneider. 1989. *Cloth and the Human Experience.* Washington, DC: Smithsonian Press.

–3–

Branding Festive Bodies: Corporate Logos and Chiefly Image T-Shirts in Ghana

Lauren Adrover

The annual Fetu Afahye festival celebrated in Cape Coast, Ghana, unfolds within a highly commodified space. Across the streets are banners with images of Unilever products such as Royco tomato paste, Blue Band margarine, and Close-Up toothpaste. Large posters of Guinness products including Star Beer, Gordon's Gin, and Smirnoff Ice are glued to the walls of buildings. Kiosks overflowing with commodities, branded promotional gifts, and print media feature colorful images advertising telecommunications firms such as Tigo, Vodafone, and MTN.

The commercial ambience of the festival is punctuated by strikingly dressed bodies that move about the town. Commercial logos decorate not only public space, buy they also adorn bodies on T-shirts displaying corporate logos. The production and distribution of branded T-shirts is a key marketing strategy for firms and companies that sponsor the event. During the festival's climax, the bodily display of brand names and logos creates a striking visual effect. The T-shirts imprinted with corporate logos are rivaled by a competing T-shirt style which features a photograph of a chief within Cape Coast, presenting spectators with an alternative form of branding that is underpinned by local politics. Dressed bodies displaying the competing logos assert two distinct forms of power: The chiefly logo is based on local political affiliations while the corporate logo is based upon external commercial relations. The use of embodied logos by chiefs suggests new ways of procuring and asserting political authority while raising questions about legitimate relations between social and economic networks.

T-shirts are a decidedly unspectacular form of dress. Endlessly reproduced and circulated in contemporary public arenas, they are deployed by mass media and local communities to inscribe commercial distinction, social difference, and collective affiliation. Increasingly, these material forms are incorporated into ceremonial settings. During many Ghanaian festivals, branded T-shirts have become a uniform. An exploration of this contemporary dress practice will alert us to other socially significant transformations within the field of cultural production and how they interact with broader global processes. The overwhelming presence of T-shirts emblazoned with logos from companies like Guinness and Coca Cola demonstrates the active role of sponsors in the production of festivals. Such T-shirts also alert us to the ways in which local political leaders evaluate corporate sponsorship. Chiefs disagree over the implications of branding in the sphere of festivals. Some argue corporate logos are not "traditional" or "culturally appropriate" and should be substituted with chief image T-shirts. By advertising people and products, identifications and affinities, these garments afford an opportunity to examine the role of dressed bodies as critical sites where political networks and economic interventions are articulated and evaluated within particular performance contexts.

Because T-shirts are inexpensive and easy to reproduce, they enjoy a prominent place both in the public sphere and individual wardrobes. Recognizing the unique materialities of dress, I explore the performative efficacy of T-shirts and their brand imagery to capture how they achieve social ends, facilitating public identifications and differentiations that link both the wearer and the distributor to other people, places, and companies. In effect, these urban dress forms are highly significant material embodiments that assert affiliations between community members, economic agents, and political leaders. Since the value of T-shirts stems, in part, from the images emblazoned on them, I focus on these inscriptions—corporate logos and chiefly images—treating them as dual forms of branding. I extend a definition of logos or brand names as "visual forms that condense and convey meaning in commerce" to include the sphere of politics (Coombs 1996: 203). Garments representing chiefs have a logic of signification that is not exclusively commercial. These two forms of festive T-shirts suggest critical differences in the ways chiefs seek to articulate their authority. While commodity-specific garments link chiefly power to broader economic networks, T-shirts with chiefs' images highlight a form of political recognition that honors kinship, lineage, and the chief's own positioning within chieftaincy networks.

This chapter examines the production, distribution, and indexicality of branded T-shirts within the visual economy of festival display. I examine two key forms of branding, linking the semiotic variability of different types of T-shirts to claims about social and economic networks, chiefly authority, and culturally appropriate modalities of display. Focusing on the relationship between branding, dressed bodies, and public display, I seek to capture the dynamics of how sartorial practices articulate new processes of social evaluations as they actively take shape through festive events. In 2006, I examined the planning and performance of the Fetu Afahye festival, interviewing traditional leaders, members of the planning committee, performers, and spectators. I regularly attended festival planning committee meetings and observed various festival events. I focus on the 2006 celebration while incorporating data collected during celebrations in 2009 and 2011.[1]

THE FETU AFAHYE FESTIVAL, 2006

The setting is the Fetu Afahye festival celebrated in Cape Coast by the Fante-speaking Akan.[2] As one of the most prominent festivals in Ghana, it draws people from many regions, as well as visitors from overseas, and serves as a homecoming event for residents living outside the locality. The festival is valued for its role in commemorating the yam harvest and reproducing the political status of Cape Coast chiefs. The annual royal ritual centers on the paramount chief or *omanhen* and is a time for the validation of his ancestral political status, which is recognized through carefully orchestrated public performances (Apter 2005; Gilbert 1994). Because chiefs have lost much of their former judicial power, Fetu Afahye is one of their few remaining opportunities to represent their authority to a broad audience.

The festival culminates on the first Saturday of September with a procession of chiefs through the streets of the town. On the morning of the procession, the town's narrow and meandering streets steadily fill with nearly three hundred thousand spectators, doubling its population. The mood is exciting, with music blaring from small shops and bars, and friends and passersby calling out the customary greeting: *"Afehnyia Pa!"* (Greet the new year). The crowded streets are jammed with people who come to witness displays of drumming, dancing, and songs that remember the past and evoke ancestral deities. *Asafo* companies[3] lead the procession with collective song and dance, drumming and gunfire.

The seven asafo companies parade in separate groups, each exceeding one hundred persons. Most asafo members wear T-shirts of a particular color that identify them with their company. The first company, Bentsir, appears as a mass of bodies in red shirts, many donated by companies with the same color-specific brand affiliation as Coca-Cola or Vodaphone. The presence of asafo groups signals the arrival of chiefs and queen mothers who follow in hierarchical succession. To begin, lower division chiefs process on foot, while higher-ranking leaders are uplifted in regal palanquins.

The procession climaxes with the arrival of the paramount chief, whose public appearance is noted as "the most spectacular" display of all (*Oguaa Fetu Afahye Journal* 2004: 24). The paramount chief has been in power since 1998 and holds a full-time position as an accountant for a civil engineering company. During the procession, he demonstrates his authority through visible signs of affluence. The omanhen rests in a palanquin carried by four men. Wearing a brightly colored, hand-woven *kente* cloth that symbolizes pride and wealth, he is adorned with abundant gold regalia such as necklaces, rings, bracelets, armbands, and a crown. An extensive, uniformly dressed entourage accompanies him. During the 2006 celebration, each person surrounding the chief wore a branded Paramount Gin T-shirt: The men who carried him and drummed behind him and the women who fanned him with their cloths and called out his name all embodied the corporate trademark as if symbolically uplifted by the force of the commodity (see Plate 3).

STRUGGLES FOR AUTHORITY

Since British colonial rule, chiefs adapted to several political economic transitions, forcing them to restructure their economic allegiances to maintain wealth and power. As early as the middle of the nineteenth century, Fante chiefs participated as independent traders and agents of British commercial houses, exploiting economic networks to expedite the flow of resources from outside (Arhin 1983: 15). Although some chiefs held privileged positions within administrative branches of the colonial government, colonial officials passed ordinances that restricted chiefs' right to rule and claims to land, initiating a long process of chiefly subjugation (Arhin 1983). Colonial officials exerted forms of surveillance and control over chiefs and their subjects, and in 1932, British administrators passed a Peace Preservation Ordinance which banned the celebration of Fetu Afahye, resulting in thirty years of nonobservance (Blankson 1974: 2). The ban marked another defeat for Fante chiefs, who were experiencing the destabilization of their reign over people and places.

Following Ghana's independence in 1957, president Kwame Nkrumah continued the process of dismantling the institution of chieftaincy by stripping chiefs of judicial and administrative functions, redirecting chiefs' land revenues toward the central government, and allowing state officials to recognize and revoke chiefs' status (Rathbone 2000: 125). Nkrumah effectively undercut the formal power of chiefs by depriving them of wealth and prestige. Chiefs, in turn, selectively extended their political allegiances to extract funding from the central government.

When J. J. Rawlings, the president in the early 1980s, agreed to a series of neoliberal economic reforms, local political leaders eager to tap into flows of international finance capital began to forge new relations with networks that, to varying degrees, bypassed the state (Chalfin 2010; Shipley 2004). Increasingly, chiefs cultivated direct relationships with corporate institutions that play a key role in Ghana's liberalized economy. For well over a century then, chiefs have accessed capital flows in new and innovative ways with little support from a central government. Since chieftaincy positions garner few direct financial rewards, many raise funds and pursue creative income-generating activities to finance their political responsibilities. In some areas, stools (political and social organization coterminous with the territorial jurisdiction of a chief) have sources of income from gold mines, oil, or businesses on stool lands, while others have nothing. Chiefs are charged with stewardship over the land within their jurisdiction, maintenance of ritual objects that belong to the stool, and the supervision of annual customs such as festivals. While the chiefs take pride in owning their festivals, the costs of production and participation are far too high for them to bear alone.

FESTIVAL FUNDING AND THE DEVELOPMENT OF CORPORATE SPONSORSHIP

Since 1963, when Nkrumah lifted the colonial ban on the celebration of Fetu Afahye, chiefs have scrambled for funds. Donors ranged from local shop owners to wealthy relatives. In the 1970s, commercial companies began to take interest in the event as evidenced by festival brochures of the time which feature advertisements, for example, for Pioneer Tobacco and Accra Breweries. In video footage from celebrations during this period, participants wear T-shirts donated by national beverage companies. When I asked chiefs about the beginnings of commercial sponsorship, most of them remarked, "Sponsors have always been here." Yet they also insisted that today sponsorship is different. Whereas in the past sponsorship was diverse, now a smaller number of large international companies provide the bulk of the funding. Chiefs also noted that in recent years sponsors' marketing tactics have become more aggressive. As a senior chief noted, "We need to put our foot down with the sponsors. They are taking advantage of us. They are threatening the beauty and the artistry. We want people to appreciate the finest things in us, in the Afahye. How sponsors brand the place, the festival, the whole town, it's too much, it's not traditional" (Interview July 2011). While some chiefs flaunt their connections with companies as a signal of their own power, others accept sponsor contributions but condemn their aggressive marketing tactics.

Large-scale corporate sponsorship began in the early 1980s, a period of severe national economic upheaval. With mounting financial woes, chiefs found it difficult to extract levies from their subjects. The variety of networks they had tapped in the past, including regionally based businesses, local entrepreneurs, and wealthy kin, had dried up. Beginning in the 1980s, brewing companies, tobacco firms, and other organizations funded almost all festive expenditures. The shift followed Rawlings's support of liberalizing reforms and his call for every possible source to subsidize the state. As sectors of the government looked to external funding, so did chiefs. They welcomed the support of international companies and foreign-owned Ghanaian businesses and, to varying degrees, accepted the demands placed on them by sponsors.

Chiefs' festival participation requires buying new attire, festive regalia, and compensating the people who accompany them during the procession. Chiefly entourages, including drummers, palanquin bearers, and praise singers, must be paid, fed, and clothed. Other aspects of festival production add to the costs, such as renting chairs, shade structures, and "refreshing" people who come to visit chiefs in the palace. Older chiefs noted that in the past individuals offered their labor by customary obligation, free of monetary compensation. Now, one chief lamented, "They won't even waste one day to help you!" Donations by fishermen, famers, market women, and others helped reduce costs. I witnessed many donations of food and beverages arrive at the offices of the traditional council, yet the total volume of such donations accounted for less than 10 percent of the planning committee's projected expenditures. As one chief put it, "The costs have become too high for us. This is why the sponsors are heavily relied upon. We cannot do it alone. We need them. We welcome all sponsors" (Interview August 2006). Corporate sponsors enable the production of the festival year after year. Regardless of whether they viewed corporate funding as a problem or welcomed it, all chiefs I spoke with accepted such support as an inescapable aspect of festival production.

The festival planning committee incorporates chiefs' participation costs into an annual budget that is sent to a wide range of prospective sponsors, from local businesses to international companies. The committee is comprised of six officers who are divisional chiefs and six members with different organizational allegiances such as the tourist board and Cape Coast Municipal Assembly. Once sponsors' donations are confirmed, the committee distributes cash allowances to chiefs in amounts that vary by their rank. Chiefs agree to the demands of sponsors by accepting donations, the results of which can be seen on dressed bodies.

T-SHIRTS, CORPORATE AND CHIEFLY LOGOS

In the following section I examine the role and uses of T-shirts, focusing on the two primary types: chiefly logo T-shirts that depict an image of a chief alongside their name, title, and area of jurisdiction (see Figure 3.1), and corporate logo T-shirts that feature a brand name or commodity image (see Figure 3.2). I consider their circulation, production, distribution, and what they mean for those who wear them. Then I compare the performance strategies of two chiefs to explore the motives that drive T-shirt production and distribution. The two cases I have selected exemplify two dominant and contrasting

Figure 3.1 T-shirt with chiefly logo featuring image of queen mother. 2006 Fetu Afahye Festival. Photo by Lauren Adrover.

modes of evaluation. How people attribute meaning to the shirts they wear is important, but I also stress that chiefs determine how to dress their entourages, carefully orchestrating the visual consumption of embodied imagery to assert their influence and political distinctiveness. The sartorial dimension of festive performance is a primary medium by which chiefs articulate their representation in the public sphere.

Chiefs parading in the festival's procession wear wrapped cloth, ranging from handwoven *kente* to factory-produced wax prints. T-shirts are most popular among nonelite festival participants, unlike other localities in West Africa where commemorative factory printed textiles are common (Bickford 1994). By the early 1990s, T-shirts began to displace more expensive forms of printed cloth that chiefs customarily provided to festival performers and participants. The low cost of T-shirts appealed both to chiefs and sponsors. The practical efficacy of T-shirts contributes to their popularity, yet they also have a semiotic efficacy, emerging from their embodied and indexical features. The body animates the garment's communicative capacity, while the material properties of the shirt "turn the body into a billboard," emphasizing the salience of this modern garment as a public and corporeal form of branding and display (Glass 2008: 3).

Figure 3.2 T-shirt with corporate logo worn by member of *asafo* company. 2006 Fetu Afahye Festival. Photo by Lauren Adrover.

Festive T-shirts draw attention to the performative power of language and images when depicted on the dressed body. Garments inscribed with such representations convey distinct messages. Whether it is a brand name accompanied by a corporate logo or a proper name alongside a photographed image, these symbols transform the body through dress, positioning it as vehicle for asserting claims of personhood and social relations. Dress scholars have noted that the T-shirt may serve as a metaphor for the encounter between body and language, and between fashion system and communicative process. Inscribed garments and the bodies they clothe are disposed toward communication (Calefato 2006: 140). In effect, T-shirts may be perceived as a medium through which people broadcast claims about themselves and the presentation of others.

Scholarship on the display of designer brand names and logos in popular fashion also provides some insight. The notion that there is "a logic of distinction fundamentally linked to brand names" has particular relevance here (Calefato 2006: 141). An important relationship exists between the garment's logo and its symbolic valence. What is revealing in the case of festive T-shirts is not solely a matter of the semantic connotation of the inscription, but rather its semiotic implications. Although people wearing T-shirts attributed different meanings to the garment dependent on the particularity of the inscription, they associated possessing and embodying the garment itself, despite its inscription, with a privileged form of inclusion and participation. The logo of the T-shirt, its distinctive marker, did in fact add to its social value as wearers often expressed deeper attachments to chief image shirts.

For chiefs, the form of distinction asserted by the brand, whether political or commercial, was key to its efficacy. They carefully employed textual and graphic references, using the visual and sensorial impact of dress, to actively draw attention to their authority. In effect, chiefs adopt distinctive modes of branding to transform the mundane properties of T-shirts into a corporeal means of achieving social, political, and economic ends (Kuchler and Miller 2005), while also enabling the production and performance of personhood (Hansen 2000).

Corporate T-shirts feature a brand image or textual representation of the company's logo. Often including an inscription with the name and year of the festival, T-shirts affiliate both corporate brand and the wearer with the event. The T-shirts are distributed free of charge to individual chiefs who have established relations with particular sponsors. Sponsoring companies provide chiefs with an agreed upon number of shirts, which chiefs distribute to the people who accompany them during the procession on the morning of the festival. Although chiefs often make demands on sponsors concerning the production of T-shirts, sponsors rarely oblige. Usually, chiefs expect that the color of shirt will match the brand. Coca-Cola, for example, provides red T-shirts. Both the color and logo of T-shirts are constant areas of contention. In one case, I witnessed a chief's assistant open a large box of black Guinness T-shirts only days before the festival. The chief was outraged: "I can't believe this! I told them no black. We are celebrating a festival, not a funeral!" Regarding the specific logos, most chiefs who request T-shirts agree to promote the brand as part of the exchange. Most chiefs in this category approve the presence of a logo. Chiefs who are critical of corporate advertising may request changes to be made of the size and the positioning of the logo on the garment.

The other dominant T-shirt style features a photographic representation of a chief with full name, political title, and area of jurisdiction. The chief depicted on the garment commissions and funds the production of such T-shirts. A chief will work with a local printer who uses a photograph of the chief to create a silk-screen effigy that is featured on the front of the garment. By placing one's image on highly visible bodies, chiefs assert their political rank for spectators to acknowledge and to inspire acts of homage and recognition. This sartorial convention enables chiefs to project their own position within the chieftaincy hierarchy, reasserting the role of local politics within a space saturated with commercial marks of trade.

THE WEARERS OF FESTIVAL T-SHIRTS

People wearing corporate or chiefly logo T-shirts had two reactions to these garments. First, people like the T-shirts and value the garment because of its relation to the festival. Second, T-shirt possession signals a direct social relation with a chief or other well-positioned person. Shirts are valued because they broadcast affiliations, linking the wearer to a specific individual, the event, or a sponsoring organization.

Wearing a shirt affiliates you with its donor, marking your inclusion within his or her network of social relations. In my interviews, people who displayed corporate logos rarely referenced their chiefs, what they thought of them, or how the shirt linked them to a specific individual. They mentioned the name of the chief when asked of the origin of the garment but did not make additional comments. By contrast, people who wore chiefly logo shirts mentioned family allegiances, friendships, or professional affiliations with the photographed person, often adding positive evaluations. For example, "He is a good. He has done a lot for our community, especially for the youth. We support him." Or simply, "I adore him. He is my chief!"

People wearing corporate logo shirts were more likely to note that the T-shirts communicated their participation and inclusion in the festival in general. One woman said she liked how her corporate T-shirt cited the festival name and year. In fact, those wearing corporate logos shirts were unlikely to highlight their identification with the brand or company. And when asked if they preferred a T-shirt with a chief or corporate logo, most preferred chiefly images.

Friends living in Cape Coast often remarked that festival participants who wear corporate shirts care little about their inscriptions. "They just want a free shirt!" they urged. Yet accounts by T-shirt wearers suggested otherwise. In some cases, participants related positively to brands, proudly displaying their logo. As a man in a blue Tigo shirt and told me, "I love Tigo. They are the best. They are here, supporting Cape Coast and our chiefs. We can rely on them!" Indeed, some expressed ambivalence, shrugging their shoulders or nodding and smiling in response to my questions. When pressed further, however, people reflected on T-shirts in nuanced ways, mediated by the form of branding depicted on the garment.

The way people maintain and use shirts after the festival illustrates the privileged position they occupy in their wardrobe. Many told me that they save T-shirts for future celebrations, storing them and not incorporating them into their regular dress routines. Keeping a shirt from a previous year enables you to participate in the event during future celebrations. Many hoped to acquire a new T-shirt each year and some boasted that they had been gifted several T-shirts in years past. People protect their shirts from overuse so that they can reuse the shirts to communicate the wearers' inclusion in the event and their relation to some person with a prominent role in the performance. An observant spectator can readily spot shirts recycled from previous celebrations based on yearly inscriptions, logos from inoperative businesses, or garments that look faded or sun worn from years of washing or overuse.

While most owners of festival T-shirts told me that they would handle their T-shirts with care, other respondents said that they might give their shirt away, wear it at home, or relegate it to the depths of their closet. Others said they would incorporate it into everyday dress because they took pride in the event and/or the chief depicted on the T-shirt. One man told me he liked wearing it because it enabled him to share his festival experience with others. To be sure, T-shirts circulate in various post-festival ways. More research is needed to analyze the ways in which T-shirts are removed and reinserted into different spatiotemporal contexts and how such forms of circulation are conditioned by the material and symbolic properties of specific garments.

THE QUEEN MOTHER AND POLITICAL DISTINCTION

Each year, the queen mother of Cape Coast commissions T-shirts that bear her image. As she told me, "These shirts adhere to traditional protocol." For her, T-shirts with chief logos constitute an appropriate mode of adornment because they focus on local political identities. Her choice to commission T-shirts at her own expense is strategic and fulfills several functions. By asserting her political identity, textually and visually, the garment projects her allegiance to her subjects while simultaneously asserting her own political persona. Her decision to display this type of T-shirt also signals an opposition to the role of corporate sponsors in the field of festive production. I questioned the queen mother about the marketing tactics companies deploy during the festival. She expressed her dismay with sponsoring agents and commodity-specific T-shirts:

> Many of us didn't take kindly to those things because the companies' products or brands are in focus more than the festival. There needs to be a forum about this, because our tradition is being lost in these festivals, lost to the companies. It's time we sat with these companies and went into a proper agreement as to what should be done . . . about what is traditional and what is not traditional. It's not right. Eventually the festivals importance and essence will be lost (Interview September 2006).

Using images of chiefs on T-shirts enables chiefs to express the importance of cultural heritage and its connection to the political structure of chieftaincy. The queen mother's assertion that commodity "brands that are in focus more than the festival" suggests that previous conventions are being violated and exploited by corporate interests. She views T-shirts with corporate logos as privileging the interests of commercial organizations in ways that compromise the appropriate reproduction of tradition and chiefs' self-presentations. While T-shirts with images of chiefs who "own" the festival assert their public personas, corporate logo shirts divert the attention of participants and spectators, obscuring forms of political recognition. For the queen mother and other critics of corporate marketing tactics, the dominance of sponsors' brands compromise the communicative capacity of chiefs' self-presentations.

Despite their high costs of production and chiefs' limited budgets, T-shirts with chiefs' logos have grown in popularity. In 2006, corporate T-shirts outnumbered chief image T-shirts two to one, whereas chief image T-shirts nearly equaled the number of corporate shirts during the 2011 celebration. This growing trend is a political maneuver by chiefs who seek to inscribe festive performances with special meaning—that is, the marks of their own political distinction. As one chief explained, "That's about the only time that you showcase yourself to your people, you showcase your authority. We need to use it, it belongs to us, it is our festival."

Discussions about corporate logo T-shirts invoked critiques from numerous chiefs who shared the queen mother's position. For them, corporate T-shirts indexed the increasing control sponsors exerted over chiefs who depend on the sponsors' economic patronage. Chiefs lamented that the visual dominance of corporate logos severed festive performance practices from their political relations of production. Chiefs with this view said they could no longer regulate festival aesthetics, ensuring they adhered to customary demands. The beauty of the procession, one chief noted, "was the chiefs and their entourages proceeding in their regalia, with entourage members in their traditional colors, or at least with shirts that advertise their chief" (Interview September 2006). The comment affirms that chiefs are critical of corporate affiliations while illustrating the efficacy of T-shirts with chiefly logos and their multiple valances. According to the chief, these garments have the capacity to assert a tacit resistance to the interventions of sponsors while maintaining the "customary" beauty of the procession despite its quintessentially modern, mass-produced form.

THE PARAMOUNT CHIEF AND COMMERCIAL DISTINCTION

The garments worn by the paramount chief's entourage during the 2006 celebration projected his close ties with corporate affiliates. The commodity-specific T-shirts he distributed placed the Paramount Gin logo in clear view. Paramount Distilleries, a Ghanaian beverage company with global operations, provided the garments and a cash donation. According to the chief, there are "strings attached to the T-shirts," which had to be produced according to the demands of chiefs (Interview September 2006).

The paramount chief described how chiefs require sponsors to print T-shirts in specific colors. Each chief is associated with a particular *asafo* company and affiliation is marked through T-shirts in colors such as red, blue, white, or yellow. Chiefs are said to make demands on sponsoring agencies requiring them to provide garments that display chiefs' communal and political affiliations. When they do so, corporate sponsors must adjust their own marketing strategies to conform to appropriate forms of chiefly display. Many leaders articulated this point, yet the dress practices of chiefs who branded their entourages with corporate logos showed little evidence of such negotiations. In some cases, chiefs aligned themselves with sponsors whose brand color was shared by their asafo company, and in other cases, chiefs dressed their entourages in corporate colors that did not match their community affiliations.

The paramount chief suggested that the relationship between chiefs and sponsors was mutually productive. Since sponsors benefit from the marketing potential created by festival publicity and participation, they are more likely to respond positively to the chiefs' demands. Publicly promoting corporate products serves this end, establishing relations between chiefs and specific companies and maximizing the likelihood that these companies will continue to provide chiefs with economic support in future celebrations. Sponsors benefit from identifying their products with festivals, increasing sales and brand affiliations. Situating corporate images within local spheres of cultural production also enables sponsors to present themselves as socially responsible institutions, invested in the reproduction of collectively valued cultural expressions (Shipley 2004: 125).

In only two cases were chiefs able to cite instances where relationships built with sponsors during the course of festivals yielded economic gains in alternate spheres. In one instance, a chief described how his town was made the site of a "corporate social responsibility" initiative by a leading telecommunications firm. For the project, the firm created infrastructure for pipe-born water at two schools. Another chief explained how a different telecom company provided building materials for the reconstruction of his chiefly residence and administrative center. He said the exchange was not made public but "was a result of friendship and reciprocity." Although I could not confirm this account, I observed the chief's retinue parading the company logo during the festival over three consecutive years, suggesting that the chief is still nurturing the friendship and the possibility of future support.

The display of corporate logo T-shirts functions as a means to a practical economic end. After all, corporate logo T-shirts are distributed free of charge, an appealing option for chiefs with limited economic means. Acquiring corporate T-shirts, however, is a time-consuming process. Relations with sponsors must be established and cultivated. Chiefs must send petitions to representatives at sponsoring agencies to request T-shirts. Such written appeals require chiefs to state their claims for support, verify their political positions, and include a description of T-shirt sizes, colors, and quantity. Often, pleas for garments are rejected unless a chief has close ties to members of a sponsoring agency.

Even in the case of the well-connected paramount chief, obtaining corporate T-shirts for the 2006 celebration was a laborious process. Although he was closely acquainted with a high-ranking Paramount Distilleries representative, the work of acquiring shirts involved multiple phone calls, meetings, and long periods of waiting. The garments were hastily delivered just hours before the festival's commencement. Chiefs' willingness to engage in the forms of labor required to obtain corporate T-shirts reflects the value that some attribute to them. Flaunting connections with economically powerful and well-positioned corporate agents offers the opportunity to convey prestige that may yield symbolic and economic capital in alternate domains. Social connections as well as the labor expended in the process of acquiring corporate shirts are imbued in the garment itself. Here again, the efficacy of the garment emerges in its embodied form: When displayed on dressed bodies uplifting chiefs through crowded streets, the value of festive T-shirts materializes, conveying political prestige, broad social networks, and access to economic resources.

The display of corporate T-shirts in the politically charged context of processional performance reflects how local leaders evaluate the potential gains resulting from self-presentations. Corporate logos inscribed on dressed bodies that physically and symbolically uplift political leaders demand that chiefs' status be recognized in relation to the corporate identity mimicked through the body. The commercial brands that festive T-shirts exhibit simultaneously become markers of chiefs' political identity. In effect, the corporeal display of corporate brands can allow local leaders to broker a self-identity that is both globally constituted (signified by logos that confirm chiefs' relations with external economic networks) and locally situated (signaled by processional performance and chief status).

To briefly demonstrate my point, I return to a description of the paramount chief's processional performance. While people gather near the chief to visually acknowledge how he represents his wealth, political authority, and social prestige, spectators are confronted with multiple images of a single corporate logo depicted on the bodies of the men who uplift him. All participants in the chief's entourage wear crisp, white, Paramount Gin T-shirts. By performing his authority alongside the uniformity of dozens of corporate T-shirts, the chief presents spectators with an alternative representation of the exchange relations that underpin political authority. Although he occupies the highest-ranking position within the chieftaincy institution, the dressed bodies surrounding the chief make no explicit reference to local political identities as distinct, superior, or even relevant. His decision to enact and embody corporate logos rather than his own image points to an emergent form of prestige associated with the ability to display individual connections within corporate structures of power. The chief demonstrates that political authority can be legitimated through an alternative modality, expressed by showcasing external social relations that link individuals, however precariously, to flows of global economic capital.

Chiefs do not agree about how to evaluate corporate sponsorship. In fact, tensions between chiefs and sponsors are growing. More chiefs have become publicly critical of sponsor participation in festival events, especially of the aggressive marketing tactics. Chiefs repeat the interchangeable notions of "traditional protocol" and "customary demands" again and again as a set of dictates about festival aesthetics that are constantly violated by sponsors and the chiefs who promote their brands. And dress is a readily identifiable way to police and participate in discourses of aesthetic legitimacy. At the same time, the increasing popularity of T-shirts with chiefs' images demonstrates how dress is used as a medium to resist sponsor impositions. Such T-shirts lighten the visual impact of corporate logos while reinscribing the space of the festival with distinctive forms of political affiliation.

NOTES

1. The research upon which this chapter is based was supported by a UCLA International Institute Global Impact Research Grant (2006), Northwestern University Hans E. Panofsky Summer Research Travel Grant (2009), Buffet Center for Summer Research Award (2009), and a Fulbright-Hays doctoral dissertation fellowship (2011).
2. The matrilineal Akan population in Ghana consists of several linguistically related groups including the Fante of Cape Coast. For more on the history and development of Akan political systems, see Allman (1993), McCaskie (1995), and Wilks (1975).
3. *Asafo* originated as military organizations with patrilineal membership and now function as social and political entities presiding over the installation of chiefs, festivals, and other community activities. For a discussion of the history and political organization of asafo companies, see Datta (1972), Ross (1979) and Labi (2002).

REFERENCES

Allman, Jean. 1993. *The Quills of the Porcupine.* Madison: University of Wisconsin Press.

Apter, Andrew. 2005. *The Pan-African Nation: Oil and the Spectacle of Culture in Nigeria.* Chicago: University of Chicago Press.

Arhin, Kwame. 1983. "Rank and Class Among the Asante and Fante in the Nineteenth Century." *Africa: Journal of the International African Institute* 53(1): 2–22.

Bickford, Kathleen. 1994. "The A.B.C's of Cloth and Politics in Cote d'Ivoire." *Africa Today* 41(2): 5–24.

Blankson, Samuel. 1974. *Fetu Afahye.* Cape Coast: University Press.

Calefato, Patrizia. 2006. "Fashion as a Sign System." In Jan Brand and Jose Teunissen, eds., *The Power of Fashion: About Design and Meaning,* 126–151. Warnsveld: Terra Uitgeverij.

Chalfin, Brenda. 2010. *Neoliberal Frontiers: An Ethnography of Sovereignty in West Africa.* Chicago: University of Chicago Press.

Coombs, Rosemary. 1996. "Embodied Trademarks: Mimesis and Alterity on American Commercial Frontiers." *Cultural Anthropology* 11(2): 202–224.

Datta, Ansu. 1972. "The Fante Asafo: A Re-examination." *Africa: Journal of the International African Institute* 42(4): 305–315.

Gilbert, Michelle. 1994. "Aesthetic Strategies: The Politics of a Royal Ritual." *Africa: Journal of the International African Institute* 64(1): 99–125.

Glass, Aaron. 2008. "Crests on Cotton: 'Souvenir' T-Shirts and the Materiality of Remembrance Among the Kwakw*aka*'wakw of British Columbia." *Museum Anthropology* 31(1): 1–18.

Hansen, Karen Tranberg. 2000. *Salaula: The World of Secondhand Clothing and Zambia*. Chicago: University of Chicago Press.

Kuchler, Suzanne, and Daniel Miller, eds. 2005. *Clothing as Material Culture*. Oxford: Berg.

Labi, Kwame. 2002. "Fante Asafo Flags of Abandze and Kormantse: A Discourse Between Rivals." *African Arts* 35(1): 28–37.

McCaskie, T. C. 1995. *State and Society in Pre-Colonial Asante*. New York: Cambridge University Press.

Oguaa Fetu Afahye Journal. 2004. Cape Coast: Nakrod Press.

Rathbone, Richard. 2000. *Nkrumah and the Chiefs: The Politics of Chieftaincy in Ghana, 1951–1960*. Athens: Ohio University Press.

Ross, Doran. 1979. *Fighting with Art: Appliqué Flags of the Fante Asafo*. Los Angeles: University of California Press.

Shipley, Jesse Weaver. 2004. "The Best Tradition Goes On: Audience Consumption and the Transformation of Popular Theatre in Neoliberal Ghana." In Brad Weiss, ed., *Producing African Futures: Ritual Reproduction in a Neoliberal Age*, 106–140. Leiden: Brill.

Wilks, Ivor. 1975. *Asante in the Nineteenth Century: The Structure and Evolution of a Political Order*. New York: Cambridge University Press.

PART II

Material Culture, Visual Recognition, and Display

–4–

Bazin Riche in Dakar, Senegal: Altered Inception, Use, and Wear

Kelly Kirby

In Senegal, *sañse,* a Wolof-French-Creole term, means "a total outfit of dress, hair, and jewelry" as a noun (Mustafa 2002: 189 fn. 6). Sañse, as a verb, means "to dress up" (Heath 1992: 1 fn.1). As an act of adornment sañse constructs and maintains social relationships through the embodiment of jewels and high-quality cloth. *Boubous* (loose fitting robes worn by both men and women), along with embellished *taille basse/ pagne* combinations (taille basse are fitted tops or blouses most often embellished on the front with embroidery, and pagnes are skirts or wraps), and *ndokets* (loose fitting dresses with flounced sleeves that are often embroidered) are the most preferred form of dress worn for sañse, the style of which was influenced by a postindependence Senegalese nationalist ideology that framed it as "traditional" African dress. In a deeper historical context, sañse is linked to Wolof notions of honor, discretion, and service. For example, reputation is not only based on what people have, but more so on what they have to give others (Heath 1992: 20–23). The social settings for sañse in Senegal are baptisms, religious ceremonies, marriages, and various other social events.

Since the 1980s, the most prominent textile used in the construction of sañse in Senegal has been *bazin riche*—a high-quality damask cotton cloth mass-produced in Europe exclusively for West African consumption. Bazin riche receives what Heath describes as an "overlay of tradition after it arrives in Africa" (1992: 21). What this means is that bolts of undyed bazin riche are converted and customized by African men and women in accordance with local aesthetic preferences once they reach Africa. Colors are manipulated through dyeing, textures are enhanced through starching and pounding, and constructed garments are often heavily adorned and embellished with embroidery, thus augmenting its quality and transforming it into public displays of social identity and wealth once it is assembled and worn as a garment. The wear and display of brilliantly colored, starched, and embroidered dress made of this particular textile has become increasingly fashionable over the last several years in Senegal, as well as in many other cities and towns across West Africa (Heath 1992; Rabine 2002; Schulz 2007).

Fashion thrives in Senegal despite decades of economic decline. After the postindependence political and economic success in the 1960s, countryside droughts during the 1970s caused significant peanut production decreases prompting expansive rural migrations to Dakar. Subsequently, during Abdou Diouf's presidency in the 1980s, World Bank IMF structural adjustment programs and the privatization of previously state-owned enterprises caused an extreme devaluation of the CFA franc, sharp increases in the cost of living in Senegal, and the breakdown of educational institutions and employment opportunities for the middle and lower classes (Diouf 1996). The country continues to struggle economically as a result of Senegal's previous president, Abdulaaye Wade, who followed a political agenda reminiscent of Diouf's (Ross 2008; Mustafa 2002). Hope resides, however, with the recent inauguration of a new President, Macky Sall. Even with these currently ongoing economic problems, fashion shines brightly in Dakar where many people from both younger and older generations invest substantial time, energy, and resources into looking stylish, sometimes beyond their financial means.

These investments in "looking good" have led anthropologists to examine the importance of this phenomenon as it relates to modesty, morality, sociality, display, and generation in Dakar. Hudita Mustafa suggests that an overwhelming embrace of fashion has been a collective response to the dire economic situations confronted by many people in Dakar (1998: 15). As such, dressing well is one way of coping with economic adversity in a "dignified manner" (Mustafa 2002: 190 fn.7). This is not to say that these circumstances incite only confinement, however, but that they frequently also cultivate innovation and creativity for both creators and wearers (Grabski 2009; Rabine 2002: 5). Moreover, for many married women and young adults whose husbands, fathers, and uncles have left the economically compromised country in search of work, dressing up has become a way of maintaining kin relations with those afar and those left behind. Urban identities are fueled and maintained through local kin networks, transnational circuits of exchange, and the innovative use, wear, and trade of clothing and accessories from other places (Buggenhagen 2001, 2003; Scheld 2003, 2007). In this chapter, I build on the extensive repertoire of literature on cloth and dress drawing from my own research carried out in Dakar during the summer of 2008. Research methods included participant observation and open-ended interviews.

In order to adequately pursue this endeavor, I begin first by establishing a foundational definition of dress, one that encompasses the production process, the end result, and the intent of the creators and wearers. Following Hansen, I use the term dress in this chapter to be inclusive of both cloth and clothing (2004: 371). I also build upon Barnes and Eicher's definition of dress as "an assemblage of body modifications and/or supplements displayed by a person in communicating with other human beings" (1992: 15; see also Hansen 2004; Schulz 2007). Explicit in this definition is the essential notion that dress is both individual and social, that it is "imbued with meaning understood by wearer and viewer" (Eicher and Roach-Higgins 1992: 15). But what role does the creator play in this process? I propose that, in the case of the production of bazin riche, embedded in this relationship are human intentions that contribute to the creation of dress and the enhancement of its value, ultimately influencing how individuals imagine themselves communicating with others. I draw from Georg Simmel's definition of fashion to make a final distinction between dress and fashion. Simmel suggests fashion is "a form of imitation and so of social equalization... The elite initiates a fashion and, when the mass imitates it in an effort to obliterate the external distinctions of class, abandons it for a newer mode" (1957: 541). Thus, according to Simmel, individuals have minimal freedom as adherents to fashion yet are liberated from having to make personal choices about what to wear (1957).

I investigate *fashion* in this chapter by building on the premise that dress holds meaning for *creator, wearer,* and *viewer.* Drawing from and building upon Alfred Gell's (1998) theory on the technology of enchantment and the enchantment of technology, I suggest that inquiry into fashion (the use and wear of dress), while often viewed as a process by which people emulate and incorporate other people's ideas, must also acknowledge that ideas originate from many sources. Therefore, I propose that an examination of the use and wear of bazin riche must consider "intent," not just of the wearer but also of the creator. It is intent in this context as it plays out through the processes of creation and embodiment, that I emphasize here. The chapter begins with an investigation of how bazin riche is produced. I describe the different qualities of bazin riche, along with the production processes—carried out by the hands and through the ideas of individuals—that augment its value. I suggest that hierarchies of display, price, and style of bazin riche throughout its creation and wear reflect hierarchies of social relations and of access. I conclude the chapter by proposing that the *intent* of the creator, wearer, and observer are critical constituents of the embodied experience of bazin riche.

BAZIN: TRANSFORMATIONS AND AUGMENTATIONS OF VALUE

Bazin, a machine-made damask textile, is mass-produced in Austria, Germany, and Asia exclusively for West African consumption. There are three broad categories of bazin along with several subcategories in Senegal: bazin riche and *Mali thioup* (also sometimes referred to as *thioup riche*), "*second quality,*" and *bazin ordinaire.* The major differences between the categories are determined by raw textile qualities, finishing processes, and price. The raw material of both bazin riche and Mali thioup is white/undyed machine-woven cotton of the finest quality damask produced in Austria and Germany. The price for one meter of white/undyed bazin riche is approximately 6,000 CFA francs per meter (US$12–13).[1] Bazin ordinaire, which is produced and dyed in various countries in Asia, is the lowest quality and least expensive. The subtle motifs of bazin ordinaire are less-intricately woven and the textile in general is lightweight with a lower thread count than higher quality bazin. Typically, after one washing it is worn out and any trace of sheen is no longer observable. Its cost is approximately 1,000 CFA francs (about US$2) per meter. The "second quality" bazin is produced and dyed in Austria and Germany, yet as its name implies, is higher quality than the bazin ordinaire because it is more durable and has more shine. While there are also subqualities available within this category, the more common of this second quality is described as "number one of number two," which translates to the best of second quality. "*Second quality*" can be purchased in the market for anywhere between 2,000 and 3,000 CFA francs per meter (US$4–6). Not all bazin ordinaire and "second quality" are dyed, however. White/undyed bazin ordinaire and "second quality" is available for sale in the market either to be worn as white or to be dyed locally.

The undyed bazin riche, while occasionally worn as is, has many steps to go before its ultimate transformation—every subsequent step in this finishing process augments its value, and thus the desirability of bazin riche. Both commercially dyed and hand-dyed cloth can be purchased at the market. While both the high-quality commercially dyed cloth and the locally hand-dyed cloth are very expensive, the hand-dyed cloth is said by many to be the most beautiful because of the dyers' artistic abilities to create multiple layers of rich resist-dyed colors and motifs in intricate compositions. The informal trade of dyeing in Senegal, once primarily women's work, has expanded significantly in Dakar since the 1980s to include both women and men in informal and commercial settings (Rabine 2002: 48). While the work of male and female bazin dyers in Dakar is greatly valued, most vendors, tailors, and designers I talked with in Dakar agreed that the highest quality of dyed bazin riche comes from both informal and commercial dyeing enterprises in Mali. A common explanation was that the tap water in Dakar is not good for dyeing because it does not allow complete pigment saturation, and laws in Senegal prohibit people from using river water for dyeing. By contrast, the tap water and river water in Mali is believed to be better for this. In Mali, dyeing in or close to the Niger River is not yet forbidden by Malian law; however, there is increasing awareness that dyeing as currently practiced is extremely polluting.

Gagny Lah, Boubacar Yara for Top Etoile, and Super Soleil are the three major commercial dyers in Bamako. Gagny Lah, a family-run business, produces the largest quantity of commercially dyed bazin riche in West Africa. Gagny Lah bazin riche is especially luminescent; its colors are solid yet deeply rich, complex, and brilliant. According to one tailor, "There is something special about the Gagny Lah, and you know it when you see it." It is considered by many to be the best quality available, and many high-profile Senegalese entertainers and politicians are customers. Not surprising, it is also the most expensive: one meter of the Gagny Lah costs approximately 7,500 CFA francs (US$15). Top Etoile and Super Soleil also produce high-quality solid colored bazin riche, and prices are likewise relatively expensive (7,000 CFA francs per meter or US$14). There is one commercial dyeing enterprise in Dakar known as Bazin Gestner. Guelewar Couture, a design house with two boutiques in posh locations of the city, claims exclusive rights to the Bazin Gestner label. Prices per meter start at approximately 7,000 CFA francs. The commercial dyeing enterprises in both Bamako and Dakar are run and maintained primarily by men.

While large quantities of bazin riche are dyed by men in a commercial capacity, women also participate actively in dyeing bazin riche in the informal economy. Women in Senegal and Mali have historically been associated with particular types of dyeing. Despite the rising popularity of commercially dyed bazin riche, women continue to run and organize successful dyeing businesses out of their homes. Prices per meter are equivalent to those mentioned above. These women are admired for their keen aptitude in creating rich colors and beautiful compositions on cloth and for their extraordinary execution of skills that have been passed down from mother to daughter. Many women dyers rely on their social and extended family networks to build clientele and maintain sales (Rabine 2002). Most of what is produced in this context is *thioup,* a Wolof term for hand-dyed bazin riche (L. Rabine, pers. comm.). Certain vendors at Sandaga Market and other markets in Dakar suggest that Mali thioup is "more traditional" than the bazin riche. Unlike the solid colors of bazin riche dyed commercially, the Mali thioup is typically resist dyed by hand to create multiple layers of colors and motifs (see Figure 4.1).

After dyeing is complete, the bazin riche must be starched and beaten. First, it is soaked in starch and left to dry in the sun. Then, the beating process, *la tappe,* done mostly by men, begins by placing the bazin riche on wooden planks, smearing it with wax, and beating it with wooden mallets until it becomes luminous (Rabine 2002: 51). Once the desired look and consistency are achieved, the bazin riche is folded and prepared for sale.

Figure 4.1 Transformation from solid *bazin riche* to *Mali thioup* and the levels of resist dyeing. This cloth was purchased at a market in Bamako. Photo by Kelly Kirby.

HIERARCHIES OF DISPLAY, PRICE, AND STYLE

The hierarchies of display, price, and styles of bazin riche reflect the social hierarchies of the people who buy it, or that the person who is wearing it wishes to send a message to others that he or she can afford to buy it. While one can purchase various qualities of bazin in the market, acquisition is most often contingent upon price or socioeconomic circumstances. People who lack economic resources yet have strong desires to attain some of the bazin riche for special occasions often depend on social or kin networks to get it (Rabine 2002).[2] Others, in turn, settle for a lower quality because after all, they are still wearing bazin (Heath 1992; Scheld 2007) (see Plate 4).

Bazin riche is available for sale in specialty fabric stores, boutiques, couture houses, and at the various market stalls in Dakar. Unlike most of the other textiles, like wax prints and bazin ordinaire, which are laid out in piles or hung on walls at open air markets, bazin riche is carefully displayed by vendors in glass cabinets. In general, the highest qualities with the most fashionable motifs and colors are stacked meticulously on eye-level shelves. It is important to note that when it comes to the use and wear of bazin riche, it is not the silhouette that changes very much, but rather color and embroidery motif that stand out as indices of innovative style. Popular colors from previous years are located either at the tops or bottoms of shelves and sold for a discounted price. The "second quality" will also sometimes be displayed in a cabinet if the vendor has more than one, and if not, it is folded, placed in plastic covering, and displayed elsewhere in the stall. Often the bazin ordinaire is displayed in stacks with no protective covering. Vendors always attempted to sell me the bazin riche first and would move on to trying to sell "number one of number two" only after I convinced them that I could not afford the bazin riche.[3] Most also said they refused to sell bazin ordinaire because it was not good. When bargaining enterprises were not progressing to a vendor's advantage, I was often told that my offering was only good enough to buy ordinaire, and the vendor would then show me some to highlight its lack of quality in comparison to other qualities.

Just as there are hierarchies of display, there are also hierarchies of price and style when it comes to clothing made with bazin riche. The cloth alone may cost anywhere from 30,000 to 75,000 CFA francs (US$60–150) before it is constructed into a garment. A client must find a tailor or couturier after purchasing the textile. Price tags of finished garments can vary anywhere between 30,000 to more than 300,000 CFA francs (US$60–600). At least 4 to 6 meters of cloth are needed to make *boubous, ndokets,* or *mariniere/pagne* outfit ensembles. In some cases, up to 10 meters are needed to make *grande boubous* or multiple pieces for interchangeable outfits. Most people take their cloth to tailors since only the wealthy can afford couturier prices.

There are thousands of tailors in Dakar, mostly men. The first male Senegalese tailors were trained to sew in French military hospitals and subsequently taught their male relatives through apprenticeship. Historically a male profession in Senegal, tailoring expanded enormously in the 1970s due to the large migrations of men to Dakar from rural settings. Female involvement in tailoring increased during the 1980s when stark rises in unemployment generated growth in the informal economy and fashion-related professions. Some young middle-class entrepreneurial women, according to Mustafa, "hired male tailors and relied on their social networks for financial support and clientele" (1998: 30), and eventually became increasingly active in the trading of cloth and the tailoring of clothing (see also Rabine 2002; Scheld 2007: 241). Some of these women have become very successful. Mariama, my key informant during my pre-dissertation fieldwork in Dakar, is one of these women.[4] Mariama, an upper-middle-class, university-educated woman who is married with three children, embarked on this enterprise ten years ago by borrowing start-up funds from her husband. Her best option was to seek out a profession that started off in the informal economy since the employment opportunities for educated men and women were scarce at the time in Dakar. She was determined to pursue this goal, first, because she grew weary of having to maintain family relations by constantly housing, hosting, entertaining, and accommodating continuous requests for things by extended family members. Because of her husband's success as a university professor and a government official, many of his family members from rural areas in Senegal would visit and stay for long periods of time. By working during the day, she would have less time to interact with them. Still a more pressing reason, according to Mariama, was that she wanted to be sure she could take care of herself and her children in the event "that something bad happened in her marriage."

Mariama owns and runs two shops. In the first she sells furniture and home décor, most of which is imported from China. Traveling to China twice yearly to choose and order merchandise for her shop, she purchases large pieces of furniture—sofas, tables, and armoires—along with smaller home decorating items such as paintings, artificial flowers, and vases. She also buys a huge stock of shoes and purses to sell in her tailor shop. She does not buy any bazin in China. Her tailor shop, located in a major market in Dakar, employs a female supervisor and ten male tailors who construct clothing made exclusively from bazin riche, specializing in women's clothing. Mariama describes her clientele as well-dressed, middle-age, upper-middle-class women and men. More than twelve mariniere/pagne combinations are displayed on the shop walls as samples for women to choose from, presenting the least expensive to most expensive from left to right. Prices of these outfits are contingent upon the quality of the bazin riche and the quantity and intensity of the embroidery and embellishment. Silhouettes of boubous made for men are most often modestly adorned with embroidery, and as such, there are no samples on the walls in the room of the shop where tailors construct clothing for men. Mariama almost never has clients bring her bazin ordinaire and the lowest quality her tailors work with is "number one of number two." Even so, the least expensive outfit combination that she sells is 30,000 CFA francs (US$60), and the most expensive can be between 70,000 and 80,000 CFA francs (US$140–160).

Clients typically make choices either from the samples on the wall, images in local fashion magazines, programs and performances on television, their own ideas, or through consultation with the manager. Mariama always buys the most current Senegalese fashion magazines so that customers can see the latest colors and styles local couturiers are working with, and she makes sure to emboss each one with her signature in permanent marker to decrease the possibility of mysterious loss. Mariama's team of tailors is superb at "knocking off" styles and embroidery design motifs. A typical interaction between a client and the manager in Mariama's shop proceeds as follows. After making her decision, a woman's measurements will be taken, and then she, along with Mariama and the manager, will decide on the shape of the shirt and the skirt, or dress. While the pattern pieces are being cut from the bazin riche, one tailor will draw the desired embroidery design freehand on a piece of tracing paper. From there, the tracing paper is pinned on the front center bodice, and subsequently, a sewing machine without thread is used to poke miniscule needle holes through it. Another tailor uses the small-hole pattern as a template and works the machine to complete the embroidery. Finally, pattern pieces are sewn together, and the finished garment is ironed before the client returns to pick it up (see Figure 4.2).

A great deal of energy and ingenuity is put forth in the making of these garments, and depending on the intricacy of the embroidery, the entire construction process in this shop can take anywhere from two to four hours. When it comes to choice of dress, clients are in many ways bound by obligations to choose styles in accordance with collective aesthetics, but they are also free from having to make these decisions on their own (Simmel 1950, 1957). Intent has many implications here, as it is through the client's description that the tailor must integrate his vision and technique in conjunction with replication.

A hierarchy of tailoring shops exists in the markets of Dakar. Many, like Mariama's, are located inside buildings, though they are open for passersby to look in and see the

Figure 4.2 Woman's top made from *bazin riche*, purchased in Mariama's. Photo by Kelly Kirby.

samples and to watch what the tailors are doing. Some shops, however, are enclosed behind glass doors in the back of market stalls that sell bazin riche. While these shops have some samples on display, they are not visible from the outside, and tailors do not allow anyone to see what they have unless they are confident that the potential client is serious about buying. This is due to the high prevalence of people appropriating the ideas of others and commissioning tailors, such as those employed by Mariama, who can make copies for less money. According to Grabski, "The emphasis on developing original designs also fosters intense competition among tailors, resulting in the need to 'hide' designs before they make their public appearance" (2009: 226). Managers and tailors in some of these shops allowed me to look at the samples on display but only very briefly, and they were not interested in talking about the garments once they realized I was not there to buy. The samples in these particular shops, often made of Gagny Lah, had exquisite embroidery, fine tailoring, and price tags starting at 300,000 CFA francs (US$600).

Like the tailors working in Mariama's shop, however, those who hide their designs behind closed doors must learn to strike a balance between intent, innovation, and locally established ideas about fashion and aesthetics. Creating the latest trend, in embroidery motif or color combination, for example, is a hefty burden. While the final product must be innovative enough for it to be considered appealing to many, it cannot expand too far outside from accepted tastes. Intent, as a process of negotiation, then comes to fruition once the garment is worn and displayed on the body.

THE EMBODIMENT OF DISPLAY

Garments constructed of bazin riche are imbued with life when worn on the dressed body. The ultimate display of bazin is attained when it embraces the skin of its wearer and turns into what Terence Turner refers to as social skin (1993 [1980]). The embodiment of display shapes both individual and social identities at once, influencing what it means to the self, what it means to everyone else, and how demeanor (Andrewes 2005) and self-representation in a social setting are interpreted by the individual and the other social participants in particular and often distinctive ways. Sañse, as an enacted public display of wealth, has been described by Heath to have a double meaning: that the woman "on display" is provided with the means, most often by a husband or a male suitor, to dress up, and also that she is independent enough to be able to present herself to others with confidence and class (Heath 1992: 24). Sañse, and the ways in which women use and present their bodies in the process, Mustafa suggests, is "the creation of an elegant and refined presentation of self" (2002: 175). During a performance commemorating Senegalese tradition at a prominent theater in Dakar, Mariama, some of her friends, and I discussed this negotiating of self that Mustafa is referring to. Several musicians performed that evening and the event lasted for more than five hours. Almost all audience members, mostly middle-aged men and women (older than thirty), were dressed in the finest bazin riche, forming a sea of splendid color—in clothing, in shining gold and in constant movement. Audience members, both men and women, recognized their favorite performers by rising from their seats, walking down the aisle, and giving gifts of money. This enactment of display was particularly dynamic in that the saunter to the stage and the handing over of the bills were mini-performances in their own rights (Askew 2002). Some people, handing over at times more than 40,000 CFA francs (US$80) to performers, seemed to be assessing the social situation and crafting a setting conducive to impressing people in a particular way (Goffman 1971: 14). Mariama and her friends told me that the gift givers might or might not have the means to hand over the cash; however, it is the satisfaction experienced by individuals through this act of display, my companions suggested, that affirms their sense of self to others, while simultaneously conveying their social status and wealth to everyone else. Mariama explained to me what several others told me subsequently: "Many people buy these outfits when they can't afford them. They borrow money from family and friends just to have the best. And then, they hand over money they do not have to performers. They give it all away, and will not even have enough to buy bread for their kids in the morning."

Such embodiments and social displays of bazin riche at social events, in circulated images, and in television performances are influential in distributing ideas about popular culture and fashion in Dakar (see Mustafa 1998). So popular are they, that people will sometimes explore and pursue a variety of means in order to obtain garments made with this highly sought-after textile. Faatu, a married Senegalese school teacher, responded with the following comment when I asked her about this: "Some women will do crazy stuff to have a very expensive bazin or other kind of cloth for a social event. They might borrow money, do 'mbaraan' [it is a kind of covert prostitution] or borrow the outfit from a friend or cousin." An unmarried school teacher, Fary, also suggested, "Many women, young and old, spend a lot of money on clothing be it on bazin riche or other fashionable clothes. They borrow a lot of money to buy cloth for ceremonies even when they know they will not be able to pay it back." Comments similar to these in reference to the fashion scene in Dakar emerged from young and middle-aged adults in almost every interview setting, thereby warranting further inquiry into the diversity of intent and implementation as it relates to young-adult dress in Dakar.[5]

CONCLUSION

Jean Allman (2004) and Karen Tranberg Hansen (2004) both suggest that high-end clothing in Africa has not yet received a great deal of scholarly attention. In this chapter, I have offered a glimpse into the use and wear of high-end fashion in Dakar. My observations about the inspirations in dress practice and display in Dakar serve to qualify Simmel's (1957) understanding of fashion in the sense that fashion trends in

Dakar, often introduced by tailors who cater to the wealthy and who through their transnational connections have achieved celebrity status, are reappropriated by the masses through the circulation of objects, images, and the media (Mustafa 1998). I suggest, however, that intent—intent of the observer, of the wearer, *and* of the creator—must be considered as an important component that contributes to augmented values related to the use and wear of bazin riche. In this context, then, what Simmel's perspective on fashion lacks is recognition that no one, not even the elite can "pay" for the gift of creativity. And therefore, rich or poor, "intent" and the ability to execute it is not always contingent upon socioeconomic status. What makes bazin riche especially interesting as a locus of study is its exceptional transnational trajectory from raw material to finished product and how each step of the finishing process enhances its value—and how so many people contribute to its trajectory. These processes, carried out in most cases by individual people, are in part influenced and inspired by collective ideas about fashion and aesthetics but also through skills and visions that only few possess. When considering the intent of certain individuals in this context, ideas become valuable commodities and hierarchies of access can be broken down through the fine art of knocking off. The construction processes of bazin riche highlight the ways in which each step of the finishing process contributes to the value of the dress and by extension to the value of the individual—the creator and the wearer (see also Renne and Maiwada 2007: 29 on the labor invested in embroidered robes in Zaria City, Nigeria).

A productive way of synthesizing ideas about production, value, and intent is illustrated through Alfred Gell's (1998) theory of artistic labor power, where the art object can be theorized both from the perspective of the artist or creator as well as from the admirer or customer. Gell suggests that artists often possess certain talents that not everyone shares. This ability to create magic captivates those who do not possess the skill, contributing to the object's value because people become bedazzled when they see something they know they cannot do. "It is the way in which an art object is construed as having come into the world which is the source of such power objects have over us—their becoming rather than their being," says Gell (1998: 166). Drawing from Bronislaw Malinowski's (1984 [1922]) ethnography on Trobriand Islanders' participation in the Kula exchange, Gell uses the making and use of meticulously crafted and ornately embellished prow boards and canoes to explore the issue of intentionality. He argues that the intent of the carver in the making of the prow board is to create something that will mesmerize onlookers and will cause them to "take leave of their senses and offer more valuable shells or necklaces to the members of the expedition than they would otherwise be inclined to do" (Gell 1998: 164–165). The magnificent prow board as a "psychological weapon" with magical powers exists as a product of the carvers/artists intent. In turn, its very ambience not only generates a more productive gift exchange through its captivating powers, but it also demonstrates that the canoe owner has access to the services of a skilled carver/artist (1998: 166).

The production process of bazin riche is a collaborative effort, where the technical and creative skills, born out of the producers' intents, contribute to its ultimate transformation. Value emanates from the garment in this context because of the thoughts, intentions, and executions that went into creating it. Eliminating one step of the process would totally change the lived in, moving, embodied experience of wearing. *Sañse* then, could not be what it is without the profound influences of all those involved in its inception: the dyers who are skilled at making vibrant colors, the *tappeurs* who pound the luminosity and crispness into the cloth, and the tailors who negotiate their own innovative skills in conjunction with locally established ideas about style. Like the Trobriand prow board carver, the dyer, the tappeur, and the tailor build upon each other's talents to collaborate in a process that fosters something magical; something magical that only plays out once the wearer embodies, lives in, and displays oneself in the piece. These very processes, then, become the crucial components of enabling people in Dakar to perform sañse on both an individual and collective level.

ACKNOWLEDGEMENTS

I am thankful for the support I received from the department of anthropology at the University of Michigan in order to carry out this ethnographic research. I especially thank Karen Tranberg Hansen and Soyini Madison, organizers of the Dress, Popular Culture, and Social Action Conference and editors for this book, for offering me an invitation to participate. I am grateful for Elisha Renne, Henrike Florusbosch, and Karen Tranberg Hansen for their helpful comments on earlier drafts.

NOTES

1. As of October 1, 2012, the U.S. dollar to CFA franc conversion rate is approximately 509.40 CFA francs to US$1.
2. Many people in Senegal and Mali participate in savings groups, ceremony circulations, and take loans in order to obtain these desirable goods (McNee 2000; Rabine 2002; Scheld 2007).
3. In recognizing that vendors are at the market to sell and make a profit on their product, I committed to buying one piece of cloth each time I interviewed a vendor. This allowed for a more extensive interview and also will contribute to a collection I have been building to use for comparative purposes during my current research.
4. In order to protect her identity, I have used a pseudonym.
5. With its long history as a destination that connects people, ideas, and thoughts, Dakar continues to be a junction where many additional extraordinary fashion endeavors are being carried out through the lived experiences of youth and young adults (see Scheld 2007: 235). One such venture, the vision of a young entrepreneurial designer, Adama Ndiaye, is Dakar Fashion Week, an international yearly event that features designers from all over the world. While outside the scope of this paper, is also part of my dissertation research.

REFERENCES

Allman, Jean. 2004. "Fashioning Africa: Power and Politic of Dress." In Jean Allman, ed., *Fashioning Africa: Power and Politics of Dress,* 1–10. Bloomington: Indiana University Press.

Andrewes, Janet. 2005. *Bodywork: Dress as Cultural Tool. Dress and Demeanor in the South of Senegal.* Leiden, The Netherlands: Kininklijke Brill NV.

Askew, Kelly. 2002. *Performing the Nation: Swahili Music and Cultural Politics in Tanzania.* Chicago: Chicago University Press.

Buggenhagen, Beth. 2001. "Prophets and Profits: Gendered and Generational Visions of Wealth and Value in Senegalese Murid Households." *Journal of Religion of Africa* 31(4): 373–401.

Buggenhagen, Beth. 2003. "At Home in the Black Atlantic: Circulation, Domesticity and Value in the Senegalese Murid Trade." PhD diss., University of Chicago.

Diouf, Mamadou. 1996. "Urban Youth and Senegalese Politics: Dakar 1988–1994." *Public Culture* 19: 225–249.

Eicher, Joanne B and Mary Ellen Roach-Higgins. 1992. "Definitions and Classification of Dress: Implications for Analysis of Gender Roles." In Ruth Barnes and Joanne Eicher, eds., *Dress and Gender: Making and Meaning,* 8–28. Oxford: Berg.

Gell, Alfred. 1998. "The Technology of Enchantment and the Enchantment of Technology." In Eric Hirsch, ed., *The Art of Anthropology: Essays and Diagrams,* 159–185. Oxford: Berg.

Goffman, Erving. 1971. *The Presentation of Self in Everyday Life.* London: Penguin.

Grabski, Joanna. 2009. "Making Fashion in the City: A Case Study of Tailors and Designers in Dakar, Senegal." *Fashion Theory: The Journal of Dress, Body & Culture* 13(2): 215–242.

Hansen, Karen Tranberg. 2004. "The World in Dress: Anthropological Perspectives on Clothing, Fashion and Culture." *Annual Review of Anthropology* 33: 369–392.

Heath, Deborah. 1992. "Fashion, Anti-Fashion, and Heteroglossia in Urban Senegal." *American Ethnologist* 19(2): 19–33.

Malinowski, Bronislaw. 1984 [1922]. *Argonauts of the Western Pacific: An Account of Native Enterprise and Adventure in the Archipelagoes of Melanesian New Guinea.* Prospect Heights, IL: Waveland Press.

McNee, Lisa. 2000. *Selfish Gifts: Senegalese Women's Autobiographical Discourses.* Albany: SUNY Press.

Mustafa, Hudita Nura. 1998. "Sartorial Ecumenes: African Styles in a Social and Economic Context." In E. Van der Plas and M. Willemsen, eds., *The Art of African Fashion,* 13–48. Trenton, NJ: Africa World Press.

Mustafa, Hudita. 2002. "Portraits of Modernity: Fashioning Selves in Dakarois Popular Photography. In Paul Landau and Deborah Kaspin, eds., *Images and Empires: Visuality in Colonial and Postcolonial Africa,* 172–192. Berkeley: University of California Press.

Rabine, Leslie. 2002. *The Global Circulation of African Fashion.* Oxford: Berg.

Renne, Elisha, and Salihu Maiwada. 2007. "New Technologies of Embroidered Robe Production and Changing Gender Roles in Zaria, Nigeria, 1950–2005." *Textile History* 38(1): 25–58.

Ross, Eric. 2008. *Culture and Customs in Senegal.* Westport, CT: Greenwood Press.

Scheld, Suzanne. 2003. "The City in a Shoe: Redefining Urban Africa through Sebago Footwear Consumption." *City & Society* 15(1): 109–130.

Scheld, Suzanne. 2007. "Youth Cosmopolitanism: Clothing, the City and Globalization in Dakar, Senegal." *City & Society* 19(2): 232–253.

Schulz, Dorothea E. 2007. “Competing Sartorial Assertions of Femininity and Muslim Identity in Mali.” *Fashion Theory* 11(2/3): 253–280.

Simmel, Georg. 1950. “Secrecy.” In Kurt H. Wolff, ed. and trans., *Sociology of Georg Simmel,* 330–344. Glencoe, IL: The Free Press.

Simmel, Georg. 1957. “Fashion.” *The American Journal of Sociology* 62(6): 541–558.

Turner, Terence. 1993 [1980]. The Social Skin. In C. B. Burroughs and J. Ehrenreich, eds., *Reading the Social Body,* 15–38. Iowa City: University of Iowa Press.

–5–

Fashioning People, Crafting Networks: Multiple Meanings in the Mauritanian Veil (*Malaḥfa*)

Katherine Wiley

This chapter considers the malaḥfa (Mauritanian veil), exploring the multiple meanings of this garment.[1] I examine how the malaḥfa at times represents, constructs, and displays women's religious and national identities and their engagement with global fashion. I argue that this garment both serves as a means for women to differentiate themselves from others, while it also can be a way through which shared identities and social networks are displayed and produced. Clothing, after all, is complicated. As Deborah Durham puts it, "Meaningful objects and experience like the Herero dress seem to me rather like quantum particles: shimmering in indeterminacy, alive with a perhaps endless range of possibility" (1999: 403).

This endless range of possibility can also lead to the misinterpretation of a wearer's intentions. That clothing can signify—and perhaps create (Masquelier 2009; Mahmood 2005; Miller 2005)—multiple identities suggests that its meaning is often ambiguous. The diverse fabrics, origins, and designs of malaḥfas can therefore be interpreted in varying ways by both wearers and viewers. Webb Keane (2005) has argued that objects are composed of "bundles" of qualities—an apple is not just red, but also spherical, light, sweet, and so on. Because of these multiple attributes, he contends that objects do not have a single intrinsic meaning, but rather that their meanings are "underdetermined." Attempts by the wearer to control the semiotic properties of her malaḥfa and thus how it is understood by others can be a challenging undertaking which may involve particular performances and discourse through which certain characteristics of the dress are highlighted.

The malaḥfa is a flexible garment composed of six yards of fabric that women first tie around their shoulders to form a tunic; they then drape the remaining cloth over their heads. Since it is not pinned into place, the malaḥfa often shifts as women move throughout their days and thus requires frequent readjustments. While malaḥfas share a common shape, they are available in a large variety of fabrics and are printed or dyed in a dizzying array of colors and patterns. They range from the somber (thick black cotton cloth) to the dazzling (cloth dyed in swirls of fluorescence), from the cheap (machine-dyed imported veils) to the luxurious (imported silk veils that cost over US$100), from the plain (solid-colored veils of a bright color) to the ornate (veils, created by women locally, that are hand-dyed and decorated with thousands of tiny circles and lines; see Figure 5.1). Many of these garments, both machine-printed and hand-dyed, are decorated with a vast variety of semiabstract patterns that are often named. The numerous patterns, many of which quickly move in and out of style, further differentiate wearers and can also signify various aspects of women's identities. As in the case of the vast variation of Muslim dress elsewhere (Sabbagh 1996; Göle 1996; Sandikci and Ger 2005; Watson 1994), the diversity of the malaḫfa makes it immediately clear that it is much more than a plain uniform that simply denotes the "Mauritanian Muslim woman." Analyzing the complexity of the malaḫfa is particularly important since public discourse in recent years surrounding garments like the burka has tended to reduce female Muslim dress to oppressive garments that restrict women's movements and well-being (Ayotte and Husain 2005).

This chapter draws upon research I conducted in the summers of 2008 and 2009 in three shops that were located in major markets in or near the center of the capital, Nouakchott. Like most Mauritanian shops, all of these boutiques were small, not much bigger than large walk-in closets. One of them exclusively sold hand-dyed malaḫfas,

Figure 5.1 *Malaḫfa* designer and seller wearing a hand-dyed *malaḫfa*. Photo by Katherine Wiley.

while the other two also stocked imported malaḥfas, purses, and shoes. In addition to discussions with shop owners, employees, and customers about the patterns and designs of these garments, I conducted interviews with other women and men about dress in Mauritania and drew from observations that I made while visiting other shops and women's homes and attending weddings.

My participants were drawn from the Bīẓān and Ḥarāṭīn ethnic groups, the vast majority of whom wear the malaḥfa. Although reliable census figures are unavailable, it is estimated that together these groups compose approximately 80 percent of Mauritania's population with the other 20 percent made up of West African groups such as Wolof and Pulaar people (Simard 1996). The Bīẓān are primarily descendants of Berbers and Arabs who, since well before Mauritania's independence in 1960, have dominated the country's economic and political scene. Typically assumed to be former slaves or descendants of slaves of the Bīẓān and generally of African descent, the Ḥarāṭīn share this group's language and dress. To avoid simplifying these categories of people, throughout this paper I try to be as specific as possible as to which group of persons (Bīẓān or Ḥarāṭīn) I am referring.

PIOUS INDIVIDUALS, MODEST MAURITANIANS

As Mauritanians are citizens of an Islamic Republic, Muslim identity is important to many of them. While the malaḥfa is considered to be an appropriate form of Muslim dress and the vast majority of Bīẓān and Ḥarāṭīn women wear one inside and outside of their homes, some women further emphasize their Muslim identities through their sartorial choices and how they wear this garment. I often found that women who spoke of themselves as being especially religious were careful to keep their veils tucked tightly around their faces and fully cover their arms, explaining that modesty is an important practice in their faith. Many women also frequently chided others if their malaḥfas slipped off of their heads or arms, particularly in public.

Certain kinds of malaḥfas were also associated with pious comportment. When purchasing (and wearing) malaḥfas, some women favored more opaque types, noting that displaying their bodies in more transparent versions violated their Muslim faith. One woman complained, for example, that women who wear thin, transparent malaḥfas that display the (often sparkly) clothing that they wear underneath violate the religious function of these garments. More opaque dress, in her view, shields the body from the gaze of others and thus helps ensure modesty. This insistence that covering the body in a particular way was essential to piety was not universally accepted; other women insisted that not only could they wear particular forms of European dress under their (transparent) malaḥfas and maintain their pious comportments, but also that these garments actually increased their modesty. One woman noted that wearing tight long-sleeved shirts under malaḥfas has become popular in recent years partly because they ensure that women's arms will remain covered if their veils shift. Another man argued that women wearing pants beneath their malaḥfas—a growing trend especially among young women in Nouakchott—helps keep their legs covered, unlike skirts or dresses which may blow up in the wind revealing a calf or ankle. This is an interesting example of Western dress being interpreted in local ways. The malaḥfa, then, provides women with a means of creating a modest presentation in varied, personalized manners. But the multiple ways in which this dress can be interpreted means that women often need to explain or defend their choices to ensure that others understand their intentions.

While malaḥfas contribute to the construction of women's personal pious identities, this veil has also explicitly been linked with Bīẓān and Ḥarāṭīn culture and Mauritania's identity as a Muslim nation. Indeed from the French in the colonial period to more recent presidents, the country's leadership has frequently called upon Islam as a (perhaps the) unifying factor in this ethnically diverse nation (Robinson 2000; Gerteiny 1971). The appearance of a malaḥfa-clad woman on Mauritania's website[2] highlights the connection between this garment and national and religious identity. The introduction of alternative Muslim dress in the capital's markets, especially the *abāya,* an opaque, black robe that is worn in Saudi Arabia and other parts of the Middle East, has triggered discussions of what constitutes appropriate "Muslim" and "Mauritanian" dress (see Figure 5.2).

Figure 5.2 Abāyas for sale in Nouakchott's Marché Capitale. Photo by Katherine Wiley.

Aichetou, a Mauritanian woman with whom I spoke, noted that she would not purchase an abāya since wearing the malaḥfa is a way to be dressed "in a religious way that's part of our culture." For her, the malaḥfa had a symbolic importance; it represented both her faith and her nationality and thus marked (and connected) those who wore it as Mauritanian citizens.

There is also a sense that the malaḥfa's shape and form make it particularly well-suited for wearing in Mauritania. Women emphasized that it is a cool garment that is comfortable in the often scorching Sahara heat, and some women felt that the flexible nature of the veil made it an impractical garment for wear outside of their country. One woman, for example, told me that her husband, who was working in Spain, had instructed her to purchase an abāya for her upcoming trip to visit him. He argued that the malaḥfa is inconvenient for train travel, particularly boarding or disembarkment. While she had purchased an abāya and tried it on in my presence to get my opinion, she said that she did not feel comfortable wearing it and might put on a malaḥfa over it. The same woman gave me another example of how the malaḥfa can be impractical abroad. When she was traveling in Las Palmas with some other Mauritanian women, one of their malaḥfas caught on a restaurant's table knocking over several glasses and causing much embarrassment. There seems, then, to be literally some sense that the malaḥfa not only can represent Mauritanian identity, but that it also functions best in the particular Mauritanian context.

Aside from the malaḥfa's distinctly Mauritanian shape, many of the popular motifs that recur on hand-dyed veils often incorporate designs that are named for objects from this culture such as the *ouguiya* (the Mauritanian currency, also denoted as UM[3]), a circle that is roughly the size of a coin, and the *kās* (cup), a larger circle representing one of the small glasses from which most Mauritanians drink tea several times a day. Patterns like the ouguiya and the kās are frequently combined with other elements to create larger designs which are given different names. That these motifs signify Mauritanian material culture also links this dress to a shared national identity and culture (see Figure 5.3).

Likewise, in 2008, hand-dyed veil designs often referenced national news events, Mauritanian celebrities, or other aspects of life in this desert nation. Such patterns included the Messould, which was named after the Ḥarāṭīn president of parliament who would be the runner-up in the 2009 presidential elections; the *enveloppe* (envelope), which was related to the Mauritanian voting process; and the *mujlis 'askarī* (military council), which was released after the 2005 coup that disposed of Maaouya Ould Sid'Ahmed Taya, who had ruled Mauritania as a semi-dictator for over twenty years. Although these designs are new, it is interesting to note that Aline Tauzin also recorded political themes in malaḥfas' patterns in the 1980s including the *ceinture de Haidallah* (belt of Haidallah, the president who was in office during this period, 1985–6). Likewise, Mauritanian celebrities were often the subject of veil names. One design, which was called the *al-qlāda Dimi* (Dimi's necklace), was inspired by the jewelry of an extremely popular Mauritanian singer.

Figure 5.3 Women holding a hand-dyed *malaḥfa*. Photo by Katherine Wiley.

Its imagery (the ouguiya, the kās) explicitly establishes the malaḥfa as a national symbol, while the tremendous assortment of available designs means that there is plenty of variation for personal self-expression. Likewise, designing and sewing a veil can be viewed as a particularly individual, expressive pursuit. When she learned that I had seen a malaḥfa in another part of town that was named for the female lead in a popular Turkish soap opera (*Nūr*), a young woman who worked at a shop and who also sewed patterns into undyed veils to earn extra income proclaimed that "that is just for promotion." She proceeded to draw a design of her own unique Nūr veil which she said she might produce. Which patterns are absent is also meaningful; one woman emphatically pronounced that she would not create an Abdel Aziz (the man who overthrew the democratically elected president in the summer of 2008 and was later elected president himself in 2009) design because she did not approve of his participation in a military coup. Tauzin suggests that the hand-dyed veils were popular from the start not only because they were made of a fabric that was more durable than the imported versions, but also because the small-scale level of production meant that local designers and dyers could make rapid changes in their patterns and colors in relation to demand

(1985–6). While the malaḥfa connects women as Muslim and Mauritanian through its shared form and connotations with Islam, the variety of fabrics and patterns and the multiple ways in which it can be worn also provide wearers with a way to play with these meanings and make them their own.

FASHIONABLE WOMEN, GLOBAL WOMEN

In her examination of dress in Botswana, Durham untangles some of the complexity of Herero dress, which is "simultaneously a static icon of cultural identity and also a dynamic enactment of so-called transnational cultural flows" (1999: 390). Like Herero dress, which both serves as a symbol of ethnic identity and incorporates elements from Europe and other parts of Africa, the malaḥfa not only speaks to national identities, but it also incorporates transnational elements and provides women with a palette with which they can personalize it. In recent years, Mauritanians have had increasing access to television programs, magazines, and movies from around the world, which, as Tauzin (2007) has demonstrated, has contributed to the construction of feminine identity by exposing women to foreign styles, bodies, and trends in fashion. She argues that, while women have not rejected the malaḥfa in the period since independence in 1960, some Bīẓān women of younger generations have expressed their individuality by developing a thinner body type than their mothers' generation (fatness has historically been the preferred female build in Mauritania), embracing an ever-widening array of hairstyles, and adopting nail polish, makeup, and even new ways of sitting and moving (Tauzin 2007).

Today, many of the most popular clothing and accessories in Nouakchott are imported, as evidenced in 2008 by shops and boutiques with names indexing Europe or America—"Las Vegas Shoping [sic]," "Paris Lux," and "Salon Dallas"—and by shoppers' concerns with the origins of the items for sale, many of which, particularly dresses, shoes, and purses, often hailed from France, Italy, Dubai, and China. When shopping, it was common for women to first inquire about the origins of goods and then make quick judgments about these products based upon where they came from, noting, for example, that Italian shoes were of better quality than shoes from Dubai.

Imported clothing and accessories in this region are nothing new; cloth from both the south and the north has circulated throughout the trans-Saharan trade routes for centuries (Lydon 2009). Likewise, Europeans were involved in the textile trade in northwest Africa from at least the fifteenth century (Steiner 1985). The cloth trade was not unidirectional; Europeans imported African cloth as well (Curtin 1975). Today, the variety of items that are available in Mauritania has greatly expanded as have the many images of world fashion that Mauritanians view on television and the Internet. This increase in products is reflected in the malaḥfa itself. Although it retains its form, it is now available in a wide array of fabrics. Prior to independence, most cloth was imported, although some textiles were produced locally. At that time, the majority of Bīẓān and Ḥarāṭīn women wore an opaque veil, known as the *guinée,* that was dyed with indigo; the guinée served as a major form of currency in the region throughout the eighteenth and nineteenth centuries (Tauzin 1985–6; Curtin 1975).

In the 1960s, imported patterned cotton *gāz* or *hawza* veils were introduced, followed in the late 1970s with bolts of fabric including *kanebo* which came from Japan (Tauzin 2007). By the summer of 2008, Nouakchott's markets offered a staggering selection of malaḥfas. Kanebo and gāz veils were still widely available with the latter continuing to be popular largely because of its durability and low cost (between 800 and 1,500UM or US$3 to US$7). Other qualities of imported veils had also appeared on the market including the *sois* (silk) version which, as the most expensive, may cost more than 50,000UM or US$222. These imported veils came in a rainbow of colors and an immense variety of patterns, some of which were copies of the locally produced, hand-dyed veils (see Plate 5).

Since many Bīẓān and Ḥarāṭīn women today are extremely knowledgeable about the origins and qualities of malaḥfas, the foreign sources of many of the accessories and veils that women wear mark the women as global citizens who participate in world fashion. Women, for example, noted that the specific malaḥfa that was popular at a given time was often connected to "*la mode*"—whichever fashion was in style both inside and outside of Mauritania. A middle-age Bīẓān woman, Fatima, told me that she brought two veils and a pair of shoes as a gift when a cousin recently got married. One of the bride's friends was particularly excited with her choice of a red veil because, unbeknownst to the buyer, red was currently in fashion in Mauritania—it was "the color of the year." Wearing the "most fashionable" malaḥfa can mark a woman as fashion-savvy and chic, just as it also connects her to other women who are equally concerned with trends. Beyond what is in vogue for dress in Mauritania, Fatima noted that dress also shifts with changes in greater global fashion. She described worldwide fashion as generally becoming more "decent" after the short skirts of the 1960s, arguing that women across the globe are beginning to see themselves as more than just sexy. She said that this trend is manifested in Mauritania through women's growing attention to wearing long sleeves beneath the malaḥfa and to avoiding transparent veils. She described how, when confronted with old photos of herself in thin veils, she asks, "How could I put that on? I was half-naked." Her comments again indicate that dress can be interpreted in varying ways. While Mariam explicitly had connected long sleeves with pious comportment, Fatima viewed this shift in dress as linked to growing female empowerment worldwide. Their comments also demonstrate that, while the malaḥfa may be a symbol of national identity, its origins and links to fashion elsewhere are powerful symbols of global connections (see Plate 5).

Likewise, while the Mauritanian motifs in the veils that I described helped signal women's national identities, these hand-dyed malaḥfas were available in a range of styles that often indexed women's contemporary, global experiences. The Nūr that I mentioned previously referred to the female star of a Turkish soap opera that was popular in Nouakchott at that time, while in 2009 the Obama malaḥfa referenced the president of the United States, who was very popular abroad. Other patterns indexed contemporary objects such as the *parabole* (satellite dish) and the *pantalon* (pants), a garment that had begun to gain popularity among young women in the capital. This tremendous variety of malaḥfas enables women to dress in distinct, unique ways that signify particular interests or orientations and join them to others who dress similarly.

CREATING PERSONALIZED IDENTITIES, FASHIONING GROUPS

The number of women who select a malaḥfa for its aesthetic appeal (women often discuss which colors complement particular skin tones) or its practical purposes (women debate which type of fabric is more durable or coolest in the desert climate) must not be underestimated; however, whether or not women consciously select veils based upon their patterns, the semiotics of these garments speak to particular orientations and identities—for example, political (the Messould), modern (the satellite dish), or explicitly Mauritanian (the ouguiya). It is interesting to note that men's *darrā'as*—the flowing robes that Bīẓān and Ḥarāṭīn men often wear—show similar variations. Like the malaḥfa, the range of colors and fabrics in which these garments are available have increased in recent years, and the intricate patterns of embroidery that surround the necklines are named and rapidly go in and out of fashion. The many patterns available on the hand-dyed malaḥfas or the embroidered darrā'as provide women and men with a vehicle through which they can express their individuality, including their engagement with modernity, politics, and popular culture as they literally wrap themselves in these images, the cloth serving as "a kind of symbolic skin" (Weiner 1992).

The malaḥfa's ability to contribute to individual identity formation reflects the value that Bīẓān society places on women's self-expression. Gisèle Simard (1996) has argued that the Bīẓān woman is valorized socially not through her maternity, but rather through her ability to be *shabība*—someone who can attract others through the power of her beauty, looks, and words; this is similar to the Senegalese notion of *sañse* (Heath 1992; Buggenhagen 2004). People often commented on women who dressed well, which involved not only donning beautiful veils, but also creating distinctive looks that often included intricate color combinations of shoes, purses, jewelry, and makeup. Women were also complimented when demonstrating a talent for verbal wit. Tauzin (1990, 2001) traces how this notion of female power is frequently repeated in Mauritanian literature and how, in recent years, women have begun to express it through a particular form of poetry. Indeed, Mauritanian women have long occupied a relatively privileged position as compared to their counterparts across the Arab world (Simard 1996; Lydon 2009). Bīẓān culture has allowed women a moderate degree of freedom, and many women assume the right to speak their minds in public, demand monogamous marriage, act as heads of household, control their income, initiate divorce, and circulate freely outside of the home (Simard 1996; Tauzin 2001). Simard (1996) attributes this power to residues of the matrilineal society that was practiced by the Bīẓān's Berber ancestors and to the fact that, since Mauritania has historically been a center of Islamic learning, individuals there may claim more liberal understandings of the Qur'an.

Many women (and men) with whom I spoke emphasized the relatively privileged position that women occupy today in Mauritania, although they often made distinctions about which categories of persons enjoyed this freedom, at times arguing that it was unevenly distributed between different ethnic groups or castes. On a household level, female autonomy has increased in recent years as more women are working outside of the home and acting as heads of household due in part to the economic difficulties the country has faced, stemming from the structural adjustment programs of the 1980s and 1990s, and, most recently, the global economic crisis (Secrétariat d'Etat à la Condition Féminine n.d.; Ould-Mey 1996). These difficulties have been exacerbated by the challenging ecologic conditions the country has experienced over the past decade as a result of drought and locust invasions. Although it is important not to romanticize women's position in Mauritania, in recent years women have also become more visible on the national political level.[4] The enactment of a 2007 quota that required that women hold 20 percent of elected positions and the appointment of six female ministers after the August 2009 presidential elections, including al-Naha Bint Miknass to the post of foreign minister, further inserted them on the national (and international) stage.[5] Likewise, in a southern Mauritanian town I visited during the summer of 2009, women played major leadership roles in the presidential campaigns, organizing political meetings and canvassing for their candidates.

The process of constructing unique personas who are shabība is partially enacted through dress. Although some of the hand-dyed malaḥfa's patterns such as the satellite dish become so popular that they are widely copied and available in multiple boutiques, the small-scale nature of production means that some designs are only available in a particular shop or must be custom ordered. This wide diversity of patterns suggests that they can index the wearer's uniqueness and ability to put together distinctive looks. This can also be true with the imported veils, which now come in a vast array of colors, fabrics, and designs.

While individual identity is an important part of Bīẓān culture, the notion of social solidarity remains a significant value as well and is also reflected in the malaḥfa. Simard (1996) has argued that the *qabīla* (tribe) endures as the principal group of affiliation and social identity in Mauritania, with its members linked by a common ancestor, rules of solidarity, and shared objectives. Timothy Cleaveland (2002) rightly complicates the meaning of this term in the Mauritanian context, arguing that qabīla does not signify a "primitive" static social organization, but rather captures complex, dynamic social relations. This term continues to be widely employed today, with people frequently discussing, for example, the qabīla of elected officials. Beyond the qabīla, Mauritanians often speak of their social obligations to provide for their immediate and extended families if it is within their means. Refusing to give is considered to be a serious character flaw, illustrated by the many words in Hassāniyya for stingy (*mḥaylī, mraykhīs, markhūs*). Likewise, being called *mạalūm* (generous) is high praise and the gifts that one has given are frequently discussed with and displayed before others. Helping and maintaining ties with friends and relatives, then, remains an important part of life in both urban and rural

Mauritania as it does in many other parts of West Africa (see Cooper 1997; Masquelier 2009; Buggenhagen 2004). Mauritanian women often draw upon their social networks in order to gather the money to buy malaḥfas for themselves (or others). When they acquire such funds, women often announce it, for example, by telling friends the amount of money that a male relative gave them to purchase a malaḥfa for a holiday. Obtaining and wearing veils, and speaking about how these garments were acquired, serve women to reaffirm and construct social networks and to make their connections public.

Wearing identical malaḥfas emphasizes the wearers' shared identities. At a wedding I attended on the outskirts of Nouakchott, for example, the young female friends of the bride wore matching dark-green, hand-dyed veils decorated with complicated patterns. Their coordinated malaḥfas marked them as members of the bride's *ʿunṣur* (age-group, closest group of friends) and therefore as important participants at the celebration. Likewise, weddings are moments when veil distribution can designate a family's social group. In addition to transferring a dowry to the bride's family, the groom's family distributes malaḥfas. These veils in turn are gifted to family and friends, identifying and visibly marking the social network of the bride's family, both through this distribution and also the wearing of these malaḥfas during subsequent parts of the wedding ceremony.

The consumption process reproduces social ties. Purchasing a veil can be a long affair involving frequenting the shops of friends and acquaintances and much drinking of tea and chatting before any purchase is made. Women often buy malaḥfas from friends or clients (people whom they have consistently bought from in the past). Malaḥfa sellers often admonish their acquaintances for not frequenting their boutiques, demonstrating the expectation that women should support friends and family as they shop.

Mauritanian Bīẓān women negotiate between a position of solidarity with their families and friends and a position in which much of their social capital is a result of their abilities to construct themselves as beautiful, and subsequently powerful, women. The malaḥfa unites these two aspects of what it means to be a successful female member of Bīẓān society by simultaneously providing women with a shared dress silhouette and a subsequent reaffirmation of unity while also allowing them to express individual preferences through its unique patterns. The expanding varieties of darrāʿa that are now available suggest that male Mauritanian fashion might be developing along parallel lines.

CONCLUSION: ARE WE WHAT WE WEAR? BUNDLED IDENTITIES IN DRESS

This chapter has demonstrated the rich meanings that malaḥfa wearers tap into in varying combinations: it is a Muslim garment, a cosmopolitan outfit, and a way to mark social solidarity or assert uniqueness. While not discounting that aesthetics, practical considerations such as cost, and their own personal preferences influence what women wear, the malaḥfa reflects the political and economic context of its wearer. Dressing in patterns that are named after government leaders shows an engagement with politics, just as clothing oneself in the ouguiya speaks to the realities that women face living in increasingly difficult economic circumstances. How malaḥfas are exchanged and consumed helps create and display wearers' social networks, just as this garment contributes to identity formation, allowing people to situate themselves and others and serving as a means through which women constitute their worlds. But this web of possibilities and functions also suggests that each veil's "underdetermined" nature can lead to multiple conflicting interpretations of its meanings.

Keane (2005) argues that objects are characterized by many different attributes—an apple is round, red, sweet, and so on; multiple interpretations and semiotic principles are inherent in objects themselves. This polyvalency indicates that the meanings of objects can be destabilized, just as new objects can introduce new meanings (2005: 191, 193). Meanings of dress are therefore ambiguous. Once the wearer enters the public sphere, she cannot control how others may interpret and understand her sartorial choices. The fact that a woman's malaḥfa, with its multiple qualities, is subject to the gaze of others makes it possible for viewers to misunderstand and misinterpret her intentions. A particular malaḥfa might have the potential to signify a woman's economic status, political leanings, connections to global fashion, color preferences, pious nature, and so on. The Obama malaḥfa could display a woman's interest in politics or in the United States. It could exhibit her conception of her racial identity (in 2009, many Ḥarāṭīn women, for example, told me that Obama was "black like me"). It could demonstrate that she finds Obama (or the pattern) attractive or simply illustrate her knowledge of the newest fashion trends. It may do several of the above.

Given these challenges, trying to ensure a particular "reading" of dress becomes, in effect, a performance. The malaḥfa is not necessarily viewed as a pious garment (compared to the abāya); women have to emphasize this quality through their discursive practices and their comportment while wearing it. For example, when showing me an expensive silk veil in her collection, one middle-aged Bīẓān woman emphasized that it had been given to her before she left on a pilgrimage to Mecca. By providing this context, she drew attention to this garment as a pious object, highlighting its connection with her pilgrimage. So while the multiple designs, origins, and fabrics of the malaḥfa provide women with a wide palate of sartorial choices, the many qualities that are embedded in these garments also mean that women must expend effort if they wish to influence how others understand their dress. Controlling meaning is not a simple process; however, the numerous types and designs of malaḥfas that continue to be available in Nouakchott's markets suggest that it is one in which Mauritanian women seek to engage.

ACKNOWLEDGEMENTS

I would like to thank the Project on African Expressive Traditions at Indiana University, the West African Research Association, and the Social Science Research Council with funds from the Andrew W. Mellon Foundation for providing the financial support that allowed me to conduct this research in Mauritania. Special thanks as well to the participants of the conference on Dress, Popular Culture, and Social Action in Africa, especially the respondents to this paper, Queen Meccasia Earth Zabriskie and Melissa Minor, as well as Adeline Masquelier, Misty Bastian, and Dorothea Schultz for their helpful suggestions. Other helpful readers were Monica Foote, Sarah Gordon, and Clark Sage. The feedback from Karen Tranberg Hansen, D. Soyini Madison, and an anonymous reviewer greatly shaped this chapter, as did feedback from Beth Buggenhagen and Gracia Clark, who read earlier versions. I would also like to thank all the Mauritanian women and men who guided and taught me during this project.

NOTES

1. I have followed the guidelines from the International Journal of Middle Eastern Studies for Arabic transliteration. See http://web.gc.cuny.edu/ijmes/docs/TransChart.pdf.
2. See http://www.mauritania.mr/fr/index.php. Note that the notion of the veil as being tied to Mauritanian identity is problematic since at least 20 percent of the country's population (including Pulaar, Wolof, and Soninke) do not wear this garment.
3. The Mauritanian currency is the ouguiya (UM). In 2008, US$1 was worth 225UM.
4. Women's political participation and access to the formal sector has been and remains limited when compared to men's. Despite the 2007 quota (see note 5), men continue to outnumber women in local and national elected positions and many Mauritanians question the abilities of women who do hold office. Although many people spoke to me of the power and autonomy that Mauritanian women enjoy, many others criticized past president Abdellahi's wife for being too involved in his government. Indeed, people whom I spoke with often justified their support for the 2008 coup, which overthrew Abdellahi, by citing the rumors that his wife had embezzled funds through her nongovernmental organization and arguing that her powerful position signaled President Abdellahi's own weakness and inability to head the government.
5. See Bios Diallo for a discussion of the 2007 quota, "Des femmes et des quotas," jeuneafrique.com, http://www.jeuneafrique.com/jeune_afrique/article_jeune_afrique.asp?art_cle=LIN19116desfesatouq0 (accessed November 19, 2008). For a discussion of female ministers in Mauritania, see "Female Ministers in Mauritania a Good Sign," *The National*, August 19, 2009, http://www.thenational.ae/apps/pbcs.dll/article?AID=/20090818/OPINION/708179888/1126/rss (accessed September 20, 2009).

REFERENCES

Ayotte, Kevin J., and Mary E. Husain. 2005. "Securing Afghan Women: Neocolonialism, Epistemic Violence, and the Rhetoric of the Veil." *NWSA Journal* 17(3): 112–133.

Buggenhagen, Beth Anne. 2004. "Domestic Object(ion)s: The Senegalese Murid Trade Diaspora and the Politics of Marriage Payments, Love, and State Privatization." In Brad Weiss, ed., *Producing African Futures: Ritual and Reproduction in a Neoliberal Age*, 21–53. Boston: Brill.

Cleaveland, Timothy. 2002. *Becoming Walāta: a History of Saharan Social Formation and Transformation.* Portsmouth, NH: Heinemann.

Cooper, Barbara M. 1997. *Marriage in Maradi: Gender and Culture in a Hausa Society in Niger, 1900–1989.* Portsmouth, NH: Heinemann.

Curtin, Philip D. 1975. *Economic Change in Precolonial Africa: Senegambia in the Era of the Slave Trade.* Madison, WI: University of Wisconsin Press.

Durham, Deborah. 1999. "The Predicament of Dress: Polyvalency and the Ironies of Cultural Identity." *American Ethnologist* 26(2): 389–411.

Gerteiny, Alfred G. 1971. "Islamic Influences on Politics in Mauritania." In Daniel F. McCall and Norman R. Bennett, eds., *Aspects of West African Islam,* 209–223. Boston: African Studies Center, Boston University.

Göle, Nilüfer. 1996. *The Forbidden Modern: Civilization and Veiling.* Ann Arbor: University of Michigan Press.

Heath, Deborah. 1992. "Fashion, Anti-Fashion, and Heteroglossia in Urban Senegal." *American Ethnologist* 19(1): 19–33.

Keane, Webb. 2005. "Signs Are Not the Garb of Meaning: On the Social Analysis of Material Things." In Daniel Miller, ed., *Materiality,* 182–205. Durham, NC: Duke University Press.

Lydon, Ghislaine. 2009. *On Trans-Saharan Trails: Islamic Law, Trade Networks, and Cross-Cultural Exchange in Western Africa.* New York: Cambridge University Press.

Mahmood, Saba. 2005. *Politics of Piety: The Islamic Revival and the Feminist Subject.* Princeton, NJ: Princeton University Press.

Masquelier, Adeline Marie. 2009. *Women and Islamic Revival in a West African Town.* Bloomington: Indiana University Press.

Miller, Daniel. 2005. "Materiality: An Introduction." In Daniel Miller, ed., *Materiality,* 1–50. Durham, NC: Duke University Press.

Ould-Mey, Mohameden. 1996. *Global Restructuring and Peripheral States: The Carrot and the Stick in Mauritania.* Lanham, MD: Littlefield Adams Books.

Robinson, David. 2000. *Paths of Accommodation: Muslim Societies and French Colonial Authorities in Senegal and Mauritania, 1880–1920.* Athens: Ohio University Press.

Sabbagh, Suha. 1996. "Introduction: The Debate on Arab Women." In Suha Sabbagh, ed., *Arab Women: Between Defiance and Restraint,* xi–xxvii. New York: Olive Branch Press.

Sandikci, Özlem, and Güliz Ger. 2005. "Aesthetics, Ethics and Politics of the Turkish Headscarf." In Susanne Küchler and Daniel Miller, eds., *Clothing as Material Culture,* 61–82. New York: Berg.

Secrétariat d'Etat à la Condition Féminine. n.d. "Stratégie Nationale de Promotion Féminine, 2005–2008." Mauritania.

Simard, Gisèle. 1996. *Petites Commerçantes de Mauritanie: Voiles, Perles et Henné.* Paris: Karthala.

Steiner, Christopher B. 1985. "Another Image of Africa: Toward an Ethnohistory of European Cloth Marketed in West Africa, 1873–1960." *Ethnohistory* 32(2): 91–110.

Tauzin, Aline. 1985–6. "Des couleurs et des voiles: Pratique de la teinture chez les Maures à Nouakchott (Mauritanie)." *Littérature Orale Arabo-Berbère* 16–17: 79–100.

Tauzin, Aline. 1990. "A haute voix. Poésie féminine contemporaine en Mauritanie." In Pierre Robert Baduel, ed., *Mauritanie: entre arabité et africanité,* 178–187. Aix-en Provence: Editions EDISUD.

Tauzin, Aline. 2001. *Figures du Féminin dans la Société Maure (Mauritanie).* Paris: Karthala.

Tauzin, Aline. 2007. "Women of Mauritania: Cathodic Images and Presentation of the Self." *Visual Anthropology* 20: 3–18.

Watson, Helen. 1994. "Women and the Veil: Personal Responses to Global Process." In Akbar S. Ahmed and Hastings Donnan, eds., *Islam, Globalization and Postmodernity*, 141–159. New York: Routledge.

Weiner, Annette B. 1992. *Inalienable Possessions: The Paradox of Keeping-While-Giving*. Berkeley: University of California Press.

–6–

The *Hijab* as Moral Space in Northern Nigeria

Elisha P. Renne

> Seductibility and seduction; evil and guilt are only one end of the moral scale which connects them . . . to the good and the pure.
>
> —Georg Simmel (1997: 134)

Wearing the *hijab*—a tailored garment that covers the head and body but not the face (Figure 6.1)—reflects the particular history of Islam in northern Nigeria, as well as the relations of Muslim Hausa women and men with Islam globally and with the West. Hausa Muslim women who wear the hijab may be seen, depending on the viewer's perspective, as devout and modest followers of Islam, as subordinated women forced to hide their bodies and sexuality, or as threatening beings whose presence challenges democratic, secular ideals. This chapter considers these different meanings of the hijab in the northern Nigeria area of Zaria, where the hijab suggests both the social action and the subordination of women. MacLeod (1992: 534) has described this contradictory situation in Cairo, Egypt, as "accommodating protest," where Muslim women are active participants in social life while they also accept gendered, social constraints. While many Muslim women in Zaria, but not all, see wearing the hijab as their choice as proper Muslim women, they also note that wearing the hijab enables them to negotiate public space without fear of sexual harassment. I examine how wearing the hijab in Zaria reveals the complex meanings of the veiling there, which have been contested within the Muslim community itself, by both men and women, and which have changed over time (Abdullahi 2008; Yusuf 1991), underscoring the ways that the ephemeral quality of fashion itself parallels shifting ideas and identities (Davis 1992). Moreover, in Nigeria, recent national efforts to enforce a public dress code on university campuses and to pass an Indecent Dressing Bill, which has been proposed to federal legislators (Adaramola 2008), suggest that dress is related to national identity (Allman 2004). Thus the hijab (and related types of Muslim-associated dress) may not be the inflammatory issue it is in Europe, specifically in France (Asad 2006; Bowen 2007; Scott 2007; Werbner 2007). Rather it not only reflects national concerns about indecency (Adaramola 2008) but may also be seen as fashionable dress (Sharma 2007). While the hijab, veils, and head

Figure 6.1 Woman wearing a *hijab* made with material known as *mai gida suga*, referring to its checked pattern, Zaria City, 2008. Photo by Elisha P. Renne.

scarf remain powerful symbols, the meanings attributed to them, by different groups of Muslims, by women and men, and by the state, in Nigeria as elsewhere, are quite specific to local conditions and histories (e.g., see Atasoy 2006; Çinar 2008; Tarlo 2010). The chapter concludes with a discussion of the qualities of cloth and fashion, which helps to explain why covering women's bodies and why the hijab, in particular—with its potential for seductive beauty and pious purity—attracts such intense, if varied, moral responses in northern Nigeria.

THE INTRODUCTION OF THE HIJAB IN ZARIA

In Mary Smith's (1954) autobiography of Baba of Karo (1877–1951), Baba wears a coiled head scarf (*gwaggwaro*) in one picture, while in another, taken approximately two years before her death, she wears a coiled head scarf *(kallabi)* over which a long cloth (*gyale*) is loosely draped. At that time, in 1949, there was nothing like the overall body covering known as the hijab in Karo, Giwa, or Zaria, where she lived. Indeed, older women living in Zaria City, the old walled section of the town of Zaria, said that the hijab was a recent introduction, unlike the large hand-woven wrappers (*zane*) women used to cover their heads in the past.

Aside from zane, other names of hand-woven cloths used as head covering worn in the early twentieth century included the kallabi (head kerchief: Lamb and Holmes 1980: 261; Ma Newman 1990: 144), *lullubi* (Ma Newman 1990: 55), and the *mayafi* (Newman and Ma Newman 1979: 90). Photographs from the early twentieth century show Hausa women in public wearing zane hand-woven cloth wrappers, at times with cloths draped over their heads (Figure 6.2). Within their compounds, married women wore kallabi or wrapped head scarves (gwaggwaro; Ma Newman 1990: 144). Bargery's (1993 [1954]: 731) definition of the terms lullubi and *lulluba*—the former, defined as "a woman's covering her head and shoulders with a cloth," relates to the latter, the verb, lulluba, which is to cover the body completely with a cloth[1]—suggests that the concept of women covering their bodies was hardly new at this time. Indeed, in her writings during the mid-nineteenth century, Nana Asma'u, the daughter of Sheikh Usman don Fodio, the religious reformer and leader of the nineteenth jihad which led to the establishment of the Sokoto Caliphate, noted the importance of women's dress in the poem *A Warning, II,* written in Hausa in 1856, which advised women "to seek knowledge" and

Figure 6.2 Women wearing *gwaggwaro*-style head ties, some with *mayafi* (*gyale*) veils draped over their head, Northern Nigeria, 1930s. Photograph from the E. H. Duckworth Photograph Archive, courtesy of the Melville J. Herskovits Library of African Studies, Northwestern University.

to "dress modestly" (vv. 20–24, cited in Mack and Boyd 2000: 83; see also Ogunbiyi 1969). The system of Islamic education for women established by Nana Asma'u during the years of the Sokoto Caliphate has continued into the twentieth century (Bivins 2007; Boyd and Last 1985). The *jaji* women teachers whom Nana Asma'u trained wore special hats[2] and covered themselves with large hand-woven cloths as they went about the city of Sokoto and its environs instructing other women in knowledge of the *Qur'ān* (Boyd 1989).

In Zaria, to the south, Nana Asma'u's influence on women's education was less-widely felt. Zaria City women indicated that they knew it was important for Muslim women to cover themselves in public, yet many women could neither correctly recite verses from the *Qur'ān* nor read Arabic or Ajami script. No special dress was associated with women's Islamic education.[3] However, this situation changed with the advent of the Islamic reform movement, Izala, during the late 1970s.

RELIGIOUS REFORM IN ZARIA

The introduction of the hijab as proper Islamic dress is associated with the Movement Against Negative Innovations and for Orthodoxy (Jama'atu Izalat al-Bid'a wa Iqamat al-Sunna, known as Izala; Umar 1993) and its support for Islamic education for married women in northern Nigeria (Kane 2002; Loimeier 1997). This movement, formally organized in 1978, was instrumental in establishing classes for adult married women (Islamiyya Matan Aure) and in encouraging women to attend them, particularly in Zaria and Kaduna beginning in late 1970s and early 1980s. Married women in Zaria City began to wear the hijab when attending the newly established Islamiyya classes for married women there.

When they were introduced in Zaria City, Izala classes for married women were considered revolutionary by some who felt that breaking the prevailing rules of seclusion would lead to immorality and dissension in the home (Callaway 1987; Renne 2004). This situation was complicated by the implicit (and at times, explicit) criticism made by the Izala leader, Sheikh Abdullahi Gumi (1992), and his followers of the two prevailing Islamic groups in northern Nigeria, the Qadiriyya and Tijaniyya orders. Heeding Gumi's advice to seek Islamic knowledge in order to better themselves as proper Muslim wives and in order to better train their children, married women attending Islamiyya Matan Aure classes also faced considerable criticism. Although women had been covering themselves with gyale cloths at that time, by wearing, women began wearing the more body-encompassing hijab in order to protect themselves and their respectability when entering public spaces to attend Islamiyya classes:

> When the hijab was first introduced, people said a lot of bad things about it. I can give you an example [from my own experience]. I have a hijab that goes to my feet, when people saw me with it they said a lot of bad things, some would say *tazarce* [like the long robes worn by the former President Sani Abacha], some would say *takunkunmin Gumi* [shackles of Gumi]

> some would say *rakata jahannama* [it will escort her to hell], and many bad things. This kind of thing happened to those who are wearing hijab (Interview June 10, 2001).

As was the case with other aspects of Izala reforms, which became internalized as proper Islamic belief and practice by the movement's followers, Zaria City women began to reevaluate what was considered proper modest Muslim comportment in their community. Indeed, it was the Izala *malamai* who encouraged married women coming to their classes to wear the hijab because of their teaching of Qur'ānic *sura* (e.g., Sura 24:30 on modesty; Ali 1994) which instructed women to cover themselves. They also supported the hijab for their students' protection, particularly when the schools first began, as one malam explained:

> There are some schools, if the women went to school, if they lived nearby, some men used to stop them on their way... the thing was serious. It was at that time that women were asked to wear hijabi and to come to school in it. Because at the beginning, [we at] the school didn't care if women were [just] going out—they could wear any cloth they wanted. But if she's coming to school, she must be wearing a uniform—the hijabi. But we didn't choose a specific cloth, she must just wear her hijabi (Interview September 1996).

This shift from wearing the gyale to the hijab reflects the tendency of religious reformers to represent themselves as purifying past practices (El Guindi 1999)—in this case, by ridding Islam of innovations *(bid'a)* that were not clearly outlined in the *Qur'ān* and *hadīth* (Kane 2002).

While the initial wearing of hijab allowed married Muslim women to extend their mobility by delineating what constituted a moral space outside of their homes in order to acquire Islamic education taught by their Izala teachers, it antagonized others for whom the wearing of the hijab had other meanings. For some, it was seen as a material symbol, not of Izala's reforms, but of Izala's critique of Qadiriyya and Tijaniyya as having incorporated un-Islamic innovative practices. For others, it was seen as contrary to Hausa culture as women had been using the shawl-like kallabi and gyale prior to the introduction of the hijab. These different readings of and reactions to women's wearing the hijab contributed to conflict over the hijab in Zaria City.

OPPOSITION AND RESISTANCE

Several women who wore the hijab in the early 1980s mentioned the hostility with which they were received in parts of Zaria City and elsewhere, where Qadiriyya and Tijaniyya prevailed and where Izala reforms[4] were reviled:

> There was a time I was going to the hospital, I stopped at one house to see one woman before reaching the hospital. A child in the house defecated on my hijabi. I gave the hijabi

> out to be washed but saw if I waited for it to dry I would be wasting my time. So I asked if there was anyone in the house who had a hijabi. There was not one, except a small one. They said, "But we have a large veil, if you can use it." The veil [gyale] was really big but honestly, I was not happy with the situation . . . because I was not used to that veil. When I was walking, the veil kept coming off, and at that time, I met my teacher Malam Habibu on the road in Kan Fage [a neighborhood in Zaria City]. I swear, I was not happy when I saw him because he always saw me with hijabi except that day (Interview April 16, 2001).

One can better understand the shame felt by this woman at being seen in public by her teacher since he had likely been the one to tell her of the importance of wearing the hijab as part of required Muslim practice. These teachings were explained by another Zaria City woman:

> The Prophet Muhammed instructed us to wear the hijabi because it completes the Islamic religion . . . Sometimes the parents don't want [her to wear the] hijabi. They may accuse the daughter because of the hijabi, but if her husband agreed for her to wear it, she should not mind about what the father is saying (Interview May 9, 2001).

As this woman's comments suggest, women's wearing the hijab also led to conflict within families. This conflict was sometimes generational, sometimes between spouses, and sometimes among women themselves. For example, when going to Islamiyya class, one woman was unable to put on her hijab until she had left her house because her father "didn't like hijab." Another woman who was married only began to wear the hijab when she moved back to her parents' home:

> Really, my husband, he didn't like hijabi but since I came back home [to her parents' house], I sewed a hijabi and started wearing it. It is three years now when I started wearing it. Nothing happened when I started wearing it. It only improved my respect. Hijabi makes a woman more charismatic [*kwarjini*], bad people will not face her (Interview May 7, 2001).

Yet despite these initial confrontations, many women persisted in wearing the hijab in public, when attending Islamiyya classes, and when praying in their houses. Indeed, as women became accustomed to wearing the hijab, they became less and less comfortable wearing the gyale head cover/veil, with some women rejecting the gyale altogether:

> Hijabi protects a woman's body because it covers her back and front; any woman who shows her body has no respect. If she wears gyale and puts it on her neck, a small boy can come and talk to her. Everywhere I put my foot, everywhere I am going, I am going with hijabi, not only if I am going to school. *I don't even know how to use gyale* (Interview May 2, 2001; my emphasis).

This internalization of proper public dress—the hijab rather than gyale—is also expressed in terms of dress aesthetics, conflating moral comportment with beautiful dress:

> The hijabi has an effect; any woman who is seen with hijabi, people will be looking at her with importance because she is not seen in ugly dress, while a woman who is seen with gyale, you see she didn't dress beautifully (Interview May 7, 2001).

For one woman, the idea of what is considered proper covering was internalized to the extent that she felt undressed in public if she was not wearing a hijab, as she noted: "Where ever I will go I wear hijab because the time I was attempting to wear gyale and cover my body, *I felt like I was going naked"* (Interview June 11, 2001, my emphasis; see also Meneley 2007: 231). This woman's comments also point to the particular gendered dynamics of public space and marriage, which are defused by the wearing a hijab. Without proper covering of their bodies, women "invite" men to make sexual advances which devalue her.

THE HIJAB, NIKAB, AND PROCESSES OF PURIFICATION

Aside from the shift from wearing the gyale, which could slide off the head, revealing the neck and arms, to covering oneself securely with the hijab, there were different types of gyale and hijab worn by women which had different connotations. For example, several women mentioned different sizes of hijab and gyale as being more proper than others:

> If I am going to school, I wear hijabi. If I am going someplace and there isn't a concrete reason [to wear it, such as school], if I will go out with gyale, I wear a big gyale that I think will not attract anyone to me (Interview November 12, 2001).

Initially, women wore large hand-woven cloths, which were subsequently replaced with machine-woven gyale cloths which were often imported, from Pakistan, India, and, sometimes, were brought back from Saudi Arabia by those who had gone there on hajj.[5] While these cloths were seen at the time as being sufficient for protecting women's modesty, they came to be seen as insufficient cover as women began attending Islamiyya classes. Eventually, even the short hijab came to be seen as insufficient cover; the long hijab, which covered a woman from head to toe, became required wear for women seeking modest Muslim comportment.

This process of purification of dress was taken a step further in the period from 2000 to 2003, when some Muslim women in Kaduna and Zaria began wearing the *nikab*—a type of veil that covers the face, except for the eyes. One woman living in Kaduna explained why she began wearing the nikab and how she learned about its importance for Muslim women:

> I think I started wearing nikab in 1999 . . . The reason why I wear nikab—there was a time we went out to do prayers. At one place, they said we could not go and pray without the nikab.

> We asked them why; they told us one verse in Suratul Azab in which God said to his Prophet to tell their wives and children and companions and women who believe in the Prophet they should cover themselves. When I heard that, I believed in what they said, and I started to wear the nikab. Nobody asked me to wear nikab; it is because I heard it from Malam Ahamed (Interview April 2003).

While not all Muslim women in northern Nigeria wear a nikab with the hijab, for those who do, they have internalized a sense of being exposed and uncovered and of being a proper Muslim woman, as was earlier the case for those who began wearing the hijab in the 1970s.

One young woman, however, observed that in her own case, it was her own idea to wear the nikab, as she'd seen it on television (Interview April 2003; Figure 6.3). While she wore it with her hijab when attending Islamiyya classes because she felt that it increased the respect that people had for her, there was also an element of wanting to be up-to-date in what was being worn by Muslim women in the Middle East. In other words, there was an element of fashion involved in her decision to wear the nikab, which may also be seen in more recent styles of the hijab worn in Zaria.

Figure 6.3 Young woman wearing *nikab* face veil, Kaduna, 2003. Photo by Elisha P. Renne.

FASHION AND THE HIJAB

Not only has the hijab been prescribed as the most appropriate form of covering worn by Muslim women, but also the cloth with which it is made should have certain characteristics. It should be made from fabric that is sufficiently thick and opaque, which "would not show the form of the woman's body" (Ibrahim n.d.: 10). Initially, hijab were made with industrially woven cloth in neutral or dark colors, which would not attract attention to their wearers—what might be described as a form of antifashion (Heath 1992). Yet because of their drab plainness, some women preferred to wear more attractive gyale to certain social occasions, as one woman explained:

> If I am going to a wedding if it in the evening. . . I have a big gyale; I will take it and cover my body. Sometimes if you go to a wedding with hijab, they will look down on you [because] you should dress beautifully (Interview May 1, 2001, Zaria).

However, more recently there have been changes in the styles of hijab available that enable women to wear them and to be "in fashion." One new style of hijab, which emerged in early 2008, is referred to as hijab-gyale; it consists of a very short hijab, made with synthetic fabric, in floral designs known as *mai flowa* and also in more muted patterns. According to one woman in Zaria, her sister received a large contract to sew hijab-gyale, which were then taken to Kaduna, where they are all the rage, to be sold. This style is particularly appealing to young, unmarried girls. For older, married women, new fabrics with more subdued woven patterns, such as waffle weave which is known as *mai gida suga* (Figure 6.1), are used to make hijab demonstrating a fashion-conscious difference (Simmel 1971). This process has continued, and in 2011, the most recent "fashion hijab" consists of a two-color head and body combination (Figure 6.4), referred to as Turai Yar'Adua, in reference to the former first lady, who wore a hijab in this style (see Plate 6).

Thus, within Zaria, there have been a range of reactions to the hijab, which have, furthermore, changed over time. On the one hand, many men and some women in Zaria initially opposed women's attendance at Islamiyya Matan Aure classes and women's wearing of the hijab when doing so. On the other hand, some husbands encouraged their wives to wear the hijab and to attend school. Some Muslim women made fun of women attending weddings wearing the hijab, asking why they could not wear gyale as they did. Other women, however, felt that wearing the hijab was part of their moral duty as Muslim women. For these women, wearing the hijab also had diverse gendered implications since those who wore the hijab to attend classes against their husbands' wishes were challenging male authority, at least at the domestic level. Yet, women who decided to wear the hijab (and nikab) as a result of instruction by Islamic leaders—such as Sheikh Abubakar Gumi—and Islamiyya teachers could be seen as acquiescing to male dominance.

Some of this contradictory behavior may be explained by adherence to different Islamic sects—with women who had accepted the teaching of Izala supporting their

Figure 6.4 Woman wearing the latest fashion hijab, called Turai Yar'Adua, Zaria, 2010. Photo by Elisha P. Renne.

decision to wear the hijab when they attended Islamiyya Matan Aure classes. Their resolve to wear the hijab also expressed a sincere sense of Muslim piety which the hijab represented (Mahmood 2004). In the majority of interviews conducted in 2001, it was this sense of the value of proper Muslim demeanor, rather than a sense of compunction (Ibrahim 2007) or of moral superiority over women who did not wear the hijab (see Mahdi 2008), that seemed to be expressed. The shift toward the "fashion hijab" has been variously interpreted. Some Islamic teachers see it as contrary to the meaning of the hijab as modest Muslim dress. Yet many women want to be proper Muslims without forsaking all sense of fashion consciousness. This shift toward fashion may be particularly appropriate with recent university dress codes, which favor the modest, yet not necessarily unfashionable, dress which the hijab can represent.[6] Nonetheless, compared with the situation of university women in Turkey where veiling is prohibited (Tavernise 2008), this support for wearing the hijab as fashionable campus wear underscores the very local nature of legitimacy of specific head and body coverings—which is also related to ideas about sexuality, gender, and cloth.

ASSOCIATIONS OF CLOTH, SEXUALITY, AND GENDER

The Hausa verbs to eat (*ci*) and to drink (*sha*) have numerous associations with sexuality and gender, which are evidenced in linguistic constructions (Gouffé 1966); ci, to eat, is associated with active activities while sha, to drink, is associated with passive ones. These constructions suggest the connections made between food, alimentation, and sexuality discussed in the anthropological literature (e.g., Delaney 1991). However, the relationship between cloth and sexuality is less frequently noted. Thus the phrase *ta ci kwalliya* (she dressed up [fashionably]), literally meaning she "eats (*ci*)/consumes" dressing up (*kwalliya*; Newman and Ma Newman 1979: 71), implies the active qualities of dressing up—pursuing fashion and presenting oneself as sexually attractive. Several qualities of cloth contribute to this particular association.

The significance of the transparency or opacity of cloth is related to sexuality in several ways. Thick, opaque cloth, which covers the body and masks its sexuality, is referred to in the names of several Hausa textiles—including types of cloth known as lullubi (related to the verb, lulluba, to cover; Ma Newman 1990: 55)—so that to cover oneself is literally to wear a lullubi cloth. Alternately, wearing thin, transparent cloth (*yane*) is thought of as being uncovered. Such dress was akin to being naked, as described in the booklet *Hijab, the Shield of the Umma:* "The clothes should not expose the form of what it wraps. The Prophet (SAW) said, 'There are, among the people of hell fire, those that have worn clothes but were naked'" (Ibrahim n.d.: 11).

Furthermore, cloth may be tailored to produce tight or loosely fitting garments, the former accentuating a woman's body, while the latter masks it. Muslim women, whose sexuality should be downplayed in public, should wear loose garments because "dress should not show parts of the body or joints, because seeing the shape [or a woman] or joints creates lust even if in clothes" (Ibrahim n.d.: 11). Similarly the hair, another source of erotic attraction (Delaney 1991; Leach 1958), must be entirely covered with cloth, as is noted in the booklet *Islam and Concept of Hijab:*

> Angel Jubril brought the Holy Prophet forth in journey where they saw some women hung with [by] their hair[s] in hell. The Prophet asked for their offense and he was told that they were the defiant ones against the convention of God who went about on earth without covering their hair. Jubril further educated the Prophet that the hair of women is like lightening with piercing and souring effect to guiding angels who prefer to stay away from such women. Thus, the grace of divine protection eludes such women and their environment (Olagoke n.d.: 36).

The point that the covering of women's bodies, including their hair, with cloth as a source of divine protection is more clearly made by Ibrahim in the following anecdote:

> In Bayero University, Kano, there was some womanizers (among whom) one day one saw a sister fully Hijabed [sic]. He then intended to try her to see whether her piety was a faked one. On going closer to her, he began to shiver when she turned and looked at him. And he stammered, '...just come to greet you and ask how your study is moving'. This man then

> walked away unable to add anything to what he had said. So brothers, just look at how Allah protected this sister, because she was obedient to Allah. That is how Allah will protect any woman from any bad man provided she fears Allah and wears Islamic dresses (n.d.: 17).

Thus while transparent cloth and scanty clothing may entice men by what it provocatively reveals, cloth that obscures the shape of a woman's body and covers her may actually repel men's advances (Ismail n.d.; Muhammed n.d.).

Cloth has other characteristics that associate it with women's sexuality, including its flexibility, its ability to serve as the foundation for attractive colored/patterned designs, its absorbency of odors, and its tactility. There are certain types of cloth—such as fine silk fabrics, for example, that are associated with the softness of women's skin—that should not be worn by Muslim men (Kunna n.d.: 62). However, silk fabrics, which cling to the body or reveal a woman's movements should only be worn in private and should not be worn in public. In other words, cloth should not only cover but also should not attract men's attention in public. Thus patterned and brightly colored cloths that may draw men's attention to their wearers, such "decorated [veils] with ostentatious colors and designs" (Abdullah n.d.: 32), should not be worn, according to some Muslim scholars.

Another aspect of cloth that is associated with sexuality is its ability to absorb the scent used by a woman, which may be noticed by strangers when she leaves her home. As is noted in Kunna's (n.d.: 15) *Miscellaneous Questions & Answers,* it is *haram* (forbidden) for women to go out wearing perfume (see also Ibrahim n.d.: 12). The logic behind this prohibition is that if a strange man smells the perfume used by a woman, it is akin to having intercourse with her.

These sexually enticing qualities of some types of cloth, its silky softness, its ability to suggest sensual movement, its colorful and patterned attractiveness, and its absorbency of alluring scent, help to explain the imagery of the Hausa proverb cited by Ibrahim: "One expects to find fire in a blacksmith's shop, but rather it is found in the weaver's shed (*Ana zaton wuta a makera, sai gata a masaka*)" (n.d.: 12). When asked to clarify the meaning of this proverb, one woman used the hijab itself in her explanation: "For example, a woman who wears hijabi—you won't expect anything bad from her [such as illicit relations with men], but she will do it, while someone wearing gyale—you will expect something bad from her but she won't do it" (Interview June 4, 2009); this suggests the moral ambiguity associated with cloth and fashion.

CONCLUSION

As Beidelman has noted, "Cloth defines the limits and possibilities of people as actors in social relations. At the same time . . . masking, hiding, and duplicity are equally important goals in the use of cloth" (quoted in Schneider and Weiner 1986: 179). In northern Nigeria, wearing the hijab has expanded the possibilities of Hausa Muslim women's respectable presence in public space, making it possible for them to go to classes for married women as well as to attend public primary and secondary schools, colleges, and universities. By covering themselves with the hijab, they have created a moral space in which their sexuality is downplayed. Yet for some Hausa Muslim women, the required wearing of the hijab underscores the limits on women's choices as compared with men, whose sexuality is not under the same sorts of social strictures. Indeed, as Bivins has observed, "The discourse of gender and power often remains in the hands of men, for whom the control of women is a fundamental requirement in the procreation of family and the community of Believers" (Bivins 2007: 134–135; see also Pittin 1991).

Despite these constraints, however, the hijab, as a symbol of Hausa women's piety and propriety, has taken on a life of its own (MacLeod 1992). With the development of the "fashion hijab" and the hijab-gyale, women have incorporated an element of fashionable attractiveness into hijab wearing that counters the rationale for its initial introduction. The insistence on women's covering themselves in public, particularly wearing the hijab when going to Islamiyya classes or when praying, has thus been adapted by women in ways that not only expand their freedom to participate in the public sphere, but also give them a certain latitude in the sorts of cloth seen as appropriate for doing so. It is this "accommodating imagination," to revise MacLeod's (1992) phrase, that perhaps best characterizes the decisions made by northern Nigerian Muslim women (see also Cooper 1997: 171).

For Hausa Muslim women in northern Nigeria (and in Niger; see Cooper 1997; Masquelier 2009), the role of the hijab reflects particular social histories and cultural contexts. As an expression of piety and as a form of fashion, the hijab serves as a vehicle with which to advance specific social strategies and to express preoccupations about morality and sexuality, piety, and attractiveness. Thus while the moral space represented by the wearing of the plain hijab distinguishes what some see as Hausa Muslim women's practice of proper Islam, this purity is nonetheless defined in relationship to the attractive seductiveness of fashionable dress, seen in the bright prints and changing styles of the fashion hijab. This interrelationship and the contested (and continually changing) meanings associated with the hijab are all the more intense because of this close association of cloth with women's sexuality and with ideas about how this sexuality is portrayed and should be controlled, which in turn reflect the distinctive configurations, present and past, of northern Nigeria social life.

ACKNOWLEDGMENTS

The author would like to thank the women of Zaria City for their cooperation and helpful interviews and to Hassana Yusuf for her assiduous research assistance over the years. I am also grateful to Alhaji (Dr.) Shehu Idris CFR, Emir of Zazzau, for permission to conduct research in Zaria City and professor S.U. Abdullahi, former vice chancellor of Ahmadu Bello University, for research affiliation. Finally, the author gratefully acknowledges funding from the National Science Foundation (2002) for research on women's Islamic education in Zaria City and to the Pasold Foundation (2009) for research on the history of head coverings in Zaria.

NOTES

1. Bargery (1993 [1954]: 731) gives the example: "He covered her with a cloth: *ya lulluba mata zane*."
2. Nana Asma'u introduced the *malfa* hat worn by women religious teachers in Sokoto. A red strip of cloth, called the *nadi*, was tied around the hat's brim, and the handing over of the red cloth to women paralleled the turbaning ceremony (*rawani*) marking the political authority of men (Boyd 1989: 50–51).
3. Schools where *allo* boards are used for copying and memorizing verses from the *Qur'ān*.
4. The reforms introduced by Izala were sometimes associated with reforms advocated by another recent Islamic group in northern Nigeria—the Shi'a. For this reason, women wearing hijab were sometimes referred to as *'dan shia*, particularly if they were wearing black hijab.
5. Women probably shifted from using hand-woven zane and head kerchiefs to the gyale after World War II. One Yoruba trader living in Zaria City market said that when his family introduced large *gele* (Yoruba, head tie) scarves in the late 1940s, Hausa women began calling them gyale (Interview June 2011).
6. Nonetheless, the hijab also has negative associations. Indeed, I was told several stories about hijab-wearing and illicit behavior such as adultery and theft.

REFERENCES

Abdullah, Abdul R. n.d. Islamic Dress Code for Women. Darussalam Research Division.

Abdullahi, Rabi Muhammad. 2008. "Hijab: A Badge of Identity Like No Other. Weekly Trust" *Daily Trust* (May 1). Available at: www.dailytrust.com. Accessed May 10, 2008.

Adaramola, Zakariyya. 2008. "Muslim Group Wants Indecent Dressing Bill" *Daily Trust* (July 18). Available at: www.dailytrust.com. Accessed July 18, 2008.

Ali, Ahmed, trans. 1994. *Al-Qur'ān*. Princeton: Princeton University Press.

Allman, Jean, ed. 2004. *Fashioning Africa: Power and the Politics of Dress*. Bloomington: Indiana University Press.

Al-Qur'ān. 1994. Translated by Ahmed Ali. Princeton: Princeton University Press.

Asad, Talal. 2006. "French Secularism and the 'Islamic Veil Affair.'" *Hedgehog Review* 8(1–2): 93–106.

Atasoy, Yildiz. 2006. "Governing Women's Morality: A Study of Islamic Veiling in Canada." *European Journal of Cultural Studies* 9(2): 203–221.

Bargery, G. P. 1993 [1954]. *A Hausa-English Dictionary*, 2nd ed. Kaduna: Ahmadu Bello University Press.

Bivins, Mary W. 2007. *Telling Stories, Making Histories: Women, Words, and Islam in Nineteenth-Century Hausaland and the Sokoto Caliphate*. Portsmouth, NH: Heinemann.

Bowen, John. 2007. *Why the French Don't Like Headscarves: Islam, the State, and Public Space.* Princeton: Princeton University Press.

Boyd, Jean. 1989. *The Caliph's Sister: Nana Asma'u, 1793–1865, Teacher, Poet, and Islamic Leader.* London: F. Cass.

Boyd, Jean, and Murray Last. 1985. "The Role of Women as Agents Religieux in Sokoto." *Canadian Journal of African Studies* 19(2): 283–300.

Callaway, Barbara. 1987. *Muslim Hausa Women in Nigeria: Tradition and Change.* Syracuse, NY: Syracuse University Press.

Çınar, Alev. 2008. "Subversion and Subjugation in the Public Sphere: Secularism and the Islamic Headscarf." *Signs* 33(4): 891–913.

Cooper, Barbara. 1997. *Marriage in Maradi: Gender and Culture in a Hausa Society in Niger, 1900–1989.* Portsmouth, NH: Heinemann.

Davis, Fred. 1992. *Fashion, Culture, and Identity.* Chicago: University of Chicago Press.

Delaney, Carol. 1991. *The Seed and the Soil: Gender and Cosmology in Turkish Village Life.* Berkeley: University of California Press.

El Guindi, Fadwa. 1999. *Veil: Modesty, Privacy, and Resistance.* Oxford, UK: Berg.

Gouffé, Claude. 1966. "'Manger' et 'boire' en Haoussa." *Revue de l'Ecole nationale des langues orientales* 3: 77–111.

Gumi, Abdullahi, with Ismaila Tsiga. 1992. *Where I Stand.* Ibadan: Spectrum Books.

Heath, Deborah. 1992. "Fashion, Anti-Fashion, and Heteroglossia in Urban Senegal." *American Ethnologist* 19: 19–33.

Ibrahim, Abubakar Saddiq. n.d. *Hijab: The Shield of the Umma,* translated by Zakariya Garba Umar.

Ibrahim, Yusha'u Adamu. 2007. "Compulsory Hijab Affects Only Muslim Students." *Daily Trust* (May 7).

Kane, Ousmane. 2002. *Muslim Modernity in Post-Colonial Nigeria.* Leiden: Brill.

Kunna, Ibrahim M. n.d. *Miscellaneous Questions & Answers for the Muslim Women.* Zaria City: BG.

Lamb, Venice, and Judith Holmes. 1980. *Nigerian Weaving.* Hertingfordbury: Roxford Books.

Leach, Edmund. 1958. "Magical Hair." *JRAI* 88(1–2): 147–164.

Loimeier, Roman, 1997. *Islamic Reform and Political Change in Northern Nigeria.* Evanston: Northwestern University Press.

Mack, Beverly, and Jean Boyd. 2000. *One Woman's Jihad: Nana Asma'u, Scholar and Scribe.* Bloomington: Indiana University Press.

MacLeod, Arlene. 1992. "Hegemonic Relations and Gender Resistance: The New Veiling as Accommodating Protest in Cairo." *Signs* 17(3): 533–557.

Mahdi, Hauwa. 2008. "The Hijab in Nigeria, the Woman's Body and the Feminist Private/Public Discourse." Paper presented at the African Studies Centre, Leiden.

Mahmood, Saba. 2004. *Politics of Piety: The Islamic Revival and the Feminist Subject.* Princeton: Princeton University Press.

Ma Newman, Roxana. 1990. *An English-Hausa Dictionary.* New Haven: Yale University Press.

Masquelier, Adeline. 2009. *Women and Revival in an African Town.* Bloomington: Indiana University Press

Meneley, Anne. 2007. "Fashions and Fundamentalisms in Fin-de-Siècle Yemen: Chador Barbie and Islamic Socks." *Cultural Anthropology* 22(2): 214–243.

Muhammed, Ramatu. n.d. *Moral Virtuous for Women.* Kano: Flash Printers.

Newman, Paul, and Roxana Ma Newman. 1979. *Modern Hausa-English Dictionary.* Ibadan: University Press.

Ogunbiyi, I. A. 1969. "The Position of Muslim Women as Stated by cUthman b. Fudi." *Odu (n.s.)* 2: 43–60.

Olagoke, S. A. n.d. *Islam and Concept of Hijab.* Ibadan: SAO Multiventures.

Pittin, Renee. 1991. "Women, Work, and Ideology in Nigeria." *Review of African Political* Economy 52: 38–52.

Renne, Elisha. 2004. "Gender Roles and Women's Status: What They Mean to Hausa Muslim Women in Northern Nigeria." In Simon Szreter, Arunachalam Dharmalingam, and Hania Sholkamy, eds., *Qualitative Demography: Categories and Contexts in Population Studies,* 276–294. Oxford: Oxford University Press.

Schneider, Jane, and Annette B. Weiner. 1986. "Cloth and the Organization of Human Experience." *Current Anthropology* 27(2): 178–184.

Scott, Joan W. 2007. *The Politics of the Veil.* Princeton: Princeton University Press.

Sharma, Ramaa. 2007. "Can the Veil be Fashionable?" *Weekly Trust* (August 25): 27.

Simmel, Georg. 1971. "Fashion." In Donald Levine, ed., *On Individuality and Social Forms,* 294–323. Chicago: University of Chicago Press.

Simmel, Georg. 1997. "Sociology of the Meal." In David Frisby and Mike Featherstone, eds., *Simmel on Culture,* 130–135. London: Sage.

Smith, Mary F. 1954. *Baba of Karo.* New Haven: Yale University Press.

Tarlo, Emma. 2010. *Visibly Muslim: Fashion, Politics, Faith.* Oxford: Berg.

Tavernise, Sabrina. 2008. "For Many Turks, Head Scarf's Return Aids Religion and Democracy." *New York Times* (January 30): A6.

Umar, Muhammad Sani. 1993. "Changing Islamic Identity in Nigeria From the 1960s to the1980s: From Sufism to Anti-Sufism." In Louis Brenner, ed., *Muslim Identity and Social Change in Sub-Saharan Africa,* 154–178. London: Hurst and Co.

Werbner, Pnina. 2007. "Veiled Interventions in Pure Space: Honour, Shame and Embodied Struggles Among Muslims in Britain and France." *Theory, Culture, & Society* 24(2): 161–186.

Yusuf, Bilkisu. 1991. "Hausa-Fulani Women: The State of the Struggle." In Catherine Coles and Beverly Mack, eds., *Hausa Women in the Twentieth Century,* 90–106. Madison: University of Wisconsin Press.

PART III

Connecting Worlds through Dress

–7–

Dressing the Colonial Body: Senegalese Rifleman in Uniform

Keith Rathbone

Kande Kamara was in Bamako, working as a driver, when World War I broke out. He returned immediately to his family's compound and asked his father's permission to join the French Army as a *tirailleur sénégalais* (Senegalese rifleman). Kamara's father, the titular chief of Kindia in French Guinée, refused to give his son his blessing and ordered him to avoid military service by fleeing into the bush. But Kamara ignored his father's orders and one morning signed up for the colonial military. As a '*bon volontaire,*' he was given a medical examination, food, 200 CFA francs, and, most importantly, a French military uniform. When he went home to his family, it was the uniform that Kande Kamara wore that elicited a strong response. He stated that his whole family reacted with surprise and anger in seeing him in the horizon-blue of the French Army—there was an "uproar, there was hysteria, there is nothing more alarming in the village than that, seeing the army uniform" (Kamara 1976: Tape 1, Side 1).[1]

Kande Kamara was not the only tirailleur who referenced uniforms in his enlistment story. In *Force Bonté,* Bakary Diallo described signing up for the colonial army. With one of his friends, Diallo approached the military garrison in M'Bala, Senegal, where he signed up. Escorted to the bureau of enlistment, he was officially admitted into the colonial army and welcomed by his fellow soldiers. The most striking visual element of Diallo's enlistment story is his continual reference to the clothing of the soldiers in the barracks, in particular to the chevrons on their sleeves. For example, the lieutenant cut a "majestic" figure with his bronze stripes on his sleeves, the attending doctor was elegant with gold stripes, and the soldiers who welcomed Diallo into the army all wore red stripes (Diallo 1926: 32–38). Why did clothing play such an important role in both Kande Kamara's and Bakary Diallo's enlistments? What does examining clothing tell about the way the tirailleur remembered the war and the French civilizing mission?

The historiography of the tirailleur sénégalais privileges the notion that West Africans were coerced into service by a violent and powerful colonial state. Historians of the tirailleur stressed that ordinary Africans wanted to avoid military service at all costs and developed complex schemes to evade enlistment. These historians assumed that the smaller number of Africans who volunteered were mercenaries. Myron Echenberg stated that tirailleurs were generally "either mercenaries or unwilling conscripts" (1991: 36). If they

Figure 7.1. Tirailleurs sénégalais with family members, Marseille 1914. Courtesy Bibliothèque Nationale de France.

admit any genuine African volunteers, historians argue that they were few in number and came only late in the war during the Blaise Diagne recruitment drives of 1918. Thus, rather than a volunteer army of citizen soldiers, historians have likened the tirailleurs to a literal or figurative slave army. David Killingray emphasized, "Many soldiers recruited were slaves or ex-slaves . . . three-quarters of the total enlistments in wartime French West Africa were slaves or former slaves" (1993: 3). Joe Lunn called the forced conscription of Africans a blood tax resulting in "the most intense expropriation of manpower for service overseas in the history of Senegambia" (1999: 33).

There is no doubt that the methods or effects of the French conscription were severe; however, a significant number of Africans, such as Kande Kamara and Bakary Diallo, did volunteer to serve with the French Army before 1917. More recent studies have placed the absolute number of volunteers between 13 and 25 percent (Fogarty 2008: 52). One must conclude that there was more widespread consent to conscription than has been suggested by previous historical narratives. The source base is admittedly limited because few tirailleur wrote or testified about their experiences; thus, I have chosen to privilege the testimonies of two of the war's most celebrated veterans: Kande Kamara and Bakary Diallo. I have supplemented those testimonies with the published excerpts of oral histories completed by Joe Lunn from *Memoirs of the Maelstrom* and the published accounts of postwar *griots* (praise singers). Using colonial uniforms as a point of entry, it became clear that there was a strong narrative of volunteerism in the testimony of many African veterans and that volunteering in fact offered West Africans benefits that historians have not fully contemplated.

Analysis of the uniforms of the tirailleur necessitated interaction with theories of dress. If the body is the "symbolic stage upon which the drama of socialization occurs," then dress is one way in which images of identity are mobilized (Turner 1980: 12). African soldiers serving with the French Army wore two different uniforms between 1914 and 1918, and at the outset of the war, there were differences between French and African uniforms. The tirailleur sénégalais wore hybridized military uniforms. Figure 7.2 shows prewar tirailleur uniforms: European-style military jackets, bloused formless pants, and the ubiquitous red *chechia* cap.

The formless pants (or even shorts) and the floppiness of the cap, in contrast to the French in their crisply pressed pants and helmets, made African soldiers appear child-like. The second tirailleur uniform was identical to that of their white counterparts: great coats, stiff pants, steel helmets, ammunition belts, and puttees. Sometimes tirailleur mixed and matched elements of both uniforms; the red chechias remained popular with Africans until the end of the war.

Uniforms embodied multifaceted individual and social meaning as a place where both individual and social identities were enacted, and by donning the horizon-blue uniform trousers and jackets of the French Army and the red chechia of the colonial soldier, tirailleur were establishing their social identity through role making and role taking. Their

Figure 7.2. Tirailleurs sénégalais in a military review during the Fête Nationale 1913, Paris. Courtesy Bibliothèque Nationale de France.

uniforms allowed the West African soldiers to appropriate the preexisting meanings of material culture and contest the significance of those meanings. Using narratives created by African soldiers that contained images of colonial uniforms as a point of entry, we can begin to understand and unpack issues of volunteerism in West Africa during World War I. By becoming embedded in the hierarchy of the military and donning French military uniforms, the tirailleur tried and were successful at undermining long-standing African and French discourses. In other words, these soldiers expanded what Jane Guyer, in her book *Marginal Gains* (2004), called their "repertoire of possibility" and were able to employ new lexicons of masculinity, hierarchy, service, and obligation to gain greater rights within the colonial nation-state.

UNIFORMS BEFORE THE FIRST WORLD WAR

Warfare in precolonial West Africa was conducted in a manner that reinforced the hierarchy of the social world, and the "uniforms" worn embodied the hierarchical nature of many African societies. The vast majority of the soldiers were drawn from people of low birth, and while their dress was not uniform, they wore a similar of style clothing.

Almost all ordinary soldiers carried similar weapons; the most common were throwing spears. By contrast, the leadership of West African armies was taken up by elites who had the available resources to acquire the symbols of leadership that materialized military and ideological power in West Africa. Swords were particularly potent symbols for soldiers in West Africa, and the sophisticated techniques required to produce them limited their availability to only the wealthiest individuals. Only notables could afford the more sophisticated weaponry such as armor, swords, shields, and, most importantly, horses that was required by the elite shock troops of West Africa.

Significantly, warfare was also the principal means through which ordinary people acquired the symbols of leadership. The strong correlation between social elites and military commanders and the ability of plunder to enrich soldiers has led some historians to conclude that in West Africa "most early chieftaincies originated in one form or other out of war leadership" (Smith 1976: 76). Oral testimony from Kande Kamara's interview supported this viewpoint. Kamara drew explicit connections between military leadership and social position by stressing that his father was a paramount chief in Kindia because of his role as a leading warrior. He stated, "Yes, [my father was a paramount chief] in Kindia . . . [Before the arrival of the French] the only people who were ruling villages and clans were warriors . . . The person who can kill the most people [and] who says *avant guard* we should fight is the paramount chief . . . The chiefs that existed were warriors" (Kamara 1976: Tape 1, Side 1).

Much like the luxury items carried by African elites in the precolonial period, European clothing held symbolic power in French West Africa. In the decades before World War I, West African men of lower birth typically wore *boubous*. Only African elites and tirailleur were guaranteed to have European clothes. For these soldiers, their uniforms materialized a variety of social and political meanings: trousers symbolized adulthood, uniforms embodied rites of passage, and various stripes and medals helped reorder familial and societal hierarchies. Bakary Diallo was raised in a Fulani village in Senegal at the beginning of the twentieth century, and he remembered that at that time trousers were still rare enough to be considered a status item. In *Force Bonté,* Diallo remembered losing his father's flock of sheep and worried that, as a consequence, his father would withhold the trousers traditionally given to sons to symbolically admit them into the community of men. He feared becoming "a man without valor," and he considered suicide (Diallo 1926: 18–19).

African volunteers often incorporated rites of passage narratives into tales of their enlistment. Kande Kamara's description of enlistment combines the anthropological notion of a rite of passage and the rejection of familial hierarchy. Returning to his family, all he saw in the village were "old people and women. All the young men my age were in the bush [hiding from conscription]" (Kamara 1976: Tape 1, Side 1). Kamara's father also ordered him to hide, but Kamara planned secretly on enlisting. Before signing up, he took all of his old and beautiful African clothes and set them out for his father, abandoning them. In abandoning his childhood clothes, Kamara literally and symbolically crossed into the liminal space between childhood and adulthood and rejected his father's authority. When he arrived at the military compound in Kindia, the first thing Kamara requested was a uniform from the French officers, and in putting on that uniform, he was enacting the post-liminal stage wherein his separation from his childhood and his father is made permanent, and he is integrated into a new community of soldiers and men.

Tellingly, Africans explicitly linked the war to other rites of passage. Kande Kamara likened the experience of the trenches with circumcision, a common rite of passage in Kindia. He stated, "To be a soldier in those days was like being circumcised . . . after you left the circumcision bush you'd be aware of a lot of thing [that you never understood before]. And that's the same parallel as warfare, as being a soldier" (Kamara 1976: Tape 5, Side 1). In the postwar period, West African praise singers also connected the war to circumcision rituals. In "Bilali of Faransekila," by Seydou Camara, Camara emphasized soldiers' masculinity by contrasting the hero with his uncircumcised enemies. The hero, Belensenjigi, promises that he is "going to the enemy / Going to the uncircumcised boys / . . . I will make the Moroccans wear the bila [a loincloth worn by boys in West African before circumcision]" (Camara 1989: lines 297–299).

Simply serving in the army allowed African soldiers to contest familial hierarchies. Kande Kamara was a second son of a second wife who had little claim to his father. However, once Kamara joined the army, his father visited him often in the barracks, giving him much sought-after individual attention and affection (Kamara 1976: Tape 1, Side 1). By entering the army, Kamara had significantly improved his place within his family hierarchy, and when he returned home after World War I, his social positioning was so improved that other males in the family felt threatened enough to plot to have him killed (Kamara 1976: Tape 6, Side 1).

During the war, younger brothers mobilized the power of uniforms against their older siblings. Hierarchies in the French Army were denoted by the rank and "stripes" exhibited on soldiers' uniforms and were based on experience rather than age. One soldier, Abdou Karim Gaye, remembers an accidental meeting with his older brother in France. At the time, Gaye was a corporal and his brother was only a private. Although he normally would have had to show his brother deference, upon meeting his brother that day, Gaye gleefully demanded that his brother salute him. He said, "We are in the army and there are no age distinctions. You are no longer my elder brother. I am your superior . . . I am a corporal and you don't have any stripes because you are a simple soldier. So give me a salute or I'll put you in prison" (Lunn 1999: 97). A similar situation happened to Kande Kamara. A chance meeting with his younger brother in France prompted Kamara to feel both pride in his brother's accomplishments and fear that his brother might supplant him in his family hierarchy. Kamara's brother had been wounded in the trenches, but he refused to be evacuated and told the doctors, "I am not going to board that [truck]. Why did I come here? I came to fight. Just come and tie my wound" (Kamara 1976: Tape 2, Side 2). For his bravery, Kamara's brother was promoted to sergeant. When he talked about his younger brother with other people, Kamara was careful to remind his interlocutors that he also had won a stripe and that "for my family, they knew I was a captain" (Kamara 1976: Tape 2, Side 2).

Joining the army and obtaining colonial uniforms also destabilized societal relationships between African elites who stayed home and the lower-born men who joined the tirailleur. There were widespread rumors throughout West Africa that the French would elevate brave soldiers to positions of authority. Kamara was certainly aware of these rumors. He stated, "[The French] had already written . . . down that every slave that went to war would be a chief when he came back . . . I was jealous of that. It was the last reason I joined the army" (Kamara 1976: Tape 1, Side 2). Other West Africans also took the threat of slaves becoming chiefs seriously. Myron Echenberg recognized that "well born families often wanted at least one of their sons to serve in the army. A good service record and the acquired ability to speak some French might help a returning veteran get appointed chief. In many regions sending a son into the army served as an insurance policy for the traditional elite" (Echenberg 1991: 63).

After the war, many tirailleurs were reluctant to give up their uniforms and the continued relevance of uniforms in West African society meant that *veteran* became a social category recognized as an alternative to traditional centers of power. Veterans preferred "European style" clothes to the traditional boubous and even wore their uniforms in largely inappropriate situations. Gregory Mann noted in *Native Sons* that "ex-soldiers were reluctant to give up any aspect of their uniform . . . even as they worked the fields, former tirailleurs continued to wear their uniform pants" (2006: 94). Tirailleurs' reluctance to part with their uniforms is understandable given the meanings that uniforms represented: adulthood, bravery, status, and close connections with the colonial state. The connection between the tirailleur and the French esteemed them in the eyes of their peers because it gave veterans access to power. Many veterans were able to take positions with the state, trading the chechia of the soldier for the hat of the *commandant de cercle* or *gendarme*. At the same time, the veteran could be threatening. Gregory Mann noted how the soldiers' red chechia came to represent "a dubious kind of worth" because of its associations with French power (2006: 94). Thus, soldiers' power came from a mixture of menace and knowledge, and soldiers coming home in uniform carried with them improvised weapons made out of wood or metal rods and "jammed the roads and cities . . . [and] roughed up villagers" (Mann 2006: 63).

In many ways, the war helped to create the universal category of the African. Before enlistment, Africans of different ethnic backgrounds often felt animosity toward each other. Joe Lunn wrote about an altercation between one Wolof tirailleur named Abdou Karim Gaye and a Bambara cook at a camp in France. The cook was being careless; flies were getting into the food. Gaye kicked over the kitchen pot saying, "We—the Wolof—we do not eat flies," and the two soldiers began to fight (1999: 98). In fact, incidents between different African ethnic groups were commonplace during the war. Nevertheless, at the end of the war, Lunn noted that many soldiers would say that "ethnic particularisms were gradually superseded by the recognition that they were 'all Africans'" and that "when you are a soldier, all soldiers are the same" (1999: 98).

Bakary Diallo's wartime experiences led him to feel a greater unity with the different peoples of French West Africa, and he often used metaphors of dress to embody that unity. Story after story in *Force Bonté* juxtaposes the homogeneity of military uniforms with diversity, reinforcing an image of unity among the tirailleur in the minds of the reader. Before he decided the join the army, Diallo met with one of his friends, named Demba, to watch a group of soldiers in uniform. The military uniforms are set in sharp contrast with the civilian clothing Diallo and his friend wore. Demba remarked that "[the soldiers] are of all the races, but order unites them. They are the children of the government . . . before the commandant they are all equal" (Diallo 1926: 31). When Diallo finally joined the army, the enlisted men surrounded Diallo and commented on the strange clothes that separated the new recruits from the military men (Diallo 1926: 38). When Diallo was with the tirailleur, one group, the Djimis, started to sing a chant. The Bambara followed the Djimis. Then the Wolof began to sing as well. Soon, all the different groups of tirailleur were singing about their histories, about ancient black soldiers, and about their exploits. Looking and listening, Diallo concluded that "despite the diversity of races, of songs, of ideas, of tastes . . . my observations show the superficiality of that called difference" (1926: 75).

By contrast, if uniforms united some groups as Africans, then they represented difference to those without uniforms. In 1920, the governor of Haut-Senegal wrote that "the fact of having been a *tirailleur* . . . constitutes a veritable profession characterized by the wearing of the uniform. The ancient *tirailleur* persuades himself that he is not like the others and he feels the need to show it" (Mann 2006: 94). The separation between the tirailleur and the noncombatant often provoked hostility between both sides; the tirailleur were often believed to be closely tied to the colonial state and frequently had special knowledge of the French that gave them social advantages. Kande Kamara's wartime experiences gave him a privileged position in his family—advantages that many of his older brothers found threatening. As noted, when he returned from the war, they plotted to kill him, and he was only able to survive by leaving his wife, family, and Guinea (Kamara 1976: Tape 5, Side 1). Treachery became a common motif in praise singers' tales about the demobilization of the tirailleur. In Seydou Camara's tale the "Balili of Faransekila," the hero of the story is killed when he returns home from the war when his rivals capsize a river steamer and "Balali lay in the treachery" (Camara 1989: lines 405–430).

REIMAGINING THE TIRAILLEUR UNIFORM

In *Orientalism,* Edward Said noted that Europeans created and managed images of the colonial, and many scholars, such as Elizabeth Ezra in *The Colonial Unconscious,* have used Said's insight to argue that the "colonial" was created wholesale within the metropole. However, there are limitations to distinguishing the ways in which Africans and Europeans mobilized dialogues of uniforms, as if the colonial nation-state hermetically sealed the metropole from the colonies. When historians focus on differences between African soldiers' dress and European soldiers' dress, they miss the opportunity to look at the ways in which similar styles of dress produced similar meanings, nor do they fully acknowledges the role that Africans play in conceptualizing themselves. Indeed, by the end of the war, French perceptions of the tirailleur had altered drastically because the tirailleur themselves mobilized complex discourses of assimilation and service to argue for additional rights within the colonial framework.

French descriptions of the tirailleur often focused on the differences between African and European soldiers' uniforms. When the French first saw their colonial counterparts in 1914, they quickly honed in on the unusual uniforms worn by the earliest tirailleurs as symbols of that difference. In Figure 7.3, one can see that, dressed in bright blue jackets and bloused white pants, the tirailleur cut a striking figure.

On top of the soldiers' heads perched the red chechia, a kind of formless cap that was useless in stopping bullets, but came to epitomize the tirailleur among Africans and French alike. French soldier André Fribourg's diary demonstrates the imagery of the exotic. While watching some tirailleurs, Fribourg remarks ironically,

> They are African troops, booted with wild beast hide, and armed with carabines. What a paradox their presence here is! What role can these swift African scouts be playing in our sinister war of "civilization?"...Some, wrapped in their great blue burnous, their cowls pulled down over their eyes, their arms crossed, and the elbows and forearms protruding under the cloth, seems as they sit almost motionless in their saddles (1918: 147).

In concentrating on the strange clothing of the Africans, Fribourg distinguished them from the civilized uniformity of European armies.

Yet, as with other "traditional" uniforms, the tirailleurs' uniforms were replaced with those designed for combat in the trenches. By wearing similar uniforms, the French and

Figure 7.3. Tirailleurs sénégalais dressed in traditional uniforms as Spahis, July 15, 1913, Dakar, Senegal. Courtesy Bibliothèque Nationale de France.

Africans shared a lexicon of power materialized through symbols such as stripes and ribbons, and for the first time in their memories, the act of "earning stripes" put Africans in positions of authority over Frenchmen. Joe Lunn states that "as Africans became promoted during the war, the soldiers became accustomed on a daily basis to seeing their compatriots exercise power over Europeans" (1999: 110). Lunn gives the example of a soldier named Galaye Gueye who claimed that he "was ranked . . . among the white men. I was even giving orders to some white men" (1999: 110). War made plenty of African NCOs and officers, and while African soldiers rarely served in the same units as Europeans, the nature of combat in the trenches meant that Africans often came into contact with their "inferiors." Kande Kamara also noted the new interaction between black officers and white enlisted men. As Kamara said,

> If the white officer was higher up than the black officer, yes, he could beat him or vice versa . . . There was nothing that could prevent it. If I am a black officer and I am told to train you, to give you the necessary exercises and you don't follow my orders, I do the same thing as was done to me before I became an officer. Even if you were white or any other color (Kamara 1976: Tape 2, Side 1).

Consequently, while it was harder for black soldiers to advance in the ranks, there were many blacks in positions of authority through battlefield promotions. Both Kande Kamara's brother and Bakary Diallo were promoted to sergeants.

The war even allowed an African to take power over the highest-ranking Europeans. Blaise Diagne became the first African representative elected to the French parliament and the commissioner general of the Ministry of Colonies. In France and in French West Africa, Diagne used his newfound authority to publically rebuke the French officers who were abusive to African soldiers. One tirailleur named Momar Candji recounted seeing Diagne in France degrading white officers who mistreated African subordinates. Candji stated, "Diagne came [and] if we said the food was not good, he called officers together and asked why. He said, 'I brought soldiers to fight for you and help you. And I don't see why you treat them like this!' So he would tear off the ranks [of insignia] of the officers and put them on the table" (Lunn 1999: 110).

Significantly, many soldiers believed that, through service, they had achieved a kind of equality with the French. Kande Kamara explicitly stated, "At the end of the war we were all mixed, because by then everyone knew that mind and their heart and no one was afraid of color except for innocents" (1976: Tape 5, Side 1). Bakary Diallo symbolized equality in a literary style by using clothing as a metaphor. The "diverse colors of the handkerchiefs" possessed by the soldiers symbolized the rapprochement between the different races in the army, all equal in service, "white, black, half-white, half-black, (and) yellow" (Diallo 1926: 59). A law passed in the last year of the war entitled soldiers who had earned a combat medal to apply for French citizenship and Bakary Diallo managed to maneuver his medal into becoming a French citizen. Another tirailleur, named Nar Diouf, remembered how decorations from the war allowed former soldiers to negotiate as equals with French colonial officials. He states,

> Wherever people...had something to contest with the French—and they do not dare do it themselves because they were afraid of them—I used to do it for them...I used to go with my decorations and arrange the situation...Whenever the Tubabs (Europeans) saw your decorations, they knew that they were dealing with a very important person...And I gained this ability—of obtaining justice over a Tubab from the war (Lunn 1999: 232).

THE TIRAILLEUR AS TRANSITIONAL FIGURE

Scholars have been cautious in examining notions of Franco-West African "equality" after World War I because of the controversial legacy of colonization. Notably, Bakary Diallo, the only tirailleur to write about the war, was accused of naïve apologies for European colonialism. Literary critic János Riesz argues, "Critical opinions about *Force Bonté*...can be roughly separated into two strands: the first attempts to use the procolonial stance of the author as colonial propaganda and the second reacts to the very same procolonial enthusiasm with discomfiture or even distaste" (1996: 157). What does examining Diallo say about the relationship between the French and the West Africans? Diallo realized the challenges that colonialism posed for Africans, and he was careful to criticize the French for treating Africans poorly. Nevertheless, he recognized the changes that colonialism brought to West Africa, citing positively improved education and medicine. Diallo was happy when he said that "the Senegalese were really transformed. Their ideas, their tastes, the way of behaving, their desires and their pleasures that they had saved and transmitted to generation after generation could not resist the processes of France" (Diallo 1926: 91).

A disinterested view of the complex relationship between the wartime and French colonial discourse is crucial to understanding the significance of sweeping changes in colonial relations brought about by the war. At the height of the war, in 1917, Blaise Diagne went on a recruitment mission around the French West Africa where he claimed that wartime service by West Africans would mean equality and after the war. He fought for the right of the *originaires* of the four communes to serve as French citizens in metropolitan units, which he won in 1916. Alluding to 1794 and 1848, Diagne told parliamentarians that during his recruitment campaign "one did not find a person who refused the call . . . at this hour, we are all together" (Cros 1961: 94–95). He told fellow Africans, "Our place as (France's) adopted children is at her side, under her flag . . . We offer to France all the vital force of our ardent youth, even its sacrifice. Would that she welcomes us in the ranks of her soldiers" (Echenberg 1991: 45). And he used uniforms to symbolize his authority. He was always escorted by a dozen handpicked African soldiers, adorned with medals, ribbons, and stripes, who had attained high ranks in the tirailleur. Diagne's recruitment mission was successful—over sixty thousand volunteers. He thought soldiers volunteered for two reasons: "in tribute to the French . . . and to gain their liberty in the future," which he saw as expanded French citizenship in Africa (Cros 1961: 73). Joe Lunn found that Diagne "informed many soldiers . . . the prerogatives to which they might aspire in the army were but an initial step towards securing similar rights in all aspects of colonial life once they returned to Senegal" (Lunn 1999: 111).

Knowledge of French discourses gained during the war was the key to the moral imagination necessary to alter colonialist discourse, and volunteer tirailleur were early adopters of that new knowledge. Volunteer soldiers were not simply the Africans who had seen the Frenchman die, not simply the Africans who had seen Europeans kill each other, and not simply the Africans who had done more than spoken with European women. These Africans came into close contact with the French (and even learned to speak French) and in doing so had been immersed in the language of republicanism as well as colonization. Kande Kamara recognized that "[France] was more or less a place that we all looked at as some place to gather knowledge . . . if we had a chance to come back, at least this was the place to gain knowledge to bring back with us" (Kamara 1976: Tape 5, Side 1). Through their experiences in France, the tirailleur became transitional figures who expanded their repertoire of possibility and their ability to make reciprocal demands on African society and the colonial state.

Changes in African self-imagination may even have helped change the way the French thought about Africans. Although the French government made efforts to prevent contact between metropolitan French and colonials, Africans routinely came into contact with people in the trenches, as well as in train depots, hospitals, and brothels. Many

African soldiers also had female French pen pals called *marraines de guerre*. Those interactions forced Frenchmen and women to complicate their image of Africans. For example, Lucie Cousturier interacted with Africans on her farm near the winter quarters of the tirailleur, and she found them to be charming, intelligent, and gentlemanly (Balesi 1979: 118–119). Analyzing a wide variety of contacts between Africans and French, Joe Lunn concluded that "the more virulent prejudices of the immediate past were ameliorated," and Africans and French "developed... intimate relationships [and] social acceptance on terms of equality" (1999: 175). Diallo received an old medal as a gift from a man on a train who had respect for Diallo's "courageous defense of France," and he also had an excellent relationship with his marriane de guerre and her family, who came to visit him when he was in the hospital in Paris (Diallo 1926: 140).

At the same time, the influence of the relatively small numbers of transitional figures should not be overestimated. There still remained many contradictions with France, its former colonies, and veterans from the colonies who served in French wars. It is unclear whether the assimilationist rhetoric of the soldiers proved too threatening to notions of French racial exclusion, but almost immediately after World War I, the assimilationist activities of the colonial state ebbed. Nevertheless, while historians have emphasized the coercive power of the French state as opposed to the agency of the tirailleur, there is a counter-history of the power of empowered Africans soldiers to comply with and contest the framework of colonial discourses. Analyzing the clothing that tirailleur sénégalais wore during World War I allows one to examine the intricate ways in which Africans reimagined their social position within African society, French society, and the framework of the colonial civilizing mission. Among Africans, uniforms enabled soldiers to contest accepted symbols of masculinity, disrupted customary age and rank, and helped fix the tirailleur as a recurring social figure that subverted and opposed traditional precolonial centers of authority. In France, uniforms were originally noted for their exoticism, but they were also used by West Africans to challenge notions of racial difference, sometimes by literally commanding European soldiers but frequently by allowing them to employ rhetoric of republican service. Nevertheless, the tirailleur were only so successful at employing the discourse of the civilizing mission and embedding that within the material culture of uniforms. In Africa, uniforms also became associated with violence and collaboration, such that many veterans found themselves displaced from their homes and communities. Similarly, in France, new themes of association came to dominate colonial discourse, undermining the power of assimilationist rhetoric and assuring that whatever gains were made by the West African soldiers were limited.

NOTE

1. The Kande Kamara interview was conducted by Joseph Opala and translated from the Susu by Abdul Kamara. The original recording of the interview is deposited in the Archives Nationales du Sénegal. Many thanks of Joe Lunn for providing transcripts of the interview.

REFERENCES

Balesi, Charles. 1979. *From Adversaries to Comrades-in-Arms: West Africans and the French Military, 1885–1918.* Waltham, MA: Crossroads.

Camara, Seydou, song writer. 1989. "Bilali of Faransekila." In "Bilali of Farensekila: A West African Hunter and World War One Hero according to a World War Two Veteran and Hunters' Singer in Mali," in *History in Africa.* Vol. 16. New Brunswick, NJ: Rutgers University Press.

Conklin, Alice. 1997. *Mission to Civilize: The Republican Idea of Empire in France and West Africa, 1895–1930.* Palo Alto, CA: Stanford University Press.

Cros, Charles. 1961. *La Parole est à M. Blaise Diagne: Premier homme d'État africain.* Aubenas, France: Les Presses de l'Impremierie Habauzit.

Diagne, Blaise, speaker. 1974. *Blaise Diagne: Sa Vie, son Oeuvre.* Dakar: Nouvelle Éditions Africaines.

Diallo, Bakary. 1926. *Force Bonté.* Paris: Redier.

Echenberg, Myron. 1991. *Colonial Conscripts: The Tirailleur Sénégalais in French West Africa, 1857–1960.* Portsmouth, NH: Heinemann.

Fogarty, Richard. 2008. *Race and War in France: Colonial Subjects in the French Army, 1914–1918.* Baltimore, MD: Johns Hopkins University Press.

Fribourg, André. 1918. *The Flaming Crucible.* New York: Macmillan.

Guyer, Jane. 2004. *Marginal Gains: Monetary Transactions in Atlantic Africa.* Chicago: University of Chicago Press.

Killingray, David. 1993. "The Impact of the First World War on African Societies, 1914–1920." Paper presented at the Centre for African Studies, Cape Town University, Cape Town, South Africa.

Lunn, Joe. 1999. *Memoirs of the Maelstrom: A Senegalese Oral History of the First World War.* Portsmouth, NH: Heinemann.

Mann, Gregory. 2006. *Native Sons: West African Veterans and France in the Twentieth Century.* Durham, NC: Duke University Press.

Riesz, János. 1996. "The Tirailleur Sénégalais Who Would Not Be a Grand Enfant." In *Research in African Literatures,* vol. 27, no. 4. Bloomington: Indiana University Press.

Smith, Robert. 1976. *Warfare and Diplomacy in Pre-Colonial Africa.* Bungay, Suffolk: Methuen and Co.

Turner, Terrence. 1980. "The Social Skin." In J. Cherfas and R. Lewin, eds., *Not Work Alone.* London: Temple Smith.

–8–

Ghana Boys in Mali: Fashion, Youth, and Travel

Victoria L. Rovine

In a single region in Mali, two styles of men's dress embody diverse routes to status, attitudes toward innovation and perpetuation of past practices, and sources of stylistic inspiration. They have in common, however, a reliance on embroidery as a means of embodying messages, histories, and identities. These embroidered garments also represent distinct approaches to style change, the hallmark of fashion. These styles also contain the traces of local as well as global networks of commodities and beliefs, literally made legible in the embroidered patterns and figures that adorn these garments.

The main focus of my analysis is on one of these two embroidery forms, known as Ghana Boy style. Garments in this style illuminate the lives and aspirations of young men in the region who seek status through affiliation with the new and the non-local rather than with past practices. These associations are evident in the style of the garments, which often incorporate embroidered depictions of figures in miniskirts and other distinctively modern, international dress. The second type of embroidery, used to create garments called *tilbi,* offers a counterpoint to the Ghana Boy style. The tilbi illuminates the deep roots of embroidery in the region because this style perpetuates longstanding dress practice even as it responds creatively to new influences. Tilbi are made in men's and women's styles; my focus here is on the role of the garment in men's dress practices. These long, flowing robes are adorned with abstract motifs that are embroidered using labor-intensive, intricate stitches. The association of the garments with local history, scholarship, and religious belief enhances their value.

A comparison of these two styles of embroidered garment enables me to draw out the motivations and sources of inspiration that have influenced their makers. My analysis of the Ghana Boy style of embroidery looks to both its roots in a region with longstanding embroidery practices, and to potential sources of inspiration drawn from far beyond the immediate cultural orbit of the young men who made these garments. Along with an exploration of the distinctive use of color, abstract pattern, and distinctive media, I offer here a tantalizing yet speculative analysis of the figurative imagery that adorns Ghana Boy garments.

FASHION ACROSS CULTURAL BORDERS

Although they are widely divergent in style, these two types of garments have many characteristics in common. The medium and the basic form are similar: both are made of cotton cloth, minimally tailored, and adorned with embroidery on front and back. Their functions and sources of inspiration have much in common as well, as both are made by and for men to be worn as status symbols; both emerge from histories of trade; and both incorporate iconographic elements that refer to the sources of their wearers' status.

An exploration of the historically important tilbi style of embroidery complements my discussion of Ghana Boy garments, illuminating the importance of embroidery in the region. The contrast between tilbi and Ghana Boy tunics draws attention to the dramatic originality of Ghana Boy embroiderers, and it also provides a framework within which to recognize the subtle but significant innovations of the embroiderers who create tilbi. The relative conservatism of the latter style may, in fact, helps to explain the dramatic inventiveness of the former. Both types of garments must be understood as manifestations of embroidery's special role in the Inland Niger Delta region and of the history of cosmopolitanism in the region, where for centuries people and goods have moved vast distances across ethnic, regional, and colonial boundaries.

Ghana Boy tunics (see Plates 7.1 and 7.2) are adorned with embroidered figures, words, and abstract patterns, all articulated using bold running stitches in brilliant colors. They are the product of a specific context of West African labor migration between an arid inland region and the forested coast, as they were created by young Malian men who traveled to Ghana in search of work. These young men are quick to create new styles of dress in order to distinguish themselves from their elders and their juniors, marking the distinct phase of newfound adulthood.

Before describing the second style of embroidery from the Inland Niger Delta, a description of one Ghana Boy tunic provides an introduction to the style and iconography of this garment. This elaborately adorned garment typifies the color, medium, and combination of figurative and abstract imagery that characterizes many Ghana Boy garments. Registers of brilliantly colored geometric patterns follow the simple cut of the tunic, across the shoulders, down the center front and back, around the neckline, and along the fringed bottom. Red pompoms and a halo of embroidered patterns adorn the two pockets, and two more pompoms emphasize the v-shaped yoke of the neck.

Amid this vibrant abstraction, four figures have been carefully articulated using thin, black outlines and broad fields of color. Two female figures on the front of the tunic are seated cross-legged, wearing miniskirts and halter tops, large earrings, and platform shoes. They have long legs, carefully styled hair, and darkly rimmed eyes that seem to indicate the use of cosmetics. Behind them float two Malian flags, each marked with the stitched word *Mali.* The words *Ghana, Accra* appear on the top left shoulder of the tunic. Two equestrian figures, one male and one female, adorn the reverse side. They wear platform heels, bell-bottom pants, wide-collared shirts, and carefully coiffed hair. The female figure brandishes a pistol, and both horses have a leg in the air as if captured in mid-trot. Beneath the horses, small numbers appear that, like the place names, seem to add to the specificity of the depiction. Each aspect of the adornment of these tunics reflects the specific moment out of which they emerged. Instead of a longstanding tradition, they represent novel experience and the perception of the "exotic."

The second type of garment, the tilbi, is firmly rooted in the perpetuation of precedent rather than in adventure and novelty, in orthodox religious practice rather than in social innovation. The tilbi is a style of *boubou,* a general term used in francophone West Africa to describe large, wide-sleeved, untailored robes worn in different styles by men and women. The style is particularly associated with the cities of Timbuktu and Djenné. In the Inland Niger Delta, tilbi are distinguished from other boubous by their complex embroidery techniques and their distinctive vocabulary of motifs, which are arranged in precise compositions in which not only the size but also the location of the motifs on the fronts and backs of garments follows longstanding precedent. They are associated with maturity, piety, and respect for established status systems.

While they are both produced in the same region, worn in the same communities, potentially even by the same people (though at different stages in their lives), these two styles of men's embroidered garments diverge dramatically in context and intention. One is an icon of "tradition," the other of the ephemeral trends that are the hallmark of fashion. The tilbi is a symbol of practices and beliefs that are conceptualized as unchanging; in principle, a tilbi made today is the same as a tilbi made a generation or a century ago. If a tilbi's embroidery is the work of a cultural insider, steeped in longstanding practice, the patterns and images stitched onto Ghana Boy tunics might be interpreted as the vision of a tourist, reporting encounters with distant places and people. The perception of these garments as either "traditional" or "fashionable" is central to the forms of status that accrue to their wearers.

SETTING THE STAGE FOR FASHION: LABOR, TRADE, AND TRAVEL IN MALI

The Inland Niger Delta region is defined by the curve of the Niger River as it reaches its northernmost point near the Sahara Desert and begins its journey south. The trade center of Mopti is the major city in the region, as are the historically important cities of Timbuktu and Djenné, along with the Bandiagara cliffs and plains, home to the famous Dogon peoples. In her analysis of trans-Saharan commerce in the nineteenth century, Lydon emphasizes the cultural diversity of the region and its long history of trade networks: "One must think of the Sahara as a dynamic space with a deep history. It was a contact zone where teams of camels transported ideas, cultural practices, peoples, and commodities" (2009: 4).

Trade across the Sahara to the north, and with the goldfields and rich agricultural regions to the south, brought great wealth to the region during its heyday in the tenth to fifteenth centuries. Leo Africanus, who visited the region in the early sixteenth century, noted that a vast amount of gold changed hands in Djenné every year, as precious metals, salt, and other commodities passed through its markets (Hunwick 2003: 278). Another important commodity that was carried on the backs of camels has particular relevance for the study of clothing and fashion: textiles. Lydon notes that "textiles of bewildering varieties and origins circulated along transcontinental trade routes" (2009: 76). Both cities were also renowned as centers of Islamic scholarship. Thus, migration for labor, trade, and education from the inland savannahs to Ghana and other countries is nothing new but instead a continuation of a history of connections across vast regions.

Today, Timbuktu and Djenné rely more on tourism than on trade or education. The cities' long, rich histories as centers of trade and learning are, however, preserved in their visual culture. The iconography and the practice of the cities' distinctive forms of embroidery, as I will describe, are deeply rooted in that past, even as the region is also home to the emphatically modern Ghana Boy style.

GHANA BOYS: WORLD FASHION, INNOVATION, AND ADVENTURE

Their multinational history and unusual iconography make Ghana Boy tunics difficult to classify and therefore elusive subjects of study; they have received only brief mention in studies of African textiles and dress (Gardi 1988, 2002, 2003). They were produced by young men from the Inland Niger Delta region during sojourns in Ghana, where they went to seek work. The cloth and the thread were acquired in Ghana; the style and iconography developed out of the distinct perspective these young Malian men brought to their encounters with Accra, Kumasi, and other Ghanaian cities and towns. Although few Ghana Boy tunics have been documented or collected, many appear to incorporate aspirational representations of Western commodities and lifestyles—the miniskirts and airplanes noted above, among other motifs. I will assert, however, that these depictions are only indirectly associated with Western products and meanings.

Many of the tunics are adorned with figures dressed in Western styles. The Ghana Boy tunics in public and private collections include depictions of figures in miniskirts and bell bottom pants, police uniforms, pompadours and afros, as well as motorcycles, airplanes, and stoplights. These and other apparent references to Western culture may be the products of diasporas that existed outside the orbit of the West, and their presence cannot be simply interpreted as a manifestation of the desire to acquire or emulate Western culture.

The dress and hairstyles of the figures locate them temporally in the recent past, and they obscure their cultural origins. Though they may have their roots in Western dress practices, the uniforms and bell-bottoms have been absorbed into dress practices around the world, becoming local everywhere. Eicher and Sumberg propose the term *world fashion* to describe such styles of dress (1995: 296). As they circulate, objects absorb new identities, and clothing is a particularly mobile and flexible medium in transcultural networks. Clothing and accessories offer visual proof of the new status these young men gained through their experience abroad, evidence of the authenticity of the journey by which they earned the name Ghana Boys.

In a discussion about Ghana Boy embroidery with several men in Djenné, the importance of such proof was clear. Even many decades after his trip to Ghana in the 1972, Kariba Bouaré described his experience in great detail. He noted every stop along the route he and his fellow migrants took from Mali through Burkina Faso to Ghana, as well as the names of neighborhoods and streets in Accra. Bouaré's narrative contained these details not because all of these locations played a role in his experience, but rather because the names themselves served as evidence of the veracity of his story. Indeed, he insisted strongly that I make note of these place-names so that my record would contain the requisite proof of his travels (Interview June 20, 2009). As a young laborer in Ghana, Bouaré embroidered Ghana Boy garments to wear on his return home. After many years as a weaver and watchman in Djenné, he returned to this style of embroidery in the 1990s, when he began to work with well-known embroiderer Ousman Traoré to produce tunics and other garments adorned with Ghana Boy embroidery, primarily for sale to tourists and other non-local consumers.

Like the iconographic details on a Ghana Boy tunic—the license plate on a motorcycle, the style of shoes worn by a well-coiffed woman, the tailfin stripes on an airplane—the names of streets and neighborhoods were evidence of first-hand experience. Bouaré explained that it was important to prove that he had actually made the trip himself by providing information that an imposter could not know (Interview June 20, 2009). Amadou Tahirou Bah, an expert on Djenné's artistic traditions, characterized the message of Ghana Boy tunics in a phrase: "This is what I saw!" (Interview June 16, 2009). Simply owning goods from Ghana was not the source of Ghana Boy status; status was attached to the experience, not the goods. One man who participated in the spirited group discussion about Ghana Boys that morning in Djenné succinctly described the distinction between the value of goods to be given away and the value of the new status: "The money is for the family, the name is for you" (Interview June 20, 2009). In other words, while everything else can be shared with one's community, a new identity cannot. One's name—a way of describing personal status—is attached to experience, not to goods; yet that experience is made visible through specific garments and accessories, including embroidered tunics.

Young men from several different ethnic groups in the region might have made the Ghana Boy tunics, including the Dogon, Songhai, Fulani, and Bozo. In his important survey of the boubou form across West Africa, Gardi notes that the large, flowing robes are made in a wide range of styles that are difficult to associate with specific ethnic groups or regions (2000: 19–20). Saad's history of Timbuktu highlights the entire region's exceptionally diverse population, declaring that the city is located in "one of the most ethnically diversified regions in Africa" (1983: 9). Some sources indicate that Ghana Boy embroidery is closely associated with the Bamana, Mali's largest ethnic group; the style is referred to as "Bambara embroidery" (*broderie Bambara*) in these contexts (Interview June 16, 2009).

Travel and adventure are time-honored routes to social status and, by extension, motivators for social action, particularly for young men. Labor migration in and from Mali's Inland Niger Delta has long been a central aspect of livelihoods. Whether for trade, animal husbandry, seasonal agricultural labor, or a wide range of other skilled and unskilled employment, young men (and, significantly though less frequently, women) from the region have traveled to Bamako, Mali's capital, to neighboring countries, to the former colonial French metropole, and, more recently, to Libya, Saudi Arabia, South Africa, and elsewhere, their choices reflecting changing economic exigencies and opportunities. Ghana has been an important destination for many of these migrants since the late colonial era. One analysis of Malian labor migration indicates that in the mid-twentieth century, the period during which Ghana Boy tunics were likely developed, approximately 20 percent of Malians living abroad were based in Ghana (Zacharia, et al., 1980).

The predominantly young men who travel in search of employment on the streets of Ghana's cities, towns, and rural areas leave home for weeks, months, or years. Grosz-Ngaté (2000: 90–91) describes Malian labor migration as an ebb and flow of forces that compelled rural agriculturalists to travel. Isaïe Dougnon's analysis of migrant labor from Dogon communities to the Gold Coast and, later, Ghana, documents the memories and the motivations of many now elderly migrants. Some recall the history of migration through modes of transportation: 1910 to 1940 was the era of pedestrians (*les piétons*); second was the generation that traveled in vehicles (1950–1980); then followed the generation of migrants' children, born in Ghana (Dougnon, forthcoming: 10). The Ghana Boy tunics were produced during the second generation of migrant labor.

Migrants were motivated by economic exigencies, often fueled by desires for new commodities. Until 1946, the French colonial administration's taxation and compulsory labor policies compelled young men to seek work abroad; in the 1950s and 1960s, new demands for manufactured goods encouraged labor abroad as a source of cash, and during periods of drought in the early 1970s and 1980s, young men went south for work (Grosz-Ngaté 2000: 91). These economic pressures were transformed into social capital, for in Mali as elsewhere, travel provided a means of seeking one's fortune, proving one's courage, and building status in the community. As they traveled between Mali and Ghana, these young men traversed linguistic, ecological, ethnic, and colonial divides. The division of West Africa into French and British colonies created separate transnational networks in which material culture and social systems circulated, enduring long after African nations gained independence. Dougnon (forthcoming: 1) labels this movement between anglophone and francophone territories "trans-colonial migration" (n.d.: 1).

Dress was a key means of visibly announcing young men's experience abroad, laying claim to their new status in public arenas. In their discussion of migration within Mali and to neighboring countries, De Hann, Brock, and Coulibaly note that "part of the money kept by the migrant—very often the major part—was spent on clothes" (2002: 50). Ghana Boy tunics are just such symbols of newfound status, handmade abroad rather than simply purchased there.

Along with clothing, language also marked the young men's experience abroad and the status they accrued. Here, the colonial history is key, for the language that marks their status is English, not Twi, Ewe, or another indigenous Ghanaian language. The name Ghana Boy—employing the English word *boy*—declares the young men's affiliation with a foreign culture. These young men used other English words to demonstrate their experience abroad. *Afloman* and *Aflowoman,* terms that combine the status of English with a reference to a hairstyle that was (and is) an element of modern, pan-African identity, were used to describe the hip denizens of Ghana's cities (Interview June 20, 2009). Detailed knowledge about the route to and the geography of Ghana, use of English, wearing distinctive clothing—all of these aspects of young men's self-presentation underscored their experience as former migrant workers and world travelers.

The style and iconography of Ghana Boy tunics reflects—and enhances—the status of young men who have successfully made the journey to Ghana, where they created these wearable insignia of identity for their return home. The basic tunic form is arguably the most common style of quotidian male dress in Mali's rural areas. Today, as in the past, these garments are usually made of strip-woven cotton cloth. To make a tunic, several strips, approximately three to seven inches wide (7 to 18 cm), are sewn together, with a neck hole cut into the center and a pocket often attached to the front. These simple, sleeveless garments are comfortable, easy to make, and, particularly, if made of strong, locally spun thread, durable.

The tunic form has been the subject of creative innovations throughout the Sahel region. Wodaabe men (a subgroup of the Fulani, who are traditionally pastoral nomads in Mali, Niger, Senegal, and Burkina Faso), wear long, elaborately embroidered tunics made of strip woven indigo-dyed cotton cloth (Bovin 2001: 18). Tunics are also elaborated by hunters of various Malian and other West African ethnic groups, dyed and adorned with protective amulets to provide spiritual protection (McNaughton 1982). The simple tunic form, thus, has a history of elaboration and cultural significance in the region, though none of these precedents resemble Ghana Boy garments.

ALFAS AND APPRENTICES: THE TILBI IN THE INLAND NIGER DELTA

While the tunic in its many forms is a sturdy, practical garment, the boubou is the region's prototypical fancy dress—large, elegant, and dramatic. Embroidery, the medium used to transform the Ghana Boy tunics, is also used to adorn boubous throughout West Africa, yet these garments reflect very different forms and sources of status. For most communities in the Inland Niger Delta region (and beyond), embroidered boubous are closely associated with forms of status that are tied to maturity and to local, Muslim identity. The strong ties between embroidery and Islamic piety are particularly vivid in the case of the tilbi (also spelled *tirbi*), a type of embroidered boubou that is closely associated with the cities of Timbuktu and Djenné, though it is worn throughout the region (see Figures 8.1 and 8.2).

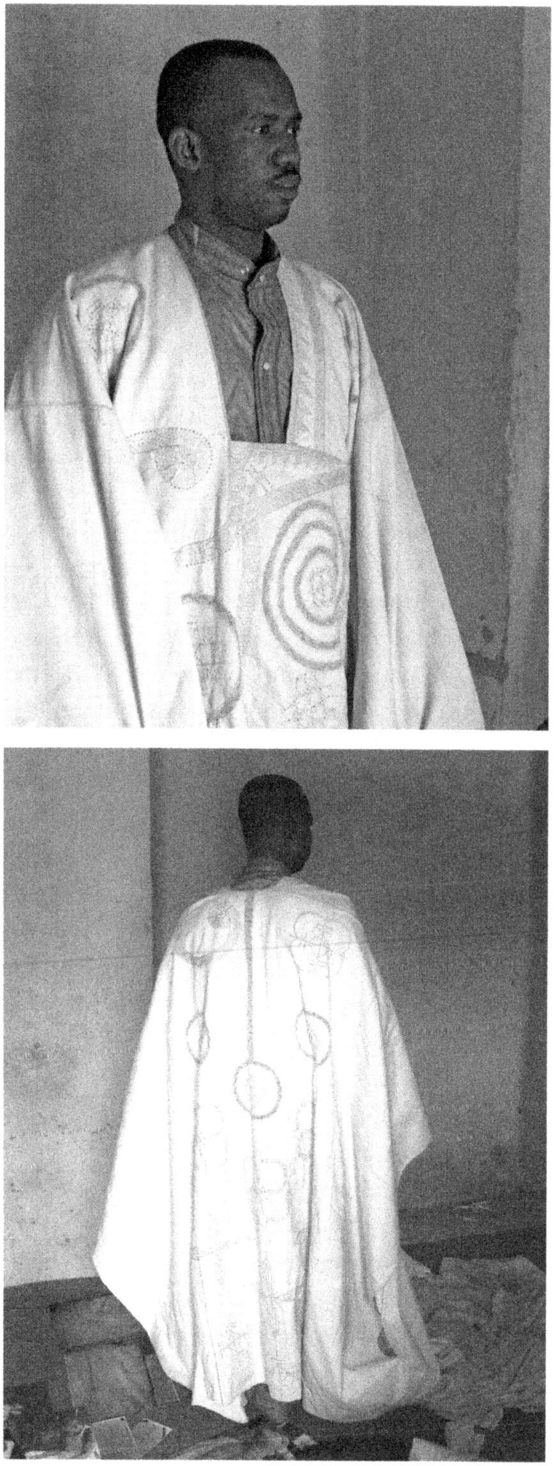

Figures 8.1 and 8.2 Baba Djitteye wearing a tilbi, Timbuktu, 2008 (front and back side). Photo by V. Rovine.

Observers of daily life in this part of Mali have long noted the distinctive dress associated with high status. Monsignor Haquard's 1900 monograph on Timbuktu identified the tilbi as the primary attire of both men and women of means, noting that the amount of silk embroidery on the garment directly reflected the wealth of its owner—a measure of tilbi quality still in use today (Hacquard 1900: 28). In 1994, Gardi also emphasized the opulence of the tilbi: "These *boubous*... are without question the most costly luxury products that have been produced by local artisans in the Niger Delta region" (Gardi 1994: 139). Their high cost reflects the tilbis' elegant forms and luxurious materials, as well as their association with high status and piety.

The tilbi's rich embroidery is characterized by the precision with which its complex motifs are delineated. According to Baba Djitteye, one of the few embroiderers still producing tilbi in Timbuktu, embroiderers both hope for and dread the commissioning of an elaborate tilbi; the labor involved is so arduous, over the course of as much as three years, that the money paid rarely covers the actual costs (Interview June 17, 2009). The ability to create painstakingly detailed embroidery is the result of many years of apprenticeship and experience.

Tilbi boubous are always made of luxurious materials, either finely spun and woven cotton strip cloth or top quality imported damask, along with imported silk thread. These elaborate garments are usually subtle in color, most commonly made of white fabric adorned with white silk embroidery. The embroidered motifs are named for elements of the natural world, including mouse teeth, cat's eye, serpent, lizard's head, and chameleon (Bah and Brunet-Jailly 2002: 103, 110–111). The styles of stitches are each named as well, designating the length of the stitches, the way they are grouped together, or the direction in which they are oriented (Bah and Brunet-Jailly 2002: 98).

Along with the layers of nomenclature by which embroiderers catalogue the elements of their work, motifs may be interpreted as references to Islamic history, belief, and cosmology. These motifs originally served protective functions and have become stylistic conventions. For example, tilbi boubous incorporate the magic square motif, found throughout the Islamic world. In her discussion of the magic square motif in Islamic West Africa, Prussin (1986: 75–80) analyzes the roots of this form in a symbolic system by which each letter is assigned a numerical value, so that numbers can be used to refer to Koranic texts, Muslim saints, and angels. The link between embroidery and religion is evident in the identities of embroiderers, who were and in many cases still are also scholars and teachers who are given the honorific title *alfa* (see Plate 7.3). Embroidery ateliers often doubled as Koranic schools at which apprentices memorized, recited, and discussed verses. In his 1921 description of professions in Timbuktu, Dupuis-Yacouba (1921: 29) noted the association of embroidery with Koranic learning, and he illustrated numerous embroidered motifs that are still in use today.

The association of embroidery with Islam continues today. During research trips to Timbuktu in 2008 and 2009, I observed and interviewed embroiderer Baba Djitteye, the members of his workshop (Hassan Soumila Cissé, Alidji Tajali Touré, Mahammane

Alkadj Djitteye, and Seydou Djitteye), and the imams of two of the city's most important mosques. Djitteye specializes in the creation of tilbi, as did his uncle and his grandfather, for whom his atelier, Alkoye Couture, is named. Djitteye and the imam of the Sidi Yayia mosque, Baba Hassey Mahamoud, who is himself a student of historical embroidery in the region, both spoke of embroidery as a form of prayer (Interviews July 23, 2008; June 17, 2009). In a vivid illustration of this link between embroidery and prayer, Djitteye and his colleagues prepare for embroidery as all Muslims prepare to pray, washing hands, feet, and face (Interview July 22, 2008).

In addition to their affiliation with Islam, tilbi are also associated with marriage, another institution that marks maturity and respectability. Gardi described the role of tilbi in marriage: the mother of the bride must provide the groom with an unembroidered white robe, preferably made of the finest thread or of luxurious imported cloth. The groom is then responsible for the adornment of the robe, either embroidering the tilbi motifs himself or paying for its adornment by an embroiderer (Gardi 1994: 144–145).

These deep roots in history, religion, and marital ritual might lead one to expect embroidery to be a conservative practice, resistant to change. In fact, Djitteye innovates constantly, inventing new combinations of motifs and garments in response to his clientele's demands. A complete transformation of key motifs or their arrangement on the garment is anathema to Djitteye, a point he made dramatically: "If one changes the motifs, it is as if one has changed something in the Koran" (Interview June 17, 2009). Yet, even within the realm of "deeply traditional" forms, alterations in style are important and reflect changing contexts and artistic creativity. Djitteye spoke of embroidery as handwriting, with every embroiderer bringing his own "hand" to the repertoire of motifs.

While the style in which an embroiderer interprets longstanding design motifs offers one realm for innovation, the creation of entirely new motifs offers another, more dramatic opportunity for creativity while still preserving the essential elements of longstanding embroidery practices. Djitteye and his colleagues created a new motif for the necklines of several styles of boubou, which they named *Tour de l'Afrique.* A monument in Bamako by the same name, which commemorates the founding of the Organization of African Unity, inspired the motif. The embroidered motifs bear no resemblance to the monument. Rings of delicate lace and groups of circular eyelets have no visual resonance with the brightly colored, massive columnar tower.

Yet, as one observer of the Tour de l'Afrique style noted, the rings of embroidery seem to echo the circle of flag poles, fences, and cement gates that surround the monument (M. Arnoldi, pers. comm., July 23, 2008). These embroiderers are pleased to receive commissions that enable them to innovate, using elements of historical embroidery to create new garments that express changing tastes. Their innovations offer continuity with the past, rather than the dramatic break with earlier practices that is the hallmark of Ghana Boy embroidery.

MAKING IT NEW: THE ICONOGRAPHY OF ADVENTURE

The deeply rooted and culturally significant practice of embroidery in the Inland Niger Delta, along with the region's long history of labor migration, provide a framework for analysis of the divergence between longstanding embroidery practices—epitomized by the tilbi—and the Ghana Boy garments. I conclude with a discussion of the potential stylistic sources that likely explain the striking originality of the Ghana Boy embroidery.

The Ghana Boy tunics employ brilliant colors, while the tilbi are extraordinarily subtle in color. One of Mali's most knowledgeable scholars of indigenous clothing and textiles, artist Kandiora Coulibaly, speculates that brightly colored thread was readily available in the regions where young men worked as a result of the important *kente* cloth industry in Ghana (Interview July 31, 2008). Kente, associated with royalty among the Akan groups of Ghana and surrounding countries, is made on multiple heddle strip looms. Its colors vary but are usually brilliant hues used in vivid combinations. Thus, the brightly colored embroidery thread may well reflect the colors of local weaving in Ghana.

The abstract patterns that adorn Ghana Boy tunics are boldly linear, with sharp-edged geometric forms in clearly defined registers. Karibe Boré, the weaver and former Ghana Boy from Djenné, equated one of the embroidered motifs with a Fulani weaving pattern called "don't hit children" (Interview June 20, 2009). I would add kente cloth, with its fields of linear patterns woven in blocks along the length of each strip, to the potential sources of inspiration for the tunics' abstract motifs. Finally, another possible source of inspiration for these abstract patterns lies in a different medium: leatherwork. Tuareg, Soninke, Bamana, and Dogon leatherworkers in the region adorn bags, pillows, horse trappings, and other products with embossed, painted, incised, and peeled abstract patterns (Frank 1998; Seligman and Loughran 2006: 102–109). The embroidery's visual resonances with all of these forms—leatherwork, woven and dyed textiles—locates it in the context of longstanding practices even as it indicates the remarkable creativity of the young men who made the tunics.

Finally, I turn to the Ghana Boy tunics' most dramatic innovation: figurative imagery. Kandiora Coulibaly, whose years of research lend his hypotheses weight, offers a convincing interpretation, though I will propose an alternative as well. Many of the young Malian migrants who went to Ghana in the 1970s and 1980s might have found work as night watchmen, a common occupation in cities of any size throughout West Africa (Gardi 2002: 27). Coulibaly notes that their occupation would have given these young men a close-up view of the lives of middle-class, urban Ghanaians. They depicted the elements of these lives that fascinated them, such as women in short skirts, legs crossed as they drank together, and sights from the streets such as elaborate motorcycles and traffic lights with their red, green, and yellow glow. Kariba Bouaré, looking at my photographs of numerous Ghana Boy tunics, said that the figures depicted the way people looked (Interview June 20, 2009).

Yet some of the tunics' imagery doesn't seem likely to have been drawn from the streets and gardens of Accra or Kumasi. The chic attire of two equestrian figures, one with gun drawn, on one tunic appears to be more Hollywood fantasy than daily life. In fact, Bollywood, the Indian film industry that has produced movies that have been exported to wide audiences in many parts of the world since the mid-twentieth century, is more likely the source of inspiration for these figures. The colonial era brought Ghana (then the Gold Coast) and India into the same networks, as part of the British Empire, so that Ghana/the Gold Coast likely had Bollywood films earlier than Mali, a former French colony. Larkin notes that Indian films were popular in Northern Nigeria by the 1950s (2008: 196). The posters and films themselves might have been a source of fascination for young men unfamiliar with the genre, which became very popular all over West Africa in the 1970s and 1980s.

The "Western"-style clothing of these figures, with bell-bottom pants, miniskirts, and halter tops, may not indicate any association with or aspiration for European or American lifestyles, but rather indicate a fascination with the "exotic" modernity depicted in Bollywood films. I want to suggest that for Malian migrant laborers, Bollywood figures were foreigners twice over. Using embroidery, a medium they associated with high status, young Malian men in Ghana depicted figures that represent the "exotic" for

Figure 8.3 Ghana Boy tunic, Mali, ca. 1980s. Arnoldi/Subler Collection. Photo by Mary Jo Arnoldi.

both Malians and Ghanaians. On their return home, wearing tunics adorned with these figures, young men vividly advertised their experience of Ghana not only through images of Ghana itself, but through the faraway visions of Indian melodramas accessible through Ghana's popular cultures.

Finally, integrated into these visions of "exotic" lives and technologies are reminders of home—Malian flags appear frequently, and the word *Mali* is stitched into garments, in one case on the tailfin of an airplane. Numbers and letters, sometimes difficult to decipher, may be insignia of literacy rather than communicative devices. Symbols of home, signs of status, and markers of experience abroad are all embedded in the adornment of Ghana Boy tunics.

I close with one final illustration of the Ghana Boy tunics' roots in the Inland Niger Delta's cultures, even as they also draw from Ghana's urban streets, and, by extension, the larger anglophone colonial world. The back of one tunic (Figure 8.3) features two motorcycle-mounted policemen; the license plates are carefully depicted.

Instead of a stoplight, the two pause before a small figure who directs traffic using two flags, one red and one green (prominent colors in the national flags of both Mali and Ghana). *Mali* is written at both sides of this highly abstract figure. It resembles—so closely as to be more than coincidence—the kanaga mask, an icon of Dogon culture that plays an important role in funerals and other rituals. Is this an assertion of the maker's pride in his national and cultural heritage, his Dogon figure controlling the "traffic" of exotically clad policemen? We might well view it that way, as part of the explosion of creativity inspired by nostalgia for home and fascination with the new cultures of Ghana. These tunics, fashion statements by youthful travelers, illustrate the power of dress to absorb layers of cultural influences, reflecting new forms of status even as they celebrate the cultures of home.

REFERENCES

Bah, Amadou Tahiroum, and Joseph Brunet-Jailly. 2002. "Métiers d'art de Djenné: la Broderie." In Brunet-Jailly, ed., *Djenné: d'hier à demain,* 97–120. Bamako: Editions Donniya.

Bovin, Mette. 2001. *Nomads Who Cultivate Beauty: Wodaabe Dances and Visual Arts in Niger.* Uppsala: Nordiska Afrikainstitutet.

De Haan, Arjan, Karen Brock, and Ngolo Coulibaly. 2002. "Migrations, Livelihoods, and Institutions: Contrasting Patterns of Migration in Mali." *Journal of Development Studies* 38(5): 37–58.

Dougnon, Isaïe. Forthcoming. "Ghana Boys and Glamour: European Clothing among the Dogon, 1920–1960." In T. C. McCaskie and Keith Shear, eds., *African at Home and Abroad: Social Aspiration and Personal Lives.* Madison: University of Wisconsin Press.

Dupuis-Yakouba, Auguste. 1921. *Industries et Principales Professions des Habitants de la région de Tombouctou.* Paris: Émile-Larose.

Eicher, Joanne B., and Barbara Sumberg. 1995. "World Fashion, Ethnic, and National Dress." In Joanne Eicher, ed., *Dress and Ethnicity: Change Across Space and Time,* 295–306. Washington, DC: Berg.

Frank, Barbara. 1998. *Mande Potters and Leatherworkers: Art and Heritage in West Africa.* Washington, DC: Smithsonian Institution Press.

Gardi, Bernhard. 1988. *Mali Land Im Sahel.* Basel: Museum fur Volkerkunde.

Gardi, Bernard. 1994. "La Broderie." In R.M.A. Bedaux and J. D. van der Waals, eds., *Djenné: Une Ville Millénaire au Mali,*139–148. Leiden: Rijksmuseum voor Volkenkunde.

Gardi, Bernhard, ed. 2002. *Le Boubou—C'est Chic: Les boubous du Mali et d'autres pays de l'Afrique de l'Ouest.* Basel: Museum der Kulturen Basel/Christoph Merian Verlag.

Gardi, Bernhard. 2003. *Textiles du Mali d'après les collections du Musée National du Mali.* Bamako: Musée National du Mali.

Grosz-Ngaté, Maria. 2000. "Labor Migration, Gender, and Social Transformation." In R. James Bingen, David Robinson, John M. Staatz, eds., *Democracy and Development in Mali,* 87–101. East Lansing: Michigan State University.

Hacquard, Mgr. Augustin. 1900. *Monographie de Tombouctou.* Paris: Société des Études Coloniales and Maritimes.

Hunwick, John O. 2003. *Timbuktu and the Songhay Empire.* Boston: Brill.

Larkin, Brian. 2008. *Signal and Noise: Media, Infrastructure, and Urban Culture in Nigeria.* Durham: Duke University Press.

Lydon, Ghislaine. 2009. *On Trans-Saharan Trails: Islamic Law, Trade Networks, and Cross-Cultural Exchange.* New York: Cambridge University Press.

McNaughton, Patrick R. 1982. "The Shirts that Mande Hunters Wear." *African Arts* 15(3): 54–58.

Prussin, Labelle. 1986. *Hatumere: Islamic Design in West Africa.* Berkeley: University of California Press.

Saad, Elias N. 1983. *Social History of Timbuktu: The Role of Muslim Scholars and Notables, 1400–1900.* New York: Cambridge University Press.

Seligman, Thomas K., and Kristyne Loughran, eds. 2006. *The Art of Being Tuareg: Sahara Nomads in a Modern World.* Los Angeles, San Francisco: Fowler Museum of Cultural History and Iris B. Gerald Cantor Center for Visual Arts.

Zacharia, K. C., J. Condé, N. K. Nair, and C. S. Okoye. 1980. *Demographic Aspects of Migration in West Africa.* Washington, DC: World Bank.

–9–

Forging Connections, Performing Distinctions: Youth, Dress, and Consumption in Niger

Adeline Masquelier

In Niger, young men often declared to me that dress was a matter of personal choice, not something that should not be dictated by religion, politics, or parental expectations. Despite being largely unemployed and having limited resources, they take great care to cultivate a fashionable appearance. "You dress a certain way because that's who you are," twenty-year-old Habibou told me. His friend Moussa elaborated:

> Wearing an outfit is about desire. It's a personal thing. I may want to wear a certain type of dress that isn't going to please everyone. Let's say I enter the mosque with my T-shirt and I pray...My prayer will be accepted. What's unacceptable are T-shirts with designs that attract your neighbor's attention. Instead of concentrating on his prayer, he'll focus on the picture on your shirt.

Although the overwhelming majority of young men in Niger identify as Muslim, many of them—regardless of whether they are religiously observant—eschew locally tailored "Islamic" attire to adopt mass-produced Western T-shirts (or tailored shirts) and pants. In contrast to the previous generation for whom dress signaled a specific Muslim affiliation, they often dismiss the notion that dress is an index of religious identity. Wearing Islamic dress doesn't make one a Muslim, they claim when feeling the need to defend themselves against accusations of religious laxity.

Dress, young men claim, is about self-expression, not conformity to religious or cultural norms. A young man known to his friends as Ronaldo often wore a green jersey advertising his fondness for the Brazilian national soccer team. "I took the name Ronaldo after my favorite player in my favorite team—Brazil," he told me. "My friends and I watch a lot of soccer. So I wear the team's jersey, it's who I am." Yet even as male youth claim that dress communicates "who [rather than what] they are," they also long to be transformed via some act of consumption into desirable others. By providing access to foreign media and commodities, the liberalization of the country's economy in the 1990s has facilitated the emergence of a local consumer culture. Many young people have embraced this burgeoning consumerism. Acutely aware that their expectations of social mobility are imperiled by the country's continued economic decline,[1] they draw on the world of fashion as a resource for enhancing themselves and distinguishing themselves from their supposedly poorer, less cosmopolitan counterparts.

Previously young men achieved adulthood by seeking employment, marrying, and starting families. Since economic shifts produced by structural adjustment programs and liberalization policies have derailed Niger from a developmental trajectory, those who attended school on the assumption that education led to economic stability and social empowerment have experienced that they cannot find secure employment. Unable to move out of their natal homes and set up households of their own, they are "stuck in the compound" (Hansen 2005). Regardless of their chronological age, they remain *samari*—youth (Masquelier 2005). Yet the very conditions that impede their becoming *cikaku mutane* (full persons) enable them to push boundaries and experiment with a range of identities before settling into mature social roles. These processes of experimentation and creativity are particularly visible in the domain of dress and fashion. Young men invoke their status as *petits* (juniors) to justify their adoption of trendy looks and their reluctance to dress like their parents. Dress therefore provides a lens through which to explore their practices of identity fashioning as they struggle to achieve social mobility while also capitalizing on their youth.

British cultural studies have emphasized the role consumption practices play in the formation of youth cultures resisting parental values and capitalist culture (Hall and Jefferson 1976; Hebdidge 1979). More recently, scholars have examined consumer culture as a site of gendered participation, enjoyment, and constraint through which young people remake themselves as youth, citizens, and social actors (Fadzillah 2005; Gandoulou 1989; Gondola 1999; Hansen 2008; Ivaska 2004; Lukose 2005). Meanwhile, Fernandes (2006) and Cole (2008) have demonstrated how the emergence of class is materially and discursively tied to economic liberalization and globalization. In his account of middle-class culture in Nepal, Liechty defines class as "not a thing, or a set of characteristics to be defined and measured, but as practice and process" (2006: 27). As a performative, contested identity, middle-class emerges out of the constitutive interplay of consumption, fashion, media, and youth. Building on these various studies, I consider how Nigérien youth, and young men in particular, harness fashion to claim distinction and cope with social exclusion. I examine how they draw on the semiotic power of dress to carve a place for themselves in the world at a time when Niger's media-saturated, globally inflected cultural economy encourages people to imagine alternative ways of being and belonging (Appadurai 1996). Drawing on Liechty's notion that class should be understood as a "constantly renegotiated cultural space—a space of ideas, values, goods, practices, and embodied behaviors in which the terms of inclusion and exclusion are endlessly tested, negotiated, and affirmed" (2003: 15–16), I highlight the shifty, intersecting, and occasionally unwitting ways that young men produce socioeconomic distinctions. The settings for my ethnographic study are Dogondoutchi, a provincial town of some forty thousand heterogeneous Hausa-speakers, and Niamey, the country's multilingual capital.

WE ARE *BRANCHÉS*: FASHION, CONNECTEDNESS, AND CONTEMPORANEITY

Dress has long been a vehicle through which people on the periphery constitute themselves as modern cosmopolitans (Martin 1995). Even more so now that consumption has become the most visible means of asserting one's participation in global modernity. Far from being frivolous or sinful (as conservative Muslims claim), young Nigérien men's pursuit of "the latest" is motivated by a genuine desire to develop themselves by acquiring competitive skills and the material accouterments that bespeak middle-class prosperity. Because dressing fashionably presupposes one has financial resources and access to information about the latest trends, youth who through sartorial investments distance themselves from so-called tradition can claim to be *branchés* (plugged in). One conventionally speaks of *brancher* an electric appliance by connecting it to a power source. By the same token, *se brancher* is to connect oneself to circuits of information via technology. In slang, to be *branché* is to be at once connected, oriented, and informed while *brancher* someone is to connect this person to someone else or arouse his or her interest.

According to twenty-five-year-old Issoufou, "un branché is someone who eats well, dresses well, attends parties, then returns home to do nothing." Issoufou's definition of branché captures the experience of educated youth who, like him, remain unemployed rather than engage in low-paying work. Elders may see the branché youth returning home to "do nothing" as lazy and unproductive, but to his peers, he embodies, through dress, consumption, and leisure, the very essence of success. Being branché, then, is not about enjoying financial stability so much as it is about projecting a stylistic savoir-faire enabled by one's consumerist engagements and grasp of current fashions. When socioeconomic conditions have simultaneously excluded youth from the labor market and targeted them as consumers, the branché's strategy is to resort to "virtual consumption." Convinced that social mobility implies participating in the drama of Western progress, young men obtain consumer goods in an effort to display standards of living they cannot afford (Jeffrey 2010). Lacking economic capital, they strive to acquire other forms of capital in their determined efforts to embody success.

Despite his limited income, Issoufou thus spent comparatively vast sums of money to acquire fashionable clothes and equip his girlfriend with similarly modish outfits. He kept up with trends by buying secondhand clothes when he couldn't afford new ones, borrowing items from friends, and even swapping goods for clothes from tourists. He once showed me a pair of fancy shoes and an expensive cell phone he claimed to have bought with the cash earned working for a shop owner for a few months. Keeping abreast of fashion, he intimated, was a constant struggle. In contrast, his friend Salissou largely expected his parents to finance his appetite for fashionable things. The privileges he enjoyed (while his lifestyle was subsidized) gave him a sense of entitlement and a savoir-faire that his less fortunate peers could not claim. It is through the possession of this kind of social capital that class distinctions emerge, Bourdieu (1984 [1979]) argued. Far from enmeshing them in a new "consumerist middle-class," as Liechty (2003) claims is the case for Nepalese youth, the diverse strategies young Nigérien men employ to access commodities often mobilize oppositions that reinstate social divides.

Scholars have recently examined the complex linkages between globalization and youth culture, arguing that processes of globalization cannot be adequately understood without a consideration of the pivotal role of youth (Cole and Durham 2008b; Maira and Soep 2005; Nilan and Feixa 2006). This perspective highlights ways in which the notion of development informs both analyses of youth culture (through a focus on "maturation") and the study of globalization (through a focus on "progress"). Yet neither maturation nor progress can be framed as temporal stages along a forward-moving continuum, Maira and Soep (2005: xxiii) note. Far from homogenizing the world, the movement of people, goods, and images across national borders is predicated upon and has further produced deep inequalities. These inequalities, in turn, have upset the "neat chronologies of the modernist life cycle" (Cole and Durham 2008a: 11), making it impossible for many youth to successfully mature into social adults. Despite these failures, the dream of development is alive and well in Niger. There, technologies of self-fashioning such as dress are an important modality through which youth attempt to secure prospects in what Castells (1996) calls the "network society."

Young men choose from a variety of vestmental styles, but none of these are complete without a *salula* (cellular phone). As both a technology for forging connections and the ultimate symbol of connectivity, the salula is an indispensable accessory of the branché's accouterment. As part of one's *zamani* (modern) look, it must be prominently displayed: young men clip their cell phones on their belts or hang them around their necks. Those who cannot afford the real thing purchase the plastic toy version at local markets, wearing them prominently on their chests and going as far as borrowing them from each other when posing for photographs. The blue and pink toy phones hanging from the necks of jobless youth do not deliver actual calls but call attention to their wearers, highlighting the struggles these youth face as they aspire to be included in the ever-expanding universe of mobile telephony.

Although few youth can afford to call each other (when they do, conversations are remarkably short[7]), ownership of a salula nonetheless signals membership in the privileged society of branchés individuals. It sets one apart from those lacking these means of communication. Urbanites and educated individuals are anxious to distinguish themselves from the supposedly backward *ruraux* (country folks). Abdou, a university graduate sent to teach primary school in a distant village, spoke of the terrible isolation he endured in a place where there was no network: "The worst is that I can't use my cell phone to call my girlfriend or receive news from my parents."

"Owning a cell phone is an obsession for [Nigérien] youth. They go to great extremes to procure one. When they succeed they make sure everyone sees it" (Baba 2003: 13). Not all cell phones are created equal, however. The price of available devices varies greatly. Top-of-the-line cell phones can cost as much as US$1,000. Those wishing to distinguish themselves from the average salula owner purchase phones with the latest features (special text messaging formats, glow in the dark, and so on). The value of cell phones does not reside solely in their capacity to impress: they are also used as a money reserve. When strapped for cash, owners sell their expensive phone and buy a cheaper model, which they'll trade in for a nicer one in flush times. It is not uncommon for young men to possess as many as three or four cell phones. Ironically, while this strategy enhances the illusion of connectivity,[3] it often hinders communication: networks are overburdened, callers forget on which phone they saved a callee's number, and so on.

Cell phones, even if they have restricted connective capacities, bespeak young people's desire to hook up with the world. They are an essential tool of romance: one cannot hope to attract a girl's attention without displaying a cell phone clipped to one's belt. A local youth was rumored to have borrowed a substantial sum to purchase a cell phone that would impress his girlfriend. According to a high school student, "Some people don't even have a goat but they get indebted to buy a salula and seduce girls." The cell phone, twenty-two-year-old Moussa explains,

> is a symbol. To show off. If a girl sees you with a 50 000FCFA [$500US] cell phone and nice clothes, she'll think, "Oh, an *alhaji*[4] [wealthy trader]" or "Great! A *boss, je vais croquer* [I'm going to eat]."

Young women require a cell phone from their boyfriends both as a measure of the young men's attachment to them and a means of evading parental control when setting up romantic rendezvous. According to Moussa, "Girls use their phone to ask for things. They send you a text message: 'Hey, you, I need this. Please send me 2000 CFA francs.'" Lest young women be reduced to the status of gold diggers, it is worth pointing out that while young men complain that romantic relationships are often mediated by money, their female counterparts describe them as unfaithful partners who like to sample other women. In the end, both young men and women are ambivalent about love and marriage. Lovers, they say, frequently betray each other, and it is difficult not to let material concerns overshadow sentiments.

Recall that those who are branchés "dress well." For many young men, this means adopting the chic ghetto look of rappers they see in the media or during live performances (see Plate 8). In Niger as elsewhere, hip-hop fashions are synonymous with "modernity, cosmopolitanism, and a certain degree of savvy" (Moyer 2003: 101). Note that the Hausa term *zamani* (period) translates as *modernity* but also refers to fashion and trendiness. *Shina cikin zamani* (he is in the times) means *he is fashionable.* "We like novelty, it's in our nature to be attracted to new clothes," a young man told me. The up-to-date-ness evoked by zamani reinforces for Hausa speakers the sense that fashion is about connectedness and contemporaneity—that is, about situating oneself in time and space so as to catch up with the world. For Nigérien youth who routinely speak of the shame of being last (Niger ranks at the bottom of the UN scale of human development), fashion strategically bridges the disconnect between the world of poverty and underdevelopment they live in and the world "out there" filled with tantalizing, yet distant possibilities. As in Dakar where youth classify people on the basis of their shoes' provenance (Scheld 2003), foreign clothes or footwear signal the consumer's connections to other places around the world: Timberland boots or All-Star high tops "speak" of the U.S., whereas a Lacoste polo shirt or a soccer jersey bearing the colors of FC Barcelona suggests one buys "European."

SOCIAL TIES AND SARTORIAL INVESTMENTS

To appreciate young men's intense concerns with fashion, let's widen the lens momentarily and consider the role of clothing among the wider population. In Niger, men and women share an intense preoccupation with clothes, have an elaborate conception of what it means to be dressed stylishly, and spend comparatively vast sums of money to acquire fashionable outfits. Clothes are not mere adornment, however; they are centrally implicated in the creation and maintenance of social bonds. Men are responsible for providing clothing for their dependents. Wives and children eagerly await Babbar Salla (commemoration of Abraham's sacrifice) when they receive new clothes.

Cloth symbolically and literally binds people together. Once the marriage has been "tied," a bride waits to receive a *valise* (suitcase filled with clothes) from the groom before entering her new marital home. One might say that a man's gift of clothing to his bride tightens the marital knot. In the past, adoption was concretized through a gift of clothing from father to child. Destroying or getting rid of clothes, on the other hand, actualizes the severance of these relationships (Masquelier 1996).

Clothing communicates information about the wearer's identity: wealth, education, adherence to Muslim values, and so on. By wearing certain sets of clothes, people signal that they are (or aspire to be) members of a particular constituency such as the *umma* or the civil service. Conversely, clothing can set people apart (Bourdieu 1984 [1979]). The distinctions that operate are not uniformly recognized, however. Those who go for the *alhaji* (pilgrim) look by wearing a *babban riga* are not necessarily practicing Muslims. By the same token, a young man's new sneakers and fancy watch may suggest that he has resources when in reality he is jobless. The deceptive potential of clothing enables people to create an appearance of wealth that contradicts their actual economic status. Dress, people say, is not always a good indicator of who a person really is. The recent adoption of *hijabi* (veil) in some Muslim households has spurred lively debates about "fake" veils, impious women, and hidden prostitution (Masquelier 2008). Deceptive or not, appearances "speak" (Barthes 1983). Youth are proficient in the language of fashion; they scrutinize each other's outfits to evaluate how much money was spent. A young man enumerated for me the value of the clothes his friend wore to visit his girlfriend: the khaki fatigues cost 6,000 CFA francs, his long-sleeved polo shirt could be had for 3,500 CFA francs, and his imitation Gucci glasses sold for 2,500 CFA francs at a local market.

By putting on a recognizable brand (a Fila T-shirt or Adidas shoes), a young man exposes himself to his peers' discriminating gaze. Friends will "read" his outfit to determine his sartorial worth and whether he deserves respect. To successfully compete, young men pester their parents for cash to keep themselves in fashion. Any money they earn through sporadic employment goes to replenish their wardrobe (or their girlfriends'). Some sell drugs to satisfy their yearnings for consumer goods. Others steal or engage in illegal commerce. In 2004, a reputedly "good-for-nothing" youth stole most of the content of a bag of rice from his mother before disappearing from sight. A few days later, he returned wearing brand-new sneakers. There was no doubt in anyone's mind that he had bought the shoes with money obtained from the stolen rice.

Reading the value of clothing off of someone's body is a skill young women develop as they look for suitable boyfriends who will keep them fashionably attired. Lavishing gifts of cloth on a young woman demonstrate not only the genuineness of a suitor's intentions but that he can provide for a wife (Masquelier 2009). Despite widespread claims that romance is independent from finance, young people admit that the strength of a man's attachment to his girlfriend can be measured by the quantity and quality of her outfits. One day, an altercation occurred between a taxi driver and the young woman he courted over a large bill sent to the young man by a cloth saleswoman. Unbeknownst to him, the object of his affection had ordered large quantities of costly fabric from the saleswoman and sent them to a tailor. She wished to appear at the next round of wedding and naming ceremonies in brand-new outfits befitting her future rank as a middle-class housewife. Her suitor would pay for everything, she told the *commerçante* and the tailor. Their relationship had been tested by her extravagant spending. The young man knew he would have to contribute to his fiancée's wardrobe, yet the price he ultimately paid to secure her commitment was higher than anticipated.

Because it is a husband's duty to clothe his wife, a woman feeling inadequately provided for may ask for a divorce—or she may pressure her husband to buy her additional clothes. Women are sometimes accused of ruining their husbands to satisfy their lust for cloth and compete with their peers. Because, as the Hausa adage goes, a wife reflects the glory of her husband, men may have no recourse but to satisfy their wives' demands if they want to remain married. Upon leaving her husband of two years, Bibata told me that her dissatisfaction with the marriage stemmed primarily from his failure to equip her with new outfits. She could not bear the shame of attending social events dressed in drab, washed-out clothes when her friends wore brand-new, crisp attires. Besides reminding us that clothing indexes wealth, Bibata's story exemplifies how worn-out clothes speak of the quality of a marriage. Since clothing actively mediates husband-wife relations, women wearing tattered outfits in public visibly display their husbands' lack of marital commitment or their state of impoverishment.

The same logic dictates that a woman who remains married without receiving new clothes be perceived as strongly (and perhaps excessively) attached to her husband. Upon noticing that her niece Bassira, who previously received generous gifts of cloth and money from suitors, had been wearing the same worn outfits for some time, a friend exclaimed, "She must be truly in love!" Only genuine love, my friend implied, would keep Bassira in a relationship with a man who could not afford to substantially reward her for the favors he presumably enjoyed. Cloth and clothing, these cases remind us, "anticipate, acknowledge, constitute, recall and memorialize relationships" (Miller 2005: 17). They also highlight the gendered dimension of consumption and the tensions emerging when young women's visions of middle-class prosperity do not mesh with their suitors' social aspirations.

KEEPING UP WITH FASHION IS HARD WORK

At dance parties, young men and women dress with utmost care and invest a great deal of time and money in the creation of the total look: the "rapper" look for most young men, the "sexy" look for young women. These gender-mixed gatherings are widely condemned by conservative Muslims as sites of immorality and decadent consumption. In this overwhelmingly Muslim country, many believe that veiling, seclusion, and other practices aimed at limiting women's mobility and protecting their integrity should be more strictly enforced and that dancing and music should be altogether banned. To escape opprobrium and avoid having to tell their parents where they go (and what they wear) on Saturday night, young girls attending dance parties engage in clever subterfuges. Dressed in conservatively outfits covering much of their bodies, they walk to a girlfriend's house after informing their parents that that is where they'll spend the evening. There they change into the racy outfit they brought with them: a *mini-jupe* (knee-length pencil skirt) and *baya* (tight tank top) or a pair of curve-hugging *pantalons pattes* (bell-bottom jeans) over a T-shirt with a low-cut neckline—and for the really adventurous, a clingy, sleeveless dress with a thigh-high slit, a hooded jacket, and high-heel mules (see Figure 9.1).

Young men face less pressure to conform to local norms of modesty and rarely hide their sartorial acquisitions and whereabouts from elders. They may nonetheless encounter disapproving stares as they leave the house in full hip-hop gear to attend a social event: in the eyes of conservative Muslims, young men wearing modern clothes (*tuffafin zamani*) of Western inspiration act in disregard of Qur'anic teachings. True, all young men own at least one Islamic article of clothing: usually a simple *jaba*, more rarely the more expensive *babban riga*—the lingua franca of male Hausa dress. Yet the large majority rarely wears this item outside of wedding receptions and prescribed Muslim festivals where everyone in town visibly affirms their membership in the Muslim community through dress and diet. Because the *alhaji* look (achieved by wearing a babban riga) connotes piety, wealth, and respectability, young men adopt it whenever they wish to put the accent on their Muslimhood. Thus, youth do not stick to one performative script but instead shift from among several available performances ("urbanite," "rapper," "Muslim," or "relaxed") depending on the occasion. Each performance strategically situates them within a distinct social field, mobilizing class oppositions through the display of stylistic difference (rural/urban, alhaji/nonpracticing Muslim, educated/uneducated, etc.).

Figure 9.1 Young women wearing matching pencil skirts at a dance party with a male friend. Photo by Adeline Masquelier.

Dance parties are opportunities to impress but also compete with one's peers, and this is why one wears trendy and preferably new clothes. Twenty-three-year-old Ali'ou explains: "For celebrations, wedding receptions, and dances, we like to *sapper* [dress fashionably]. Me, I wear baggy pants and Paladium tennis shoes." For many young men, the de rigueur dress at dance parties includes baggy jeans (or khaki pants), oversized T-shirts adorned with the name of a widely popular rap artist (such as Eminem or 50 Cent) or the face of President Obama, a baseball cap, and high tops (or Timberland boots) (see Figure 9.2). Accessories (silver chains, bandanas, earrings) are part of the look many aim for. Other young men go instead for the *coupé-décalé* style, a controversial fashion (associated with a dance music and hedonistic culture of the same name) from Côte d'Ivoire that has earned a substantial following among youth striving to channel meager resources into self-enhancement. Wearing sleeveless jackets worn over clingy T-shirts or tight shirts and close-fitting bell-bottom jeans, they emulate coupé-décalé performers who "carve out spaces of *jouissance* in the face of diminished opportunities and real precarity" (McGovern 2010: 90). The world of easy money, decadence, and hipness conjured by coupeurs-décaleurs has been denounced by critics as "all style

Figure 9.2 Young men dressed as rappers posing at a dance party. Photo by Adeline Masquelier.

no substance." Not only does it lack the authenticity of hip-hop, some argue, but it has fostered an immodesty many find troubling. Those who reject hip-hop and coupé-décalé fashions and opt for the classic look (long-sleeved shirts, pleated pants, and dress shoes) associated with educated urbanites take no less care to polish their appearance: Shirts are impeccably clean, pants are neatly pressed, and shoes shine.

As elsewhere in Africa (Ferguson 2002; Newell 2005; Scheld 2007), young Nigériens employ creative strategies to "appropriate, gatecrash, cushion, subvert or resist the effects of their exclusion" (Nyamnjoh 2004: 39) from the world of wages and entitlements. Demonstrating one is a *'dan zamani* (modern person) by keeping up with the latest sartorial styles takes skill and dedication. Buying new clothes is best. Some youths obtain clothes from suppliers in Niamey or buy them directly from traders returning from Tripoli or Dubai. Those who cannot afford new clothes (referred to as *qualité*) purchase secondhand *bosho* clothes (from *Boston*). Local *fripperies* (secondhand stores) sell a range of bosho, from ski jackets to baggy jeans and gangsta-style shorts to dress shirts as well as stuffed animals (see Figure 9.3). Originally, bosho clothes were known as *kaya matatu* (dead people's things). Like hair extensions thought to be

Figure 9.3 Young man selling used baggy pants in Dogondoutchi. Photo by Salifou Hamidou.

dead people's hair, they were spurned by local consumers. With the loosening of restrictions on used clothes imports and the continued impact of the economic crisis, bosho gained popularity among youth: "You can find nice pants for 750 CFA francs at the *fripperie* but the same ones will cost you 3,000 CFA francs if you buy qualité," a young man explained. In contrast to bosho items hanging from racks and trees or piled on the ground, qualité clothes come folded in crisp plastic bags. Bosho is thought to come ("on a boat") from the United States whereas qualité products are supposedly manufactured in China. The latter are judged to be of lesser quality than their vintage counterparts although their design follows changing trends more closely.

Young men complain about the shoddy quality of locally available consumer goods, highlighting the perceived contrast between life in Niger and life in wealthier countries, where everything from school bags to cell phones is allegedly of better quality. Hamissou explained,

> The stuff you buy here doesn't last. Our *salula* stop working after a few months. The shoes and shirts you buy fall apart quickly. Whereas your products are good quality. Even the soap we use is inferior. It's called SoKlean but isn't like the real Omo. You can tell by the lather, when you wash your clothes, it doesn't foam right.

Hamissou's description of how soap "doesn't foam right" because the local version is a pale imitation of the real thing provides a measure of the gap young Nigériens feel between the world they live in and the elsewheres they fantasize about. As Weiss notes in his ethnography of marginality in urban Tanzania, this poignantly illustrates how "the dynamism and force of the global world constructed by these . . . actors are clearly felt to lie elsewhere" (2009: 127).

Regardless of its quality, one must keep one's wardrobe clean and fresh-looking: sneakers should remain in pristine condition (a problem with "cheap" knockoffs is that soles quickly come unglued), and clothes shouldn't lose their sheen after two washes. Aside from being able to select items from a vast array of stuff of differing origin, quality, and value, "clothing competence" (Hansen 2004: 174) involves learning how to preserve the crisp and clean appearance of one's clothes. To that end, young men (and young women) avoid wearing their best clothes on a daily basis, especially if they are engaged in potentially sullying activities. One wears one's good clothes when it is important to be elegant. Before visiting their girlfriends, young men wash and iron their nicest clothes—borrowing items from a friend if necessary. Although none of them ever put it to me that way, young Nigériens would probably agree with their Zambian counterparts that dressing for self-enhancement is "hard work" (Hansen 2009: 118).

THE FUN OF DRESSING

Lest my discussion of fashion be construed solely as work, let me say in conclusion that Nigérien youth also perceive dressing up as a fun, pleasurable, and occasionally irreverent endeavor driven by the desire to challenge the status quo as well as the perception that all things, including having fun, are ephemeral. Thus, "fun" provides a useful lens through which to explore young people's relationship to global consumer spaces. Lukose notes, however, that "it is difficult to formulate precisely how one can rescue the 'fun' of fashion from its simultaneous demonization by the protectors of 'tradition' and by critics of capitalism who locate 'fun' as a mere diversion, a market-driven, consumer, middle-class subterfuge" (2005: 930–931). Recuperating the playful in young men's fashion practice implies recognizing that play is both experimentation and escape from the world of labor, adulthood, and social responsibilities. Firmly located in the here and now and unburdened by a sense of the past, "fun" is a mode of self-fashioning that privileges newness. It is marked by the tension between a desire to belong and a desire to "distinguish [one]self before others" (Simmel 1950: 338). In the way that it channels their middle-class aspirations, it is a means of contradicting the rhetoric of failure that has come to define young men in this era of job scarcity.

Given the condemnation that youth's fashion exuberance draws from elders (for whom youth practices are often synonymous with triviality and immodesty), those seeking to affirm their maturity take pains not to dress like rappers or coupé-décalé fans. A young policeman in training explained, "When I was younger I dressed as an MC with baggy jeans, chains, and earrings. Now that I am a gendarme, a monsieur, I cannot dress like that. When I go out, I wear a three-piece suit. I must look respectable." Dress here was an inescapable dimension of the middle-class values the young man felt he typified now that he was gainfully employed. When I offered to buy a friend a pair of jeans as a goodbye present, he refused saying that he wanted his students to respect him. He too was well aware that youthful performances were scripted by a "politics of fun" (Bayat 2007: 433) that contradicted the kind of responsible personhood he wished to embody. Although he could barely sustain his wife and daughter on his meager salary as a temp high-school teacher, he strove to project through dress and deportment an appearance of maturity in keeping with his new status as a "full" adult.

Much of the value of being fashionable, Finkelstein (1991: 143) notes, rests upon successfully eliciting respect, approbation, and envy from others. Nigérien young men who, through their deliberate choice of fashion, articulate desirable social identities would probably concur. As they wait for adulthood and its attendant rights and responsibilities, they use dress as a personalized mode of conveying who they are or aspire to be, mapping out desired itineraries from unemployed citizens of the world's poorest country to fashion-savvy, branchés consumers. Focusing on their sartorial experimentations thus provides a window into the workings of social class. At a time when traditional mechanisms of social mobility are threatened and consumption is the most visible means of self-enhancement, understanding how socioeconomic identity and difference are staged and performed through fashion-centered practices is more relevant than ever.

NOTES

1. Niger's economy experienced a short-lived boom in the 1970s and early 1980s but has performed poorly ever since.
2. To save money, callers "beep": call and hang up after the first ring. By utilizing the cell phone's technological capabilities, the aborted call's recipient finds out who called and interprets the message accordingly.
3. By making their phone numbers differentially accessible to interlocutors, young men appear to be well-connected individuals receiving a high volume of calls. Moreover, "You only give out all your phone numbers to important people."
4. A pilgrim returning from Mecca is called alhaji. Because wealth and piety presuppose one another, wealthy businessmen are called alhaji regardless of whether they have been to Mecca.

REFERENCES

Appadurai, Arjun. 1996. *Modernity at Large: Cultural Dimensions of Globalization.* Minneapolis: University of Minnesota Press.

Baba, Naïm Ahmat. 2003. "Un cellulaire pour la frime." *Tel Quel* 13: 13.

Barthes, Roland. 1983. *The Fashion System.* Berkeley: University of California Press.

Bayat, Asef. 2007. "Islamism and the Politics of Fun." *Public Culture* 19(3): 433–459.

Bourdieu, Pierre. 1984[1979]. *Distinction: A Social Critique of the Judgment of Taste.* Cambridge: Harvard University Press.

Castells, Manuel. 1996. *The Rise of the Network Society.* Oxford: Blackwell Publishers.

Cole, Jennifer. 2008. "Fashioning Distinction: Youth and Consumerism in Urban Madagascar." In Jennifer Cole and Deborah Durham, eds., *Figuring the Future: Globalization and Temporalities of Children and Youth,* 99–124. Santa Fe: School for Advanced Research Press.

Cole, Jennifer, and Deborah Durham. 2008a. "Introduction: Globalization and the Temporality of Children and Youth." In Jennifer Cole and Deborah Durham, eds., *Figuring the Future: Globalization and the Temporalities of Children and Youth,* 3–23. Santa Fe: School for Advanced Research Press.

Cole, Jennifer, and Deborah Durham, eds. 2008b. *Figuring the Future: Globalization and the Temporalities of Children and Youth.* Santa Fe: School for Advanced Research Press.

Fadzillah, Ida. 2005. "The Amway Connection: How Transnational Ideas of Beauty and Money Affect Thai Girls' Perceptions of Their Future Options." In Sunaina Maira and Elisabeth Soep, eds., *Youthscapes: The Popular, the National, the Global,* 85–102. Philadelphia: University of Pennsylvania Press.

Ferguson, James. 2002. "Of Mimicry and Membership: Africans and the 'New World Society.'" *Cultural Anthropology* 17(4): 551–569.

Fernandes, Leela. 2006. *India's New Middle Class: Democratic Politics in an Era of Economic Reform.* Minneapolis: Minnesota University Press.

Finkeltsein, Joanne. 1991. *The Fashioned Self.* Philadelphia: Temple University Press.

Gandoulou, Justin-Daniel. 1989. *Dandies à Bacongo: Le culte de l'élégance dans la société congolaise contemporaine.* Paris: L'Harmattan.

Gondola, Ch. Didier. 1999. "Dream and Drama: The Search for Elegance among Congolese Youth." *Africa Today* 42(1): 23–48.

Hall, Stuart, and Tony Jefferson. 1976. *Resistance through Rituals: Youth Subcultures in Post-War Britain.* London: Hutchinson.

Hansen, Karen Tranberg. 2004. "Dressing Dangerously: Miniskirts, Gender Relations, and Sexuality in Zambia." In Jean Allman, ed., *Fashioning Africa: Power and the Politics of Dress,* 166–185. Bloomington: Indiana University Press.

Hansen, Karen Tranberg. 2005. "Getting Stuck in the Compound: Some Odds Against Social Adulthood in Lusaka, Zambia." *Africa Today* 51(4): 3–16.

Hansen, Karen Tranberg, ed. 2008. *Youth and the City in the Global South.* Bloomington: Indiana University Press.

Hansen, Karen Tranberg. 2009. "Youth, Gender, and Secondhand Clothing in Lusaka, Zambia: Local and Global Styles." In Eugenia Paulicelli and Hazel Clark, eds., *The Fabric of Cultures: Fashion, Identity, and Globalization,* 112–127. New York: Routledge.

Hebdidge, Dick. 1979. *Subculture: The Meaning of Style.* New York: Methuen and Co.

Ivaska, Andrew M. 2004. "Anti-Mini Militants Meet Modern Misses: Urban Style, Gender, and the Politics of 'National Culture' in 1960s Dar es Salam." In Jean Allman, ed., *Fashioning Africa: Power and the Politics of Dress,* 104–121. Bloomington: Indiana University Press.

Jeffrey, Craig. 2010. *Timepass: Youth, Class, and the Politics of Waiting in India.* Stanford: Stanford University Press.

Liechty, Mark. 2003. *Suitably Modern: Making Middle-Class Culture in a New Consumer Society.* Princeton: Princeton University Press.

Liechty, Mark. 2006. "Building Body, Making Face, Doing Love: Mass Media and the Configuration of Class and Gender in Kathmandu." In T.J.M. Holden and T. J. Scrase, eds, *Medi@sia: Global Media/tion In and Out of Context,* 25–43. New York: Routledge.

Lukose, Ritty. 2005. "Consuming Globalization: Youth and Gender in Kerala, India." *Journal of Social History* 38(4): 215–235.

Maira, Sunaina, and Elisabeth Soep, eds. 2005. *Youthscapes: The Popular, the National, the Global.* Philadelphia: University of Pennsylvania Press.

Masquelier, Adeline. 1996. "Mediating Threads: Clothing and the Texture of Spirit/Medium Relations in *Bori.*" In Hildi Hendrickson, ed., *Clothing and Difference: Embodied Identities in Colonial and Post-Colonial Africa,* 66–93. Durham: Duke University Press.

Masquelier, Adeline. 2005. "The Scorpion's Sting: Youth, Marriage, and the Struggle for Social Maturity in Niger." *Journal of the Royal Anthropological Institute (Man)* 11: 59–83.

Masquelier, Adeline. 2008. "When Female Spirits Start Veiling: The Case of the Veiled She-Devil in a Muslim Town of Niger." *Africa Today* 54(1): 39–64.

Masquelier, Adeline. 2009. *Women and Islamic Revival in a West African Town.* Bloomington: Indiana University Press.

McGovern, Mike. 2010. "This is Play: Popular Culture and Politics in Côte d'Ivoire." In Anne-Maria Makhulu, Beth A. Bugenhagen, and Stephen Jackson, eds. *Hard Work, Hard Times: Global Volatility and African Subjectivities,* 69–90. Berkeley: University of California Press.

Miller, Daniel. 2005. "Introduction." In Susanne Küchler and Daniel Miller, eds., *Clothing as Material Culture,* 1–19. Oxford: Berg.

Moyer, Eileen. 2003. "Keeping Up Appearances: Fashion and Function Among Dar es Salam Street Youth." *Etnofoor* 16(2): 88–105.

Newell, Sasha. 2005. "Migratory Modernity and the Cosmology of Consumption in Côte D'Ivoire." In Lillian Trager, ed., *Migration and Economy: Global and Local Dynamics,* 163–190. Walnut Creek, CA: AltaMira.

Niang, Abdoulaye. 2006. "Bboys: Hip-Hop Culture in Dakar, Sénégal." In Pam Nilan and Carles Feixa, eds., *Global Youth? Hybrid Identities, Plural Worlds,* 167–185. New York: Routledge.

Nilan, Pam, and Carles Feixa, eds. 2006. *Global Youth? Hybrid Identities, Plural World.* New York: Routledge.

Nyamnjoh, Francis B. 2004. "Globalization, Boundaries, and Livelihoods: Perspectives on Africa." *Identity, Culture, and Politics* 5(1/2): 37–59.

Scheld, Suzanne. 2003. "The City in a Shoe: Redefining Urban Africa through Sebago Footwear Consumption." *City and Society* 15(1): 109–130.

Scheld, Suzanne. 2007. "Youth Cosmopolitanism: Clothing, the City, and Globalization in Dakar, Senegal." *City and Society* 19(2): 232–253.

Simmel, Georg. 1950. "Adornment." In *The Sociology of Georg Simmel,* 338–344. New York: Free Press.

Weiss, Brad. 2009. *Street Dreams and Hip Hop Barbershops: Global Fantasy in Urban Tanzania.* Bloomington: Indiana University Press.

–10–

Fashion, Transnationality, and Swahili Men

Tina Mangieri

In Kenya, clothing choice has, until recently, been largely circumscribed—limited primarily to secondhand garments (*mitumba* in Swahili) in the aftermath of the collapse of the local apparel-manufacturing sector.[1] Newly produced clothing in Kenya, all of it made in a dwindling number of factories located in Export Processing Zones (EPZs), is unavailable to local consumers due to legal requirements forbidding the sale of EPZ goods in the domestic market.[2] In this setting of mitumba and garments for export (Mangieri 2008), a varied, informal, and expanding apparel marketplace of new clothing imports from Dubai has emerged (known locally as *Dubai clothes*). In this evolving system, those able to participate as consumers and entrepreneurs may exploit various clothing options to "fashion" new, or strengthen existing, transnational relationships. This countervailing effect creates consumer and entrepreneurial subjectivities rooted in local understandings of identity, faith, and the visual performance of both via clothing, while transforming transnational apparel systems in which they are a part. This consumption is itself tied to specific transformations in the regional political economy of the Indian Ocean and the particular sartorial resonances of transnational trading networks within which Kenya and Kenyans are situated.

In this chapter, I detail practices surrounding Muslim/vernacular fashions within and in relation to Kenya's Swahili community with a focus on Swahili men. Swahili have long utilized the flexibility of clothing to assert particular sociocultural affiliations, framed both locally and regionally. Thus, for Swahili, clothing consumption promotes assertion of particular Islamic subjectivities. I address recent trends in Muslim fashion among Swahili, particularly transnational narratives expressed in and through clothing choices made by coastal residents. I aim to highlight mutually constitutive ways in which taste, fashion, and culturally meaningful patterns of Swahili consumption offer men multiple sartorial possibilities and attendant sociopolitical identities, while contributing to transformations in regional apparel trade systems.

DATA AND METHODOLOGY

This research is situated in a broader framework exploring the changing South-South connectivities between Africa and Asia currently reformulating through clothing (Mangieri 2007). The discussion is based on research conducted in Kenya (2002, 2004,

2006), the Sultanate of Oman (2006), and Dubai, United Arab Emirates (2006, 2008), on transnational apparel systems linking Africa and Asia. This chapter draws primarily from twenty-five semi-structured interviews of sixty-five total conducted in Kenya (Nairobi and Mombasa) in 2006. Analysis draws from several emergent themes over the course of these conversations: specifically, the subject's own gendered and Muslim understandings of dress; the clothing selected to meet these perceived imperatives; and historical and contemporary connections Swahili have to other Muslims elsewhere, particularly in Arabia. A pervasive subtext evolved indicating the contested place of the Swahili community (and Muslims in general) within Kenya and two strategies offering possibilities to position/reposition Swahili.

Firstly, Swahili research participants drew upon long-standing links with Asia, particularly the Arabian Peninsula, to detail the cultural importance of a shared Islamic legacy and regional family ties. This framing places Swahili, who express their faith through dress, at odds with a Kenyan government waging a U.S.-backed "war on terror" in which Muslim men are viewed with suspicion. The second narrative, by contrast, focuses on the rapid repositioning of Kenya's economy as increasingly intertwined with Asia. Here, the then-booming economy of Dubai, particularly, offers Kenya a regional trading partner of global importance. Swahili ties with Arabia perceived as disadvantageous with respect to the common practice of Islam are thus inverted to offer Swahili entrée into the lucrative economic possibilities with which Dubai was, and is, associated despite global economic instabilities since 2008. These seemingly antithetical positions circulate, in part, around textiles and clothing.

SITUATING DRESS AS PRACTICE, MATERIALITY, COMMODITY

Dress is a conspicuous identity marker. In coastal East Africa, clothing has provided immediate information on status, class, and ethnicity (Prestholdt 1998, 2004; Fair 2001, 2004). Given its capriciousness—as expressed in the fleeting temporality of the term "fashion"—dress is similarly flexible, fluid, and performative, offering wearers myriad opportunities to publicly declare particular affinities (Tarlo 1996; McRobbie 1997; Entwistle 2000). While the literal and figurative superficiality of clothing is evident, each garment is embedded in a series of political, economic, and cultural systems—from design conception to sourcing of production materials, to manufacture, distribution, taxation, advertisement, consumption, to, in some cases, recasting as secondhand garments (Hansen 2000; Dwyer and Crang 2002; Dwyer and Jackson 2003; Dwyer 2004).

In Muslim communities, as elsewhere, clothing animates discussions and debates on gender, identity, modesty, and modernity (Dwyer 1999; White 1999; Secor 2002, 2005; Gökariksel 2003). Women remain the primary focus of academic, political, and popular narratives concerning Islam and clothing, particularly regarding debates over veiling politics (El Guindi 1999; Secor 2002, 2005; Gökariksel 2003; Gökariksel and Mitchell 2005). Despite the importance of this research, it reinforces a striking imbalance. Women remain the focus of fashion and Islam, "even though socioeconomic changes and Islamic revival have changed Muslim men's dress as well" (Hansen 2000: 382). In her review of research on clothing and apparel, Hansen laments the absence of attention to Muslim men and fashion, noting that normative and pervasive gendered perceptions of dress tend to confine research to women (not only within Muslim communities but globally), thus perpetuating this anomaly.

Bodies as gendered and Muslim are among the understandings Swahili bring to their choice of dress. Clothing is, likewise, a commodity, and interviewees detail ways in which values associated with commodities are expressed via consumption. This approach to commodities signals shifts underlying the (re)emergence of the concept as an important analytic, beginning with the work of Appadurai (1986) and intersecting a number of social science fields (Gereffi 1994; Gereffi and Korzeniewicz 1994; Cook and Crang 1996). Economic practices associated with the production, distribution, and consumption of garments are seldom brought into dialogue with this approach, although Hansen's work on secondhand clothing in Zambia is a notable exception (1995, 1999, 2000, 2004). Research attentive to cultural economies—specifically various symbolic and corporeal understandings of fashion and its meanings with respect to political economy—is increasingly generated through the analytic of consumption (Dwyer and Crang 2002; Dwyer 2004; Dwyer and Jackson 2003; Leslie 2002; Mangieri 2007).

While attention to transnationality has grown (Glick Schiller et al. 1992; Appadurai 1996; Mitchell 1997a, 1997b; Ong 1999; Crang et al. 2003; Mitchell 2003; Pratt and Yeoh 2003; Cravey 2005), scholars bring multiple understandings to the term. Given its breadth and scope, transnationalism "has provided a broad, flexible conceptual apparatus that has been adopted across disciplines to examine interconnections between global economic restructuring, the politics and cultures of diasporas, ethnicity and race, class, community, gender, and the nation" (Olsen and Silvey 2006: 805). Sharing this focus, I explore sartorial practices whereby economic and cultural processes, together with an intervening and insinuating identity politics, contribute to newly emergent linkages between Africa and Asia performed, in this case, by Swahili men.

DRESSING SWAHILI IDENTITIES[3]

Though emerging from the cultural specificities of the East African coast, Swahili are associated with several distinct styles of dress commonly worn in the Arabian Peninsula and by fellow Muslims worldwide. Swahili women's clothing consists of loose dresses of synthetic fabric (known as *kanzu, gauni, direh,* or *jalabiya*) worn with the addition of *leso/khanga* at home and in prayer, for added coverage. Leso—the preferred term in coastal Kenya—are brightly colored rectangular cotton cloths, which are sold as single pieces, and cut and hemmed to form an identical pair, with a four-sided border, distinctive designs, and a boxed Swahili text near the garment edge. Outside the home, women wear *buibui,* black synthetic cloaks, over their dresses with *hijab* (head scarf) and increasingly a *niqab* (face veil, known colloquially as *ninja*). Presently, buibui are primarily imported from the Gulf states, where they are known as *abaya.*

While Swahili women's normative public dress is defined by buibui and hijab, Swahili men have multiple options when it comes to self-presentation. These possibilities reflect, in part, neoliberal shifts in Kenya since the 1980s and their consequent sartorial effects. Trousers, jeans, shirts, jackets, suits—new and secondhand—are widely available and worn. These clothes do not, however, distinguish the wearer as Muslim. By contrast, dress distinctive of Swahili men, including *kanzu, kikoi,* and *kofia,* is associated with Islam and shares similarities with garments worn by fellow Muslims globally. Kanzu (the word is also used above, albeit less commonly, to indicate a woman's dress) have long sleeves, a large opening at the neck with a button or snap closure, and fall to the wearer's ankles. Kanzu are made of cotton and cotton blends—wholly synthetic kanzu, unlike buibui, are rare. As is true for gold worn by men, several hadith (collections of sayings and acts by the Prophet Muhammad) ban men from wearing silk (*hariri* in Swahili). Swahili use the word hariri to designate not only true silk but silky fabrics (including nylon and polyester). According to interviewees, this faith-based injunction forbidding silk for men is a likely explanation for the persistence of cotton kanzu.

Often white, kanzu are nevertheless available in a range of muted colors, from lavender to grey and various shades of brown (see Plate 9). Regardless of color, kanzu must be scrupulously clean, whether worn for work, prayer, or relaxation. Cleanliness is a critical component of Islam and characterizes dress specifically. Issues surrounding cleanliness animate Swahili men's debates about proper kanzu length—whether hems should

Figure 10.1 Kofia for sale in souq al Moutrah, Muscat, Oman. Photo by Tina Mangieri.

rise above or below the ankle. According to Islamic scholars in Kenya interviewed for this research, kanzu hems should fall to mid-calf—a length rarely seen—to avoid soiling the fabric on the street.

Under kanzu, men wear undershirts and either loose cotton trousers, ending at or below the knee, or *kikoi*—a cotton or rayon wrap. Kikoi are similar to waist-wrapped garments worn by Indonesian men (*sarung*), in Yemen (*futa*), and elsewhere varyingly in the Muslim world (including Somalia and Oman) (Alpers 1983). Kikoi available for purchase in Mombasa and Nairobi are of three dominant styles: rayon Indonesian sarungi, sewn to form a tube to fold around the body at the waist; rectangular Swahili-style kikoi, machine-made in India or hand-woven of cotton, with fringe on each short end; and, rarely, large, hand-woven, heavy cotton kikoi or *banadir,* named for the area of manufacture in Somalia until the chaos of local conditions ended this production and trade in the mid-1990s (Omar, May 28, 2006, Mombasa).

Whether wearing kanzu, kikoi, or jeans and T-shirt, Swahili men may wear an embroidered cap, or *kofia,* although only required for prayer (Figure 10.1). Young men in jeans and trousers with kofia in hand hurrying to mosques is a frequent sight on Friday afternoons in Nairobi. While kofia are not always worn with Western clothing, they are always paired with kanzu, according to interviewees. In Dubai, by contrast, young Emirati men wearing the equivalent of Swahili kanzu (known locally as *dishdasha*) combined it in 2006, and less frequently in 2008, with designer "trucker caps"—baseball-style caps with a fabric front and mesh back/side sporting stylish brand names including Von Dutch or designs by Ed Hardy. Among Swahili, however, a proper kofia is de rigueur.

Kofia styles are both regional and distinctly classed, as reflected in the wide disparity in their pricing. While Zanzibari and Omani styles are commonly worn, knit kofia (similar to skullcaps or *thagiya* in Saudi Arabia, where they are worn under white head-coverings or *gutra*) are increasingly available, and even red fezzes or *tarboush* are present in local shops though seldom worn. Handmade, indigenous Swahili kofia of the Lamu archipelago (northern Kenyan coast) boast the best quality and most attractive designs (according to multiple interviewees), and highest prices. Whereas the least expensive kofia (either knit or sewn) may cost 200 to 300 Kenyan shillings (Ksh) minimum (US$2.85–US$4.28, at 70 Ksh equals US$1), kofia from Lamu may cost upwards of 5,000 Ksh (US$71). Taken together, these styles form a particular sartorial regime of the Swahili male, contributing to an individual's projected identity on any given day, in any given social setting.

SWAHILI MEN: FASHIONING FAITH, TRANSACTING IDENTITIES

In interviews with Swahili men regarding clothing, older informants sought—first and foremost—to historicize dress, offering examples and descriptions of what was once worn. In an interview conducted with Ahmed—a Swahili man in his late sixties originally from the coast but residing in Nairobi—this history was projected as far back as the nineteenth century. In this narrative, even his earliest descriptions of Swahili clothing were understood as transnational:

> In the far past the Bajuni [Swahili from the Lamu archipelago, bordering Somalia] had their own clothes...called *misare.* Misare are sheets of cloth, which used to be worn over the shoulders. There were also *kikoi* named *banadir.* Banadir is a region in Somalia. Both kikoi and misare came from Banadir, Unguja [Zanzibar] and Singapore. Thus, a typical man would wear a banadir kikoi on the bottom, wrap *msare* [sing.] from Unguja covering one shoulder and leave the other open. [My grandfather] used to wear kikoi and a long shirt. He also put on kanzu...and kofia [embroidered cap worn by Swahili men]. All Swahili- or Bajuni-made kofia have names. Old names include *kulabu, kopa, pini, kibao cha mpiara.* New kofia designs are called *jani, zulia, couch,* and *ijasi.* Kofia names are determined by their stitching patterns...Omani kofia have no names. They [Omanis] truly love our kofia. Omanis of personality always wear our [Swahili] kofia and not theirs (Ahmed, April 3, 2006).

Older East African men have long been associated with the wearing of kanzu, even as younger generations sought to distance themselves from this look. Summing up a common observation in late 1960s Tanzania, Hino reports that although "middle-aged and older men of Ujiji generally wear the costume called kanzu...the majority of younger men generally dress themselves in western style clothes" (1968: 110–111). The older research participants in this study all wore kanzu with some regularity (in several cases daily, while others donned theirs several times a week and always on Fridays) and expressed their decision to wear (or not wear) kanzu as based on a sense of their obligations that day, the level of comfort they desired (the garments were described as particularly cool in warm weather), and with whom they would likely be spending time. "You see, we are not like Omanis," said Mombasa-based Said, who traveled frequently between the two places. "They are always in kanzu, always, and always in kikoi. They know how best to dress for Islam. They are committed. We Kenyans have been corrupted. But their kofia cannot be compared. They have lost the art. While here things are not what they once were, still our kofia are prized even in Oman!" (June 6, 2006).

In interviews, younger men explained that wearing kanzu varied: it could be a weekly obligation for Friday prayers or, when worn with greater frequency, a way of expressing pride in their identity and devotion to Islam. This choice was not without ramifications. One young Muslim woman, a college student in Nairobi originally from Mombasa who herself wears hijab but not niqab, described a dress ban at her private college not for young women but rather, for young Muslim men: "They [fellow Muslim male students] were told by our professors, 'You cannot come here wearing your pajamas! That is not allowed in the classrooms!' We were very upset by this news and very sad for them. Their language—pajamas!—was so offensive" (Ashura, May 20, 2006).

Due to their immediate association with Islam, kanzu wearers at times bear the brunt of ignorance and condemnation, as the banning above suggests. More publicly, in the "humor" column "Men Only" in Kenya's *Sunday Standard,* Tony Mochama conflated

Islamic dress for men with impending terrorist attack in the following "advice" for travelers: "Check out the person next to you. Is he bearded, muttering from some holy book, and has wires sticking out of his '*kanzu*'? If the answer is in the affirmative, maybe you don't want to be friends!" (2006: 15). This sentiment expressed in print suggests the issues confronting those (young) Swahili men who choose to wear kanzu. Despite this notoriety (or perhaps because of it) more young men are opting to wear kanzu, more often. This observation and comments by research participants are further supported by the recent availability of secondhand kanzu from the United Arab Emirates, and the sharp increase in value of such imports (Mangieri 2007).

In their recollections, several interviewees spoke at length about kanzu they had had as children—often only one garment—and their responsibility to have it washed and pressed on Thursdays in preparation for prayers each Friday. One interviewee originally from Malindi, who attended boarding school in Nairobi as a child, remembered even this laundry chore with fondness, commenting on how special the garment was, though modest, and how he cherished his single kanzu. Now that his closet was full (of kanzu and other clothing), he no longer did his own washing (it was done by a "houseboy"), and the connection he felt with the garment was somehow diminished by this lack of engagement. The domestic worker responsible for washing these kanzu, who is Muslim but not Swahili, acknowledged that he owned one kanzu, which he obtained as a gift from his employer. The employer in turn indicated that he periodically purchases secondhand kanzu to give as gifts to those Muslim men he knows would not otherwise be able to afford the garment.

Whereas buibui worn by Swahili women are not readily available as secondhand garments or mitumba (one interviewee, a man, explained this absence by noting what he perceived as women's strong relationships to their clothes: "Women would never give away their buibui!"),[4] the recent appearance of secondhand kanzu in Nairobi and Mombasa offers a stark contrast to the wholly Western image associated with used clothing in sub-Saharan Africa. On side streets off First Avenue in Nairobi's Eastleigh Estate and at several locations on Digo Road around MacKinnon Market in Mombasa, secondhand kanzu are now readily available.

Stacks of neatly folded kanzu, some individually wrapped in clear plastic, crowd together on small roadside tables. Sizes vary from infant to adult, and available colors are primarily white and cream. While prices are considerably lower in comparison to new kanzu available elsewhere in both cities, the excellent quality of these mitumba kanzu is noteworthy, making them a very attractive purchase even for people who may not otherwise buy their clothing secondhand. In 2006, the price of a new kanzu (always negotiable) averaged 1,500 Ksh, while good quality used kanzu were selling for 300 Ksh (US$21 and US$4, respectively). This quality, as described by several wearers, is evident in the heavier weight of the garment and in the softness and luster of the fabric. While several research participants described purchasing used kanzu to give as gifts, the very existence of this secondhand trade in Islamic men's fashion came as a considerable surprise to other interviewees who, while otherwise very familiar with mitumba, knew it only as an option for purchasing Western-style clothing.

Kikoi—worn under kanzu or as a stand-alone waist wrap either in public or, often, in the home or mosque—have, conversely, declined in use among Swahili men. These garments have, however, entered a new trading space as a garment widely marketed to tourists, particularly women. The contrast of a male Swahili garment associated with Islam now promoted through a sexualized and suggestive advertisement campaign to Western women in Kenya (showing a woman strolling on a beach with a bikini top and kikoi modified to form a miniskirt) struck some interviewees as inappropriate and made them feel uncomfortable. One respondent however, when shown a magazine image of these new *kikoy* (the spelling of the item has likewise been anglicized to accommodate non-Swahili speakers), was nonplussed by the overt sexuality of the image (and the gender inconsistencies within normative Swahili practices) and instead commented on the garish colors (turquoise is common) as particularly offensive—anathema to the preferred white Swahili men's kikoi.

Clothing choice for Swahili men is rarely an either/or proposition of local/Islamic or Western wear, and is further complicated by the inclusion of new Western-style clothing designed with an awareness of such phenomena as the Iraq war. Osama bin Laden T-shirts, emblazoned with his visage, and other iconography, including graffiti, had been openly displayed in Mombasa and Lamu in 2002 but appeared to have declined as fashionable statements given their relative absence in 2006. The clothing messages, however, had become increasingly subtle, including several T-shirts I noticed in Nairobi with one word and no additional graphics: Faluja, a Sunni town (also spelled "Falluja") in Iraq (in)famous for its fierce resistance to U.S. forces in 2004. According to Saidi (twenty-eight years old and Muslim), who wore the shirt to work in a domestic shipping company in Nairobi, "I bought the shirt in Eastleigh [Somali enclave in Nairobi]. When I saw it, I liked the simplicity. It's good looking, but still it shows my support. [For whom?] Our brothers and sisters in Iraq." When I asked what shop sold the shirts and if they had more, he replied, "They are all over Eastleigh. The Somalis are bringing them in [from Dubai]. You can get one there" (Saidi, pers. comm., April 4, 2006). For Saidi, "performing" Muslim identity and connectivity is accomplished through the object of a Western-style shirt, made possible by Somali trade and investment systems in "Dubai clothes," including the establishment of shopping malls in Nairobi for the sale of new, imported apparel.

Local narratives of dress, including those projected into the past, repeatedly intersect with regional and transnational understandings of Islamic identity. Many interviewees, both women and men, were quick to point out the transnational nature of their clothing, either through (often presumed) knowledge regarding manufacturing location, the routes clothes traveled through trade, or the neighborhood details regarding its purchase and the often ethnic assumptions these imply. Both women and men made frequent mention of the relationship between Dubai and their clothing, though in only one instance was the United Arab Emirates seen as more entrepôt than place of origin. In the words of Fatuma, an older woman living in the Eastleigh area of Nairobi, who self-described as Swahili and is originally from the coast:

> We have many styles to choose from now—many fabrics, many types of dress. The ones [textiles] coming from Bangkok are favored by the poor. Those for indoor use cost very little, but there are other qualities, which cost 5,000 to 6,000 Ksh [$67–$80US]. These clothes are mainly for weddings and special occasions. They are called *hariri* [silk]. They come from London, Paris, and Bangkok, but not Dubai. They do not manufacture anything in Dubai—they just import and re-export (Fatuma, April 11, 2006).

Given the myriad clothing choices available to Swahili men, what is worn and purchased, by whom, when, where, and why, speaks to current socioeconomic and geopolitical possibilities, and individual subjectivities, forged in a deeply transnational milieu. Clothing references global Islamic movements and their regional expressions (particularly Wahhabism, cited by several young wearers of kanzu, and Tabligh Jamaat—the latter a transnational movement of Islamic revival originating in India in the 1920s and, according to research participants, experiencing recent growth in urban Kenya). The political affiliations denoted by this clothing visually marks wearer participation in networks extending beyond Kenya, yet within which Kenya and East Africa are increasingly intertwined. One description of clothing styles spanning the *umma,* or Muslim community of believers, occurred in a recorded interview between my research assistant [questions in brackets] and Sheikh:

> [Your clothes are interesting. Tell me what you're wearing.] It's a Punjabi pajama. These are for resting but I have another pair for walking around. [Why Punjabi? How did that tradition reach you?] It's common today among the Tabligh Islamic Movement. This movement is very strong in Asian countries, so Kenyan members of the movement can be found in these clothes. They're also good for insect protection from mosquitoes (Sheikh, May 2, 2006).

Other informants spoke of their frustration with the geopolitical realities of the world, most notably the war in Iraq and the perceived injustices suffered by Muslims in a global "war on terror," and sought, with clothing, to comment. The wearer of the "Faluja" shirt expressed his attraction to the garment, which he had purchased himself in a Nairobi clothing stall, as both a small act of solidarity with the people of Iraq—his "brothers and sisters"—and a visible sign of awareness of, and engagement with, the world beyond Kenya.

SWAHILI MEN AND TRANSNATIONAL IDENTITIES

Kenya and Tanzania (especially Zanzibar) are home to the most substantial Swahili communities, with smaller populations in Oman, the Comoros, and, increasingly, the United Arab Emirates, though anecdotal reports and email correspondence with project participants suggest the recent economic downturn has prompted a reversal of this trend toward Dubai in particular (Hussein, personal communication, 2011). Today, as in the past, Swahili are transnational in the palpable sense of maintaining aspects of a common cultural and linguistic identity across national boundaries. While it is not uncommon to find Kenyan Swahili who have traveled abroad to Zanzibar, Oman, Yemen, or the United Arab Emirates, transnational subjectivities emerge from collective spiritual, historical, and economic linkages across and through these national spaces, rather than via individual journeys. The expenses, preparations, and difficulties of travel thwart many trips before their realization. In this situation, memories of those who have traveled and lived (or continue to live) abroad, communications with relatives who reside outside of Kenya via mobile and Facebook, and the stories associated with both, are continually revamped to strengthen familial and social bonds across these disparate spaces. Clothing serves as an important material and imaginative connection in this setting.

While clothing materializes the social, cultural, and economic networks within which we are joined, clothing also offers its wearers opportunities to create new networks and relationships based on individual and collective exploitation of its inherent possibilities. In this way, dress constitutes "competing set[s] of discourses, linked to the operation of power" (Hansen 2000: 370). In the examples above, the conversation is ongoing, expressed via gendered local and regional conceptualizations of faith, piety, class, and cosmopolitanism. While considerable attention has been given to the myriad ways in which Muslim women of East Africa (and elsewhere) visibly express their identities and the politics these vocabularies imply (see Fair 2001, 2004 for a historical account), attention to Muslim men's fashions has been scant.

Discussion of Muslim men's fashion is limited to few scholarly references, while at the same time a popular imaginary of what "the" Muslim man looks like captivates the general non-Muslim public in the United States and elsewhere. Among published works, reference has been made to the "droop" of a man's mustache and its relationship to Turkish politics (in Secor 2002: 20) and the dialectics of moustaches and memoir in Lebanon (Daoud 2002).

While these are but two examples highlighting facial hair rather than clothing, per se, there is very little work on Muslim men's fashion. Why? Gender norms throughout much of the world equate an interest in and awareness of clothing with women. The association of women with fashion has contributed to the marginalization of research on dress, more generally, thereby devaluing the significance of dress as both cultural and economic phenomena (Hansen 2000). The perception of fashion in Muslim communities is likewise often bound up in similar distinctions, popularly perceived. This is in spite of the central but by no means exclusive role played by men in the clothing trade in East Africa.

Islamic fashions (from *jalabiya* to buibui/abaya, to perfumes and incense) enable the literal and figurative embodiment of transnational affinities in ways that are, for women, increasingly empowering. As Tima, a Swahili woman in her twenties, suggested:

> We wear buibui, but these are the same [as abaya] in places like Dubai. Now we can get what's most in fashion as soon as it's available in their shopping malls: buibui, hijab, ninja, *udi* [oil-based perfume]. We see what people are wearing [in the Gulf states], and hear about it from people who've just come back, and we Africans can [now] get these. Now Mombasa doesn't seem so far away. And, ok, some styles are not so modest [but] most give me a good feeling as a Muslim . . . I feel almost spoilt for choice (Tima, June 15, 2006).

Men find that reveling in their choice of clothing, and using it as the basis for an empowered Muslim identity, is fraught with issues of masculinity, the appropriateness of attention to appearance, and the particular gendered encounters with daily life that Swahili, and all men in varying ways, experience. As members of a community marginalized with respect to a Christian majority, and possessing an officially undefined ethnicity in a nation in which tribal affiliation has often formed the basis of people's relationships (or lack thereof) to political and economic power, Swahili men in Kenya who choose to wear Islamic clothing in situations other than Friday prayers are making a pronounced statement of personal and collective identity. Given the wider geopolitical climate, this renewed adoption of Islamic fashion is, similarly, increasingly bold. While the U.S. embassy bombings in Nairobi and Dar es Salaam in 1998 brought worldwide attention to the role of East Africa within widespread terrorist networks, it was the September 11 attacks in the United States in 2001 that visited perceptible scrutiny on the Kenyan coast particularly. Despite the softening of rhetoric following the Bush administration, in the post 9/11 global "war on terror," visibly Muslim men remain the focus of attention in areas where they are not the majority. Unlike women, Swahili men are free to choose from various styles that do not direct attention to religious identity—jeans, T-shirts, button-down shirts, trousers, suits, and so on. The adoption of Islamic clothing, particularly among younger men, both signals shifting subjectivities and highlights transnational changes in the political economy of the clothing trade in East Africa.

Implementing neoliberal policies, the government of Kenya has contributed both to the "abandonment" of its citizens to used clothing/mitumba and, at the same time, laid the foundations for a varied, highly informal, apparel marketplace, within which people with the means to participate as consumers (and entrepreneurs) may "fashion" new linkages through clothing choice. These emergent consumer (and entrepreneurial) subjectivities, rooted in local understandings of faith and its visual performance via clothing, are enabled by the presence of contemporary transnational apparel systems. For Swahili, clothing consumption thus offers a means by which to assert particular Islamic subjectivities, though these sartorial choices are both bound by and constitute the specific transnational trading networks of the western Indian Ocean. Swahili have long utilized the flexibility of clothing to assert particular sociocultural affiliations, framed both locally and regionally. Today some Swahili men, in particular, are (re)turning to historical ties with Arabia, newly conceived, and visibly expressed in/as fashion.

NOTES

1. *Mitumba* (pl.) are secondhand garments sold throughout Kenya and imported in 45-kilogram bales primarily from the United Kingdom, Canada, Germany, and the United States. Mitumba were earlier banned in Kenya in an effort to protect the now-defunct domestic apparel industry.
2. Export Processing Zones (EPZs) were established in Kenya in 1990, though export manufacturing did not start until 1993 and did not grow until passage of the American Growth and Opportunity Act in 2000, boosting export to the United States. EPZ manufacturers receive numerous tax breaks and other incentives from the government of Kenya, including duty-free imports of manufacturing inputs, with the stipulation that all finished garments are subsequently exported (see Mangieri 2007).
3. Characterizing coastal East Africans as a community with a distinct ethnicity—Swahili—has been a problem animating academic scholarship and befuddling government policymakers through to the present, though most Swahili themselves are considerably less troubled by a lack of consensus (Allen 1993; Eastman 1971; Horton and Middleton 2000; Middleton 1992; Prins 1967). The political implications of defining oneself as, for example, Swahili or Arab or Zanzibari or Kenyan, have continually transformed the cultural and ethnic landscapes of East Africa, prompting various claims of particular identities to take precedence over others (Sheriff 1987; Allen 1993; Mazrui and Mazrui 1995; Myers 1995; Prestholdt 1998, 2004; Fair 2001, 2004; Askew 2002). Recent efforts have sought to put to rest earlier debates that have centered on whether the Swahili are "Arab" or "African" by historicizing the development of Swahili communities as necessarily constituted differently, at different times, and with different sociopolitical effects (Fair 2001; Askew 2002). Acknowledgement of the social construction of Swahili identity, and its mutability, have emerged, in part, within an academic milieu in which essentialist notions of identity are rejected in favor of an understanding of identities as fluid and performative. For Swahili themselves, this fluidity has been a remarkable constant in their communities. This inclusive, situated understanding of identity reflects the diversity and tolerance characteristic of the coast. This situatedness of identity, and its performance, relies in large part on the visual dialogue of clothing.
4. Women do give away their *buibui,* as several interviewees attested, though these exchanges were noted to be very individualized acts of charity, to neighbors, relatives, friends, and house-help (Amina, May 14, 2006).

REFERENCES

Allen, James de Vere. 1993. *Swahili Origins: Swahili Culture and the Shungwaya Phenomenon.* London: James Currey.

Alpers, Edward. 1983. "Futa Benaadir: Continuity and Change in the Traditional Cotton Textiles Industry of Southern Somalia, c. 1840–1980." In Catherine Coquery-Vidrovitch and Alain Forest, eds., *Entreprises et entrepreneurs en Afrique, XIXe et XXe siècles, I,* 77–98. Paris: L'Harmattan.

Appadurai, Arjun, ed. 1986. *The Social Life of Things.* Cambridge: Cambridge University Press.

Appadurai, Arjun. 1996. *Modernity at Large: Cultural Dimensions of Globalization.* Minneapolis: University of Minnesota Press.

Askew, Kelly. 2002. *Performing the Nation: Swahili Music and Cultural Politics in Tanzania.* Chicago: University of Chicago Press.

Cook, Ian, and Mike Crang. 1996. "The World on a Plate: Culinary Culture, Displacement and Geographical Knowledges." *Journal of Material Culture* 1(2): 131–153.

Crang, Philip, Claire Dwyer, and Peter Jackson. 2003. "Transnationalism and the Spaces of Commodity Culture." *Progress in Human Geography* 27(4): 438–456.

Cravey, Altha. 2005. "Desire, Work and Transnational Identity." *Ethnography* 6(3): 357–383.

Daoud, Hassan. 2002. "Those Two Heavy Wings of Manhood: On Moustaches." In Mai Ghoussoub and Emma Sinclair-Webb, eds., *Imagined Masculinities: Male Identity and Culture in the Modern Middle East,* 273–280. London: Saqi.

Dwyer, Claire. 1999. "Contradictions of Community: Questions of Identity for Young British Muslim Women." *Environment and Planning A* 31: 53–68.

Dwyer, Claire. 2004. "Tracing Transnationalities Through Commodity Culture: A Case Study of British-South Asian Fashion." In Peter Jackson, Philip Crang, and Claire Dwyer, eds., *Transnational Spaces,* 60–77. London: Routledge.

Dwyer, Claire, and Philip Crang. 2002. "Fashioning Ethnicities: The Commercial Spaces of Multiculture." *Ethnicities* 2(3): 410–430.

Dwyer, Claire, and Peter Jackson. 2003. "Commodifiying Difference: Selling EASTern Fashion." *Environment and Planning D: Society and Space* 21: 269–291.

Eastman, Carol. 1971. "Who Are the Waswahili?" *Africa* 41(3): 228–236.

El Guindi, Fadwa. 1999. *Veil: Modesty, Privacy and Resistance.* Oxford: Berg.

Entwistle, Joanne. 2000. *The Fashioned Body: Fashion, Dress and Modern Social Theory.* Cambridge, MA: Polity Press.

Fair, Laura. 2001. *Pastimes and Politics: Culture, Community, and Identity in Post-Abolition Urban Zanzibar, 1890–1945.* Athens: Ohio University Press.

Fair, Laura. 2004. "Remaking Fashion in the Paris of the Indian Ocean: Dress, Performance, and the Cultural Construction of a Cosmopolitan Zanzibari Identity." In Jean Marie Allman, ed., *Fashioning Africa: Power and the Politics of Dress.* Bloomington: Indiana University Press.

Gereffi, Gary. 1994. "The Organization of Buyer-Driven Global Commodity Chains: How US Retailers Shape Overseas Production Networks." In Gary Gereffi and Miguel Korzeniewicz, eds., *Commodity Chains and Global Capitalism,* 95–122. Westport, CT: Praeger.

Gereffi, Gary, and Miguel Korzeniewicz, eds. 1994. *Commodity Chains and Global Capitalism.* Westport, CT: Praeger.

Glick Schiller, Nina, Linda Basch, and Cristina Blanc-Szanton, eds. 1992. *Towards a Transnational Perspective on Migration: Race, Class, Ethnicity, and Nationalism Reconsidered.* New York: New York Academy of Sciences.

Gökariksel, Banu. 2003. "Globalization and Alternative Modernities: Forging Identities in Urban Space." PhD diss. University of Washington.

Gökariksel, Banu, and Katharyne Mitchell. 2005. "Veiling, Secularism, and the Neoliberal Subject: National Narratives and Supranational Desires in Turkey and France." *Global Networks* 5(2): 147–165.

Hansen, Karen Tranberg. 1995. "Transnational Biographies and Local Meanings: Used Clothing Practices in Lusaka." *Journal of Southern African Studies* 21(1): 131–145.

Hansen, Karen Tranberg. 1999. "Second-Hand Clothing Encounters in Zambia: Global Discourses, Western Commodities, and Local Histories." *Africa* 69(3): 343–365.

Hansen, Karen Tranberg. 2000. *Salaula: The World of Secondhand Clothing and Zambia.* Chicago: University of Chicago Press.

Hansen, Karen Tranberg. 2004. "Helping or Hindering? Controversies about the International Secondhand Clothing Trade." *Anthropology Today* 20(4): 3–9.

Hino, Shun'ya. 1968. "The Costume Culture of the Swahili People." *Kyoto University African Studies* 2: 109–145.

Horton, Mark, and John Middleton. 2000. *The Swahili: The Social Landscape of a Mercantile Society.* Oxford: Blackwell.

Leslie, Deborah. 2002. "Gender, Retail Employment and the Clothing Commodity Chain." *Gender, Place, and Culture* 9(1): 61–76.

Mangieri, Tina. 2007. "Refashioning South-South Spaces: Cloth, Clothing, and African Cultural Economies." PhD diss. University of North Carolina at Chapel Hill.

Mangieri, Tina. 2008. "African Cloth, Export Production, and Secondhand Clothing in Kenya." In Lois Labrianidis, ed., *The Moving Frontier: The Changing Geography of Production in Labour Intensive Industries,* 301–318. London: Ashgate.

Mazrui, Ali, and Alamin Mazrui. 1995. *Swahili State and Society: The Political Economy of an African Language.* Nairobi: East African Educational Publishers.

McRobbie, Angela. 1997. "Bridging the Gap: Feminism, Fashion and Consumption." *Feminist Review* 55: 73–89.

Middleton, John. 1992. *The World of the Swahili. An African Mercantile Civilization.* New Haven: Yale University Press.

Mitchell, Katharyne. 1997a. "Different Diasporas and the Hype of Hybridity." *Environment and Planning D: Society and Space* 15(5): 533–553.

Mitchell, Katharyne. 1997b. "Transnational Discourse: Bringing Geography Back In." *Antipode* 29(2): 101–114.

Mitchell, Katharyne. 2003. "Cultural Geographies of Transnationality." In K. Anderson, Mona Domosh, Steve Pile, and Nigel Thrift, eds., *Handbook of Cultural Geography,* 74–87. London: Sage.

Mochama, Tony. 2006. "Men Only" *Sunday Standard [Kenya]* 9 April 9: 15.

Myers, Garth. 1995. "A Stupendous Hammer: Colonial and Post-Colonial Reconstructions of Zanzibar's Other Side." *Urban Studies* 32(8): 1436–1449.

Olsen, Elizabeth, and Rachel Silvey. 2006. "Guest Editorial. Transnational Geographies: Rescaling Development, Migration, and Religion." *Environment and Planning A* 38: 805–808.

Ong, Aihwa. 1999. *Flexible Citizenship: The Cultural Logics of Transnationality.* Durham, NC: Duke University Press.

Pratt, Geraldine, and Brenda Yeoh. 2003. "Transnational (Counter) Topographies." *Gender, Place and Culture* 10: 159–166.

Prestholdt, Jeremy. 1998. "As Artistry Permits and Custom May Ordain: The Social Fabric of Material Consumption in the Swahili World, circa 1450 to 1600." PAS Working Papers 3, Program of African Studies, Northwestern University, Chicago. Available at: http://www.

northwestern.edu/african-studies/working%20papers/wp3prestholdt.pdf. Accessed March 31, 2010.

Prestholdt, Jeremy. 2004. "On the Global Repercussions of East African Consumerism." *The American Historical Review* 109(3): 755–782.

Prins, A.H.J. 1967. *The Swahili-Speaking Peoples of Zanzibar and the East African Coast.* London: International African Institute.

Secor, Anna. 2002. "The Veil and Urban Space in Istanbul: Women's Dress, Mobility and Islamic Knowledge." *Gender, Place and Culture* 9(1): 5–22.

Secor, Anna. 2005. "Islamism, Democracy, and the Political Production of the Headscarf Issue in Turkey." In Ghazi-Walid Falah and Caroline Nagel, eds., *Geographies of Muslim Women: Gender, Religion, and Space,* 203–225. New York: Guilford Press.

Sheriff, Abdul. 1987. *Slaves, Spices, and Ivory in Zanzibar: Economic Integration of East Africa into the World Economy.* London: James Currey.

Tarlo, Emma. 1996. *Clothing Matters: Dress and Identity in India.* Chicago: University of Chicago Press.

White, Jenny. 1999. "Islamic Chic." In Caglar Keyder, ed., *Istanbul Between the Global and the Local,* 77–91. Lanham, MD: Rowman and Littlefield.

PART IV

Transculturated Bodies

–11–

Photography, Poetry, and the Dressed Bodies of Léopold Sédar Senghor

Leslie W. Rabine

My task is to awaken my people to dazzling futures
My joy to create images that nourish them, Oh luminous rhythms of the Word!

—Léopold Sédar Senghor (1991: 505)[1]

As poet and politician, Léopold Senghor put the relation between word and image at the heart of his practice. As a poet, he composed powerful images through writing. As a philosopher of Négritude, he wrote: "The Black Word is *sense* thanks to symbolic images, melody and rhythm" (Senghor 1980: 230–231). Five years after Senghor's death, Dakar photographer Pap Ba organized Senghorama in 2006 "as an event of *photo-poésie,* an exploration in the interplay of text and image in general and the dialogue between Senghor's poetry and contemporary visual production in particular" (Grabsky-Ochsner 2007: 92). This essay, interweaving readings of Senghor's own poetic images of dress and photographers' images of his dressed body, also investigates that relationship.

A thorny problem arises from an attempt to explore this relationship in general through photos of and writings by Senghor: He did not fund photography like the other arts, nor did he include it in his lists of cultural activities essential to the life of the Senegalese people (1980: 24–25). Rather, he dismissed it as a "copy" that did not attain the artistic status of creativity: "The point is not to reproduce exactly—to photograph . . . The point is to create new works" (1964: 284). Here Senghor suggests a scale of values separating photography, a mere reproduction, from art, a true creation that does not copy visible appearance: "The Black-African *image* is the *surrealist* image, or better still, the *sub-realist* [sous-réaliste] image, in the sense that it expresses the reality that *subtends* the reality of appearances" (1964: 280).

For Senghor then, photography and poetry would seem to function at irreconcilable poles of the spectrum of expressive forms. Photography would be the most utilitarian of forms, poetry the most otherworldly. The photography-poetry opposition would thus increase the divide between Senghor the politician and Senghor the poet. Indeed, this pragmatic politician (Markovitz 1969: 32) always had an official photographer document his state visits. Yet the poems Senghor wrote during his presidency most strongly emphasize the absolute incompatibility of the surreal "Royaume d'Enfance" in his poetry and "your brutal, and so very cruel, reality, Oh Civilization!" (Senghor 1991: 413).

In this, Senghor's thought fits into European theories that place photography and poetry as semiotic systems at opposite poles of the sign-referent spectrum. These theories "have given a definition of poetry as independent of any referent other than itself" (Gouvard 2001: 87). The "poetic function" in language "deepens the fundamental dichotomy of signs and objects" (Jakobson and Rudy 1981: 25). By contrast, photography attenuates this dichotomy. Roland Barthes calls photography "this pure deictic language," whose "very essence" is the undeniable past reality of its referent, "the *this-has-been*" (Barthes 1980: 16, 120). Thus Senghor's opposition between photographic and poetic imagery belongs to a larger intellectual tradition that places the two signifying forms in distant categories.

Nonetheless, I propose that detailed readings of poetic images by Senghor and photographers' images of Senghor can challenge this dichotomy. How can poetic space intrude in photographs while the referential "*this-has-been*" animates poems? To join these readings, I focus on a third "image-sign" system, that of dress (Calefato 2004: 5). Images of dress in both photographs of and poetry by Senghor open up access to the cross-penetration of these seemingly irreconcilable expressive forms.

The photographs in question are unlike the familiar close-ups of the legendary Senghor published in books. They are wide-angle shots that show Senghor's dressed body in political action, interacting with officials or surrounded by enthusiastic crowds (Figures 11.1 and 11.3). In fact, both their unexpected content and the space in which I first viewed these photos jolted me out of my assumption of Senghor as a distant seamless legend. The photos reside in an old suitcase in the Dakar home of Madame Khady Ndoye Faye and Monsieur Ibrahima Faye, regional governor in Senegal during the first years of independence. The casually jumbled photos show independence leaders interacting with Senegalese people at all manner of events from the late 1950s to the mid-1970s. An archive is a "presentational form" that shapes the way we see and interpret its photographs (Edwards and Hart 2004: 2). When the Fayes generously gave me access to their collection, I expected to find old family portraits. Instead there emerged from the old suitcase leading figures of the past such as Senghor, Demba Diop, Cheikh Hamidou Kane, and Modibo Keïta, (Figure 11.1). As they came out into the domestic chaos of a Sunday family gathering in Dakar, these figures appeared both bathed in an aura of familiarity and suddenly defamiliarized.

These political photos are, like the published close-ups of Senghor, official photographs, but differ in focal length and composition. Published close-ups seem strictly composed to illustrate Senghor's legendary stature (Mudimbe 1988: 94). Unlike the published photos, those in the Faye collection are unposed, often candid. In these photos, he does not appear as a legend. Physically diminutive and restrained, here is a figure difficult to imagine as the charismatic leader, the most popular and powerful Senegalese politician of his generation, the intellectual and literary giant. Some details of that biography will aid study of the photographic and poetic images.

Figure 11.1 President Senghor and Governor Faye with a welcoming crowd, Senegal, 1960s. Courtesy of Ibrahima, Khady, and Gnilane Faye.

BACKGROUND NOTES ON THE LIFE OF SENGHOR

Senghor began his poetic and philosophic writing by reconstructing his own autobiography and the ancient history of Africa within a mythic space. Young Léopold's maternal uncle Tokô'Waly immersed the child in "the magic world more real than the visible world" (Senghor 1964: 262). But when Léopold was seven years old, his father sent him away to Catholic school.

In 1928, he arrived as a student in Paris and wrote his first poetry in the 1930s. In 1946, Senghor left his professorial position in France to win an election as a Senegalese representative to the French National Assembly. By 1951, he became the most powerful political leader in Senegal and remained so throughout his presidency (1960–1980). In 1955, Senghor divorced his wife Ginette Eboué and, in 1956, married Colette Hubert, scion of a French aristocratic family, his assistant in Paris, and the long-time object of his passionate love.

Throughout his political career, Senghor continued to write poetry. He also continually revised his philosophy of Négritude in response to a younger generation of African artists and writers who criticized him for reproducing European racial stereotypes and later for imposing a dictatorial state policy on artistic production (Harney 2004: 20–21, 39–45; Njami 2006: 10).

Relevant to the interweaving of poetic imagery, photography, and the dressed body is Négritude's treatment of language and the "magico-mystic" space of an idealized African past. As a student in Paris, Senghor tackled the urgent necessity of constructing a self-reflective black identity from the ground of "this other exile, more heavy on my heart, the wrenching of self from self" (Senghor 1991: 392). The yearning to gain recognition from Europeans who cast Africans as uncivilized savages also motivated the early writings of Négritude (Jules-Rosette 1998: 58). From this core of black self-identity and lost African grandeur, Senghor's Négritude expanded. During World War II, it became a political theory for uniting colonized people in a transnational fight for equality. As president, Senghor made Négritude the theory of state policy. Biographical background may provide context for understanding Senghor's poetry and the Faye photographs. But empirical biography, as any writer or critic might say, is not directly reflected in either a poet's text or a politician's image.

PHOTOGRAPHIC IMAGES OF SENGHOR'S DRESSED BODY

Even when the photos in the Faye collection show Senghor as the central focus of a photo—walking through crowded streets lined with enthusiastic people or greeting officials—his diminutive figure and reserved comportment conform to his own self-descriptions "as...the person no one would notice" (Njami 2006: 309). These photos of a great African leader as deceptively unnoticeable result from the pioneering work of African photographers (Bajorek 2010; Rabine 2010).[2]

Although even more devalued in Senegal than other photographic genres, political reportage of the independence period vividly documents a new kind of public space in the new republic where Senegalese people fashioned new political self-identities through the dressed body. While Senegalese photographers continued the conventions of colonial political reportage, their style, like the style of the crowds in their photos, is more exuberant, more vibrantly in motion, and more casual in its framing. Many of the photos are caught on the fly in the animated melee of the moment.

For the first time, wide-angle photos of the 1960s represent scenes with large numbers of fashionable, politically active Senegalese people. In new and more spontaneous ways than the more famous studio portraits of the 1950s, political reportage offers yet another form of self-representation that counters colonial ethnographic and postcard photographs with their Western fantasies of race and sex (Enwezor and Zaya 1996: 21; Geary 1998; Prochaska 1991: 46). The array of fashions in group and crowd scenes span social classes and passing years, yet are anchored in a historical moment of enthusiasm and hope. The visual moment is all the more poignant for being on the cusp of a precipice into disillusionment.

Even in the midst of Sénégalaises in voluminous head scarves and male leaders in majestic *boubous,* Senghor always wore a prim and proper Western suit (contrast Figure 11.2 with Figures 11.1 and 11.3). In the context of inventive African fashions in the new republic, Senghor's suit might seem incongruous. Pre-independence West African

Plate 1 Nwanneka in one of her favorite outfits. Photo by Misty Bastian.

Plate 2 Gallery of Poems. Vlisco advertisement campaign, November 2010.
Source: http://www.vlisco.com/Gallery-of-Poems/en/page/471/ © Vlisco Helmond B.V.

Plate 3 Paramount chief of Cape Coast with his entourage of men wearing T-shirts with corporate logos. 2006 Fetu Afahye Festival. Photo by Lauren Adrover.

Plate 4 *Bazin riche* in the Sandaga Market. The second and third shelves from the top display the most popular colors for the summer of 2008. Photo by Kelly Kirby.

Plate 5 Imported malaḥfas in a Nouakchott boutique. Photo by Katherine Wiley.

Plate 6 Woman wearing the latest style of fashion hijab, *hijab alkyabba,* referencing a robe-like cape, *alkyabba,* worn by Hausa Emirs. The style is also called *mai wuya* ("owner of the neck"), suggesting the cowl-like neck covering. Zaria City, May 2012. Photo by Elisha P. Renne.

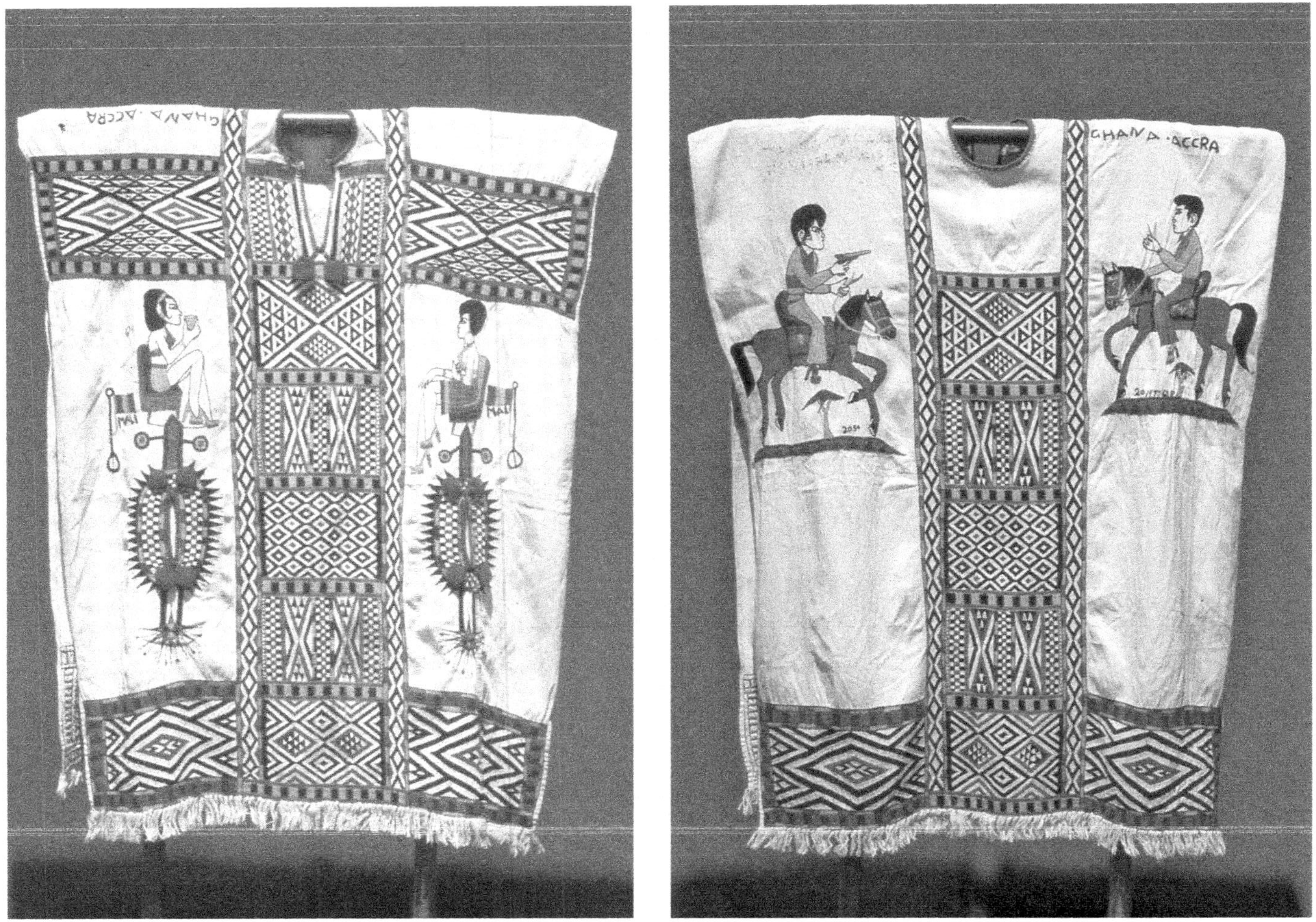

Plate 7.1 & 7.2 Ghana Boy tunic, Mali c. 198Cs. Front and back. Private Collection; photo by Steven Tatum.

Plate 7.3 Kariba Bouaré embroidering, Djenné 2008. Photo by Victoria Rovine.

Plate 8 A young man wearing jeans with a fashicnably crumpled look and a belt buckle with bling. Photo by Adeline Masquelier.

Plate 9 *Kanzu* for sale in souk al Naif, Deira, Dubai, United Arab Emirates, 2006. Photo by Tina Mangieri.

Plate 10 *Kanga* commemorative cloth from Kenya. Photo by D. Soyini Madison.

Figure 11.2 President Modibo Keïta of Mali with Madame Mariam Travele Keïta and Senegalese officials, Kaolack, Senegal, December 1966. Courtesy of Ibrahima, Khady, and Gnilane Faye.

Figure 11.3 President Senghor, media journalist, and griotte. Saint-Louis du Sénégal, ca. 1971–1974. Courtesy of Ibrahima, Khady, and Gnilane Faye.

writers describe Western dress as inscribing on the body a multiple rupture: a rift within the self, separation from one's community, and loss of continuity with the ancestors, precisely the ruptures that Senghor's Négritude fought against (Keïta et al. 1997: 12; Laye 2005: 54–55).

There are many ways to interpret the image of Senghor's suit, historically an imposition of French colonialism. The simplest concerns a sartorial religious divide in Senegal. While Catholics confine themselves to Western dress, Muslims wear boubous and caftans as well as Western fashions. Yet Senghor's suit, in the context of the Faye photos, appears too marked a choice for such a simple explanation. Cosmopolitan Senegalese Muslims pride themselves on being able to glide effortlessly and gracefully among radically different cultural vocabularies of dress—Arab, European, American, or Asian. Images of Governor Faye show him adopting with grace a Western suit or uniform, but equally comfortable and dashing in a boubou, a caftan, or a polo shirt (Figures 11.1 and 11.3). Like other Muslim officials in the photos, he displays the dexterous talent to remain anchored in a secure identity and move flexibly into any cultural guise.

In this context, Senghor's dress cannot be divorced from the charged semiotics permeating the suit's decisive role in constructing the historical identity of the European male bourgeoisie, including its colonial identity (Carter 2003: 108; Craik 2009: 144). Moreover, Senghor's suited image seems to violate in a sartorial register a basic principle of Négritude: the vehement rejection of French colonialist policies of assimilation and the insistence that Senegalese culture have the "power to assimilate" other cultures into itself. It is rather Faye's fashion practices that uphold this principle.

One might argue that fashion is too unimportant to exemplify weighty principles of anticolonialist philosophy. This dismissal, however, is itself a historically constructed, fundamental assumption of Western bourgeois fashion, one that points to the importance of dress as a text of cultural value systems. For Senegalese culture, fashion is a major form of creative aesthetic expression (Rabine 2002: 27). The Western assumption of fashion as a trifling, frivolous matter was crucial to the construction of new class and gender systems required by nascent capitalism in the nineteenth century (Hollander 1994: 79). Bourgeois men denigrated ornamental adornment as both aristocratic and feminine (Carter 2003: 108). Fashion signified women's presumed inanity, their essential inability to engage in political or intellectual life (Carter 2003: 48). The bourgeois suit became, in its "intrinsically abstract formal character," the signifier of men's seriousness, their substance, their integrity, their honesty and rationality, and, by extension, their dominance (Hollander 1994: 4, 91).

The images of Senghor's suits, by the very deliberateness of their sartorial insignificance, cannot escape this accumulated semiotic weight. Nothing could be further from this codification of the male suited body than images of dress and body in Senghor's poetry.

IMAGES OF DRESS AND BODY IN SENGHOR'S POETRY

The poetic body appears in two guises. One is a surreal "cosmic body," by which I mean the antirealistic image of a body that dissolves into fragments—heart, blood, head, hands, breasts—that fuse with the cosmos in the form of heaven, earth, or nature. An embittered poet laments to his beloved but treacherous France: "And you also tore from this too loving heart its bonds of union with the pulse of the world" (Senghor 1991: 304). The dress of the "cosmic body" is metaphoric: "Look as the night descends upon Gorée, dressed in old rose, like those long-ago signares" (1991: 473).

In the second guise of the body, Senghor's poetry transforms figures from African history or his own childhood into mythic beings. One such figure, Koumba N'Dofène Diouf, the last king of the Sine, appears in Senghor's youthful collection *Chants d'Ombre* (in English, *Shadow Songs*):

> I remember the splendor of the Sunset
> Where Koumba N'Dofène wanted the making of his royal cloak
>
> I remember funeral feasts with the fuming blood of slaughtered sheep
> The Noise of Quarrels, The Rhapsody of Griots. (1991: 296)

This poem, like Senghor's poetry generally, creates two different types of mythic figure and treats their bodies according to different creative procedures. One type includes African kings, warriors, athletes, or freedom fighters. Senghor will either sing their praises or adopt their personae, sometimes half-ironically, as allegories for his own mundane political actions. The second type is the *griot* or *dyâli,* the West African troubadours who sing the praises of their noble patrons, keep their genealogies, act as their spokespeople, and guide their righteous comportment (Diop 1981: 88–90; Hale 1998: 18–58). In his poetry, Senghor will eventually inhabit profoundly the figure of the dyâli and adopt its voice. While the kingly figures wear clothing of otherworldly splendor, like the "royal cloak" above, the griot figures, alter egos of the poet, are marked by what they don't wear.

This significant lack of sartorial description is connected to the most common use of dress in Senghor's poetry. Dress is most often a metaphor for illusion or false material values. The opposite of dress as illusion is clothing as figure of nudity. Senghor's classic, though problematic, poem "Black Woman" begins, "Nude woman, Black woman / Dressed in your color which is life, in your form which is beauty" (1991: 270).

This metaphor, appearing often in *Shadow Songs,* implies that nudity is the most, indeed the only, authentic dress. The idealization of nudity, like Senghor's theory of poetry itself, evinces European influences, as nudity expresses a traditional Christian and Western assumption summed up in the phrase "the naked truth." The association goes back to the biblical story of Adam and Eve, where clothing symbolized the fall from innocence and the attempt to deceive. This moral ideology of dress also connects to the bourgeois ideology of the suit, which signified in the nineteenth century the sober probity of its masculine wearer. In addition, the suit, as the dress of minimalist antiadornment, has an ambiguous relation to nudity (Hollander 1994: 84). As it duplicates the lines of the body and makes itself almost invisible through its uniformity, the suit becomes naturalized as a sort of second skin. It also naturalizes the meanings of class, gender, and colonial dominance invisibly woven into its positive moral meanings.

The meaning of nudity in Senghor's poetic imagery, and in fact his poetic language in general, undergoes a dramatic change in the course of World War II. In 1939, when Senghor was a lycée professor in Tours, he was drafted and classified as a common soldier in a company of Africans. Captured by the Germans, he and his comrades spent two years in a prison camp. While there, he wrote many of the poems in *Hosties noires,* his most powerfully moving collection. Simon Njami writes that these poems "bear uncompromising witness" to "the profound wound that Senghor suffered in the double Self he had composed . . . So now it happens that this agrégé knowing Latin and Greek, this being who had struggled to prove his value, finds himself demeaned to the lowest level" (2006: 171). As the poet writes in "Prayer of the Tirailleur Sénégalais": "I am presently a second class soldier among the most humble of soldiers" (Senghor 1991: 322). Senghor's fellow prisoners were "for the most part peasants snatched from their milieu by the laws of conscription, unable to pronounce a word of French . . . Like the others, he did not exist in any other way than as cannon fodder" (Njami 2006: 171).

Senghor's philosophy and poetry transform themselves through his struggle to overcome his bitterness against the betrayal by France, whose officials treated "her Sénégalese as mercenaries, making them the black mastiffs of the Empire" (Senghor 1991: 344). Poetic images of the dressed body change accordingly, as in the "Preliminary Poem" of the *Black Hosts* collection in *The Collected Poetry:*

> To you Tiralleurs Sénégalais, to my black brothers with your warm hands under ice and death
> Who can sing of you, if not your brother-in-arms, your brother-in-blood?
> I will not let the ministers and generals have the last word
> I will not—no not!—let scornful praises be heaped upon you at furtive burials. You are not dishonorable poor wretches with empty pockets. (Paris 1940, 1991: 309)

The empty pockets constitute the first time that Senghor's poetry refers to literal garments in daily reality. But as items of clothing in visible reality, the pockets are of course metaphors of illusion. As in *Shadow Songs,* visible clothing hides a deeper reality—here, the reality of the African soldiers' bodies, invisible to French officials: "Free volunteers . . . who offered their god-like bodies, glory of the stadiums, for the catholic honor of man" (Senghor 1991: 322). The epithet "glory of the stadiums" alludes to the celebrated wrestling champions in Senegalese villages and belongs to the process by which the poem transforms the soldiers into the kind of mythic hero that the poet had constructed in *Shadow Songs.*

Including these bereft and scorned contemporary soldiers in his pantheon of heroes from the glorious African past, Senghor goes far beyond the more conventional poems of

Shadow Songs. In *Black Hosts,* he also intertwines more complexly metaphoric clothing as illusion and the new realist images of clothing, in symbolism more intensely infused with bitterness, as in "The Despair of a Free Volunteer":

> They gave him garments of servitude, which he imagined the candid cloak of the martyr
> Oh naïve! Natively naïve! Fez and boots for his free domesticated feet...
>
> He rids himself of his collar—his tie hides the sweat soaking his shirt—of his somber jacket.
> He leans over a second plain saturated with fezzes and blood. (Senghor 1991: 321)

The visible fez and boots are doubly illusory: First, the French colonialists mask the conscript's nobility behind metaphoric garments of servitude; second, the conscript himself, in his nobility, misrecognizes the debasing garments as symbols of his sincere devotion. The image of the soldier undressing begins the poetic process that will transform him into a mythic figure. In this process, the red fez gradually ceases, step by step, to be a literal garment-as-illusion and becomes surreal "cosmic" clothing. The fezzes fuse with blood and then with the plains of the French battlefield, which in their turn fuse with the "high-lands of corpses" that "mask the fields over there." The poet asks, "Can he see the lost paradise beyond the horizon of that fabled time?" (1991: 321). In *Black Hosts,* even the cosmic body is unequivocally political. The symbolism of nudity likewise becomes less entangled with clichéd Western tropes: "We are... bodies deprived of hope who wither away / Declawed bobcats, disarmed soldiers, naked men" (1991: 326). As in Senghor's youthful poetry, nudity is tied to the construction of a new foundational identity from within the experience of deepest of loss and division. But rather than symbolize authenticity, nudity here connotes the rock bottom of loss and division themselves. It figures the necessary ground for constructing an identity, and this time, a collective identity.

But in the very act of exerting poetic power to overcome the split self, Senghor recreates an irreconcilable contradiction at the heart of his writing: He performs in the French language a celebration of what he considers the unique symbolic and rhythmic power inherent to African languages. The poet of *Black Hosts* inhabits directly the voice of the griot. Solemnly, he performs the forms and formulae of the griot songs to honor the dead and disdained soldiers. Yet he does so in French: "Mbaye Dyôb! I want to speak your name and your honor" (1991: 333). Within this division, the poem fuses the poet as griot and Senghor as political leader.

Although Senghor often dismisses this conflict between African and French languages in his theoretical writings, it emerges in his poetry as a painful division. The conflict flares acutely in a particularly moving poem of *Black Hosts.* The poet invokes the now familiar Senghorian metaphors of clothing and nudity:

> Here I am before you Mother, a soldier with naked sleeves
> And I am dressed in foreign words, where your eyes see only a collection of sticks and rags. (1991: 335)

The visible, and therefore illusory, clothing symbolizes language itself. The "foreign words" that dress the poet are the very words of the poem. Moreover, the poet speaks French in the act of performing himself speaking Sérère: "Mother, speak to me. My tongue slides over our sonorous hard words." Through the metaphor of dress, the poetic voice performs the rock-bottom internal division of Senghor's poetic self.

As a later poem suggests, the poet's French language is both the necessary bridge to the mystic-magic "sous-reality" and also the wrenching separation at his core: "And that other exile more heavy on my heart, the wrenching of self from self / From my mother tongue, from the Ancestor's head, from the tam-tam of my soul" (1991: 388). Every word of the poetry signifies "*la Parole nègre*" and also expresses its loss.

The poems Senghor wrote during his presidency thematize a more obvious kind of self-division, between the "Royaume d'Enfance" and the daily life of the head of state. Poetic language becomes the barrier protecting the presences of that dream world from being debased in the world of commodified material values. These poems state insistently the theme that mystico-magic presences can exist only though the absence of their positive reality. The "Nights of childhood . . . Nights palpitating with presences" (1991: 442) live only in an aura of loss.

Dress as illusion becomes accordingly more insubstantial, represented as nonexistent, especially when contrasted to the dress of the dyâli, which is not represented at all. In "L'Absente," the poet writes:

> But I am not your honor, not the impudent Lion
> My head is not golden, not dressed in tall schemes
> Without heavy bracelets my arms are just there, my hands so naked! . . .
> I'm telling you: I am the Dyâli . . .
> My greatness is to sing the charm of the Absent one. (1991: 364)

The nondescription of the dyâli's dress, marked only by what it is not, leads, through a chain of imagery, to the photographic image of Senghor's suit. The first link in the chain is the figure of "l'Absente." Since this poem is dedicated to Senghor's future wife, Colette Hubert, "L'Absente" symbolizes both the beloved lady, as in medieval Provençal poetry, and the mystico-magic presences. Simon Njami also reads into this poem Senghor's political ambition: "The poem is to be read backwards, like a code whose principle would be to invert true and false" (Njami 2006: 160–161). On one level of the poem then, the "naked hands" act as antithesis to the metaphorical dress of political grandeur and as symbol of the poet/griot's authenticity. But in Njami's code, nudity is the visible illusion masking the powerful politician.

Another link in the chain appears in a poem where the poet/president uses similarly negated figures of grandiose political dress:

> No I am not the prince in the purple headband, the classic pagne, my chest crucified with white cauris.
> I am not the red-throated bee eater of Nubia, not the yellow-crowned gonolek of Barbary
> But combassou finch of Senegal, I've donned my beige livery. (1991: 506)

The metaphor of livery, nested within the metaphor of a bird, reverses the usual direction of the poet's symbolic images.

Instead of leading to the sous-reality beyond the visible garment, the metaphor points to the literal dressed body and inadvertently recalls the realistic photographic images of President Senghor. The little beige bird conjures images of Senghor's small physical stature and inconspicuous suits. But the metaphor of "livery" also recalls the unadorned dyâli in "L'Absente." The visible uniform of a servant of "my people" masks the underlying mastery of the autocratic president.

AGAIN THE PHOTOGRAPHIC IMAGE OF THE SUIT

In the context of his own poetic imagery, Senghor's suit in photographers' images of the Faye collection appears as the antimythic garment. But it can be read poetically as the visible sign of what it is not. As such, it protects an "underlying" more real, necessarily absent mystico-magic presence. Read in the context of Senghor's poetic process of signification, the suit in the political photographs complicates the historical bourgeois meanings discussed above. Senghor's suited photographic image, like his poetic griot persona chanting in French, can appear as both the bridge linking the mundane world to sous-reality and the paradox at the heart of his philosophy of Négritude.

Yet another poetic passage brings this significance of the suit into focus. It combines a description of the poet/president's modest appearance, a reference to his language, and the mention of his griot persona:

> Lord, you have made me the Master-of-Language
> Me, the son of a trader, born gray and so puny
> And my mother named me Impudent, so much did I offend the beauty of the day.
> You granted me power of the word in your unequal justice. (1991: 448)

As in *Black Hosts*, the Master-of-Language combines the figures of griot and leader, and once again, the image of his small, gray body has a double meaning. An almost satirical, realist reminder of the president's photographic image, this insignificant body is also the visible signifier of the power of *la Parole*. Read with these multivalent poetic images, the political reportage images of the suited Senghor can also take on multiple meanings.

Although the photographs in Ibrahima Faye's archive have enormous value and emotional power as visual historical documents, only a few have artistic flair. One of the most striking, for composition, detail, mood, and dramatic storytelling, portrays, perhaps not coincidentally, Senghor and a griotte (Figure 11.3). In the photo, taken in Saint-Louis in the early 1970s, a rhythmic interplay of triangles forms the composition. They make Senghor the unmistakable central focus while also emphasizing his small physical stature. In the center, Senghor walks at the head of a large entourage. The right foreground is filled with the figure of a large griotte caught in dynamic movement. She bends forward, flinging her arms out wide as if to greet and embrace the president. Her left arm forms one side of the triangle connecting to the figure of Senghor's body.

The left foreground is filled by the figure of a man whom Mme. Faye identified as "a famous journalist." Dressed in a print Senegalese shirt, a baseball cap, heavy earphones, and sunglasses, he holds out toward the griotte a microphone connected by a heavy cord to a battery pack slung over his shoulder. The head and cord of the microphone form a mirror image of the griotte's hand and arm, as they outline the other side of the triangle connecting to Senghor's figure. Behind Senghor, the figures of Governor Faye and the mayor of Saint Louis form a reflecting triangle, which fans out from them in concentric circles of local officials, bodyguards, gendarmes, the excited crowd, and, finally, packs of boys hoisted on the walls surrounding the Governor's Palace.

A contingency of contrast creates an effect uncannily reminiscent of the "cosmic body" in Senghor's poems. His light-colored suit disappears into the white clothing of the figures behind him, leaving his head and hand visible. The head, for the only time in these photos, is animated with a joyous smile, and the hand is outstretched toward the griotte. Although Senghor is the central focus, all eyes are on the griotte. He is the almost-invisible cause and motivation of her powerful song. His enthusiastic reaction suggests that she represents a bevy of profoundly influential figures from the "Royaume d'Enfance"—his storytelling childhood nurse, Nga; the "poetesses of my village"; King Koumba N'Dofène and his splendid visits: "with a great cortège, on horseback, surrounded by four troubadours, also on horseback, who would sing his praises" (Senghor 1980: 34). The griotte figures as well Senghor's own alter ego, the being he assumed at his moments of deepest loss when he was forced to reconstruct from the bottom up his individual and political identity. In this photo, the symbolic relation to the griotte makes Senghor double. He is at once the prince whose praises the dyâli sings, and also the reflection of her.

The journalist, loaded down with technological gear, interacts with the griotte figure to signify several core values of Négritude: the power to assimilate European culture into African culture rather than be assimilated and to adapt audiovisual media to African culture rather than succumb to Euro-American cultural imperialism (Senghor 1964: 295). Together, griotte and journalist signify "the Promised Land, the land of reconciliation between Négritude and Modernity" (Senghor 1980: 234). In capturing the moment of Senghor's joyous smile and spontaneous open gesture, the photo even presents a fleeting instant of reconciliation between the "Royaume d'Enfance" and political reality. Yet beyond the visual signifiers of *métissage* between ancient African praise-singing and technological modernity, something invisible makes this photo symbolize an underlying sous-reality.

At the bottom of the photo appears the shadow of the usually invisible photographer. He developed the photo and sent prints to Governor Faye. According to Elizabeth Edwards and Janice Hart, "Photographs have inextricably linked meanings as images and meanings as objects...both of which are direct products of intention" (2004: 62). Governor Faye had these photographs produced as image and object with the intention of giving them as gifts and souvenirs to other officials in attendance and to the president. The griotte, the journalist, and the invisible photographer signify an array of modes, developed at different historical periods, for recording a historical event and preserving it for future audiences. The visual content of the photo projects a future in which the event it represents will be broadcast for radio. The invisible production of the photo projects a future in which it will become a souvenir of a past event.

This particular photo therefore dramatically portrays the temporality of Senegalese mid-twentieth-century political reportage in general. This temporality is simultaneously prospective and retrospective. The visible imagery of this photo, as it alludes to an invisible nonlinear temporality, makes the photo approach the "symbolic image" of Senghor's "Black Word."

CONCLUSION: IMAGE, TIME, AND REFERENTIALITY

Of course, the photo can only approach this status of a Senghorian "symbolic image" if it actually survives into a distant future and if it then gets viewed by people who see it across years of history and change. Only through this long and uncertain process can the photographic signs of mundane political ceremony become signifiers of mythic grandeur. In a major speech of 1959, Senghor defined myth in relation to black-African art. Art is "the imagination which, at the confluence of Desire and the real, creates *myths,* i.e. the living forms of the mystico-magic world" (1964: 283).

Some atmosphere of such a mythic space informed my research in the domestic space of Governor Faye's photo archive. As I handled and viewed the photos in their double-being as objects and images, "the physical traces of usage and time" (Edwards and Hart 2004: 3) amplified the testimony in the images. Forty years of historical change had progressively separated them from, and also connected them more complexly to, the events portrayed. In this floating temporality of separation and connection, I experienced the images through the filter of my own long-ago youthful awe. It imbued the people portrayed with the legendary status of the heroic generation that had liberated francophone Africa from colonialism. It conjured up the space and time of the late 1960s, in which I had first read the texts of writers such as Léopold Senghor and been inspired to study and teach African literature.

During my research in M. Faye's archive in 2007 and 2008, I came to realize that beyond simple temporal distance, a long process of bereavement created the mythic aura. The suitcase of historical photos insistently evoked the enormous loss since that unique period of hope and enthusiasm, which Senegalese people often talk about. This aura through which I viewed the photos is not nostalgia because one knows that nobody actually experienced this past grandeur in a lived present. It is a product of the retrospective/prospective temporality of political photo reportage, its constant relay of past and future. The fascination of the Faye photographs comes not just from their undeniable past referent (Barthes 1980: 150), but also from the gap between the original imprint of this visible referent and the images of a lost past that the photographic process was producing for (possible) future audiences.

The photos approach the Senghorian living forms of myth by representing to future viewers (at least to this one) a conjunction between image, reality, desire, and "imagining consciousness" that was necessarily absent from the lived experience in the present tense. Conversely, Senghor's most powerful and memorable poems, those of *Black Hosts,* achieve their poetic intensity precisely because they are not "self-referential" and "autonomous" (Gouvard 2001: 87). From the immediacy of their undeniable present referents—the bitter experiences of African soldiers in World War II—the poems derive their imagistic and tonal power. These are also the poems that perform most explicitly the step-by-step process that transforms the real referent into myth. In this way, the image that documents the joy of President Senghor in his almost invisible suit and the image that makes mythic "Despair of a Free Volunteer" in his blood-red fez touch each other across the divide between photography and poetry.

NOTES

1. Translations from French texts in this essay are mine. For the original French poetry, see Senghor (1991).
2. Many grateful thanks to photographers Adama Sylla and Oumar Ly for their testimony about political reportage photography for Governor Faye.

REFERENCES

Bajorek, Jennifer. 2010. "Photography and National Memory: Senegal around 1960." *History of Photography* 34(2): 158–169.

Barthes, Roland. 1980. *La chambre claire: note sur la photographie. Cahiers du cinéma Gallimard*. Paris: Gallimard.

Calefato, Patrizia. 2004. *The Clothed Body. Dress, Body, Culture*. Oxford: Berg.

Carter, Michael. 2003. *Fashion Classics from Carlyle to Barthes. Dress, Body*, Culture. Oxford: Berg.

Craik, Jennifer. 2009. Fashion: *The Key Concepts*. Oxford: Berg.

Diop, Abdoulaye Bara. 1981. *La sociéte wolof: tradition et changement: les systèmes d'inégalité et de domination. Hommes et sociétés*. Paris: Karthala.

Edwards, Elizabeth, and Janice Hart. 2004. "Introduction: Photographs as Objects." In E. Edwards and J. Hart, eds., *Photographs, Objects, Histories: On the Materiality of Images*, 202–515. London, New York: Routledge.

Enwezor, Okwui, and Octavio Zaya. 1996. "Colonial Imaginary, Tropes of Disruption: History, Culture, and Representation in the Works of African Photographers." In Okwui Enwezor, Oliu Oguibe, and Octavio Zaya, eds., *In/Sight: African Photographers, 1940 to the Present*. New York: Guggenheim Museum.

Geary, Christraud M. 1998. "Different Visions?: Postcards from Africa by European and African Photographers and Sponsors." In Christraud Geary and Virginia-Lee Webb, eds.,

Delivering Views: Distant Cultures in Early Postcards. Washington, DC: Smithsonian Institution Scholarly Press.

Gouvard, Jean-Michel. 2001. *L'analyse de la poésie*. Paris: Presses universitaires de France.

Grabski-Ochsner, Joanna. 2007. "Senghorama: Goethe Pencum, Dakar, Librarie Quatre Vents, Dakar: December 20, 2006–January 6." *African Arts* 40: 92–93.

Hale, Thomas A. 1998. *Griots and Griottes: Masters of Words and Music*. Bloomington: Indiana University Press.

Harney, Elizabeth. 2004. *In Senghor's Shadow: Art, Politics, and the Avant-Garde in Senegal, 1960–1995*. Durham: Duke University Press.

Hollander, Ann. 1994. *Sex and Suits: The Evolution of Modern Dress*. New York, Tokyo, London: Kodansha Press.

Jakobson, Roman, and Stephen Rudy. 1981. *Poetry of Grammar and Grammar of Poetry*. The Hague: Mouton.

Jules-Rosette, Bennetta. 1998. *Black Paris: the African Writers' Landscape*. Urbana: University of Illinois Press

Keïta, Seydou, André Magnin, and Youssouf Cissé. 1997. *Seydou Keïta*. Zurich: Scalo.

Laye, Camara, 2005. *L'enfant noir*. Myrna Bell Rochester, and Natalie Schorr, eds. Newburyport, MA: Focus Publishing/R Pullins.

Markovitz, Irving Leonard. 1969. *Léopold Sédar Senghor and the Politics of Negritude*. New York: Atheneum.

Mudimbe, V. Y. 1988. *The Invention of Africa: Gnosis, Philosophy, and the Order of Knowledge. African Systems of Thought*. Bloomington: Indiana University Press.

Njami, Simon. 2006. *C'était Senghor*. Paris: Fayard.

Prochaska, David. 1991. "Fantasia of the Photothéque: French Postcard Views of Colonial Senegal." *African Arts* 24: 40–47.

Rabine, Leslie W. 2002. *The Global Circulation of African Fashion. Dress, Body, Culture*. Oxford: Berg.

Rabine, Leslie W. 2010. "Fashionable Photography in Mid-Twentieth-Century Senegal." *Fashion Theory* 14(3): 305–330.

Senghor, Léopold Sédar. 1964. *Liberté I: négritude et humanisme*. Paris: Seuil.

Senghor, Léopold Sédar, and Mohamed Aziza. 1980. *La poésie de l'action: conversations avec Mohamed Aziza*. Paris: Stock.

Senghor, Léopold Sédar, and Melvin Dixon. 1991. *The Collected Poetry*. *CARAF Books*. Charlottesville: University Press of Virginia.

–12–

Transculturated Displays: International Fashion and West African Portraiture

Candace M. Keller

In the last twenty years, photographic portraiture from West Africa has captured the imagination of international audiences. Appearing in numerous exhibitions on nearly every continent, and featured in a large corpus of catalogs, monographs, fashion magazines, and news journals, these images have attracted copious attention in the realms of art and popular culture. Perhaps none have been more publicly revered and emulated than the black-and-white works of Malian photographers Malick Sidibé and Seydou Keïta. Admired for the artistry and graphic quality of their images, which showcase their subjects' flair for fashion, both photographers have been commissioned to shoot fashion spreads for some of the world's top designers and stylists, and their photographs have been referenced on textiles and CD jackets as well as in video and film.[1]

Recently, this acclaim has presented Malick Sidibé with a host of accolades, travel invitations, and exhibition opportunities, since he has taken center stage as the most internationally renowned African photographer after Keïta's passing in 2001: Sidibé became the continent's first photographer to be awarded the prestigious Hasselblad Foundation International Award in Photography in 2003. Four years later, he was honored with the Golden Lion Lifetime Achievement distinction at the 2007 Venice Biennale. The following year, he was recognized by the International Center of Photography in New York City for his lifetime achievement, and in 2009, he was decorated with the PHotoEspaña Baume & Mercier Award.

Sidibé's celebrity has also fostered new commissions. Among the most exceptional of these is an editorial fashion shoot (Figure 12.1), with stylist Andreas Kokkino, that appeared in the April 5, 2009, issue of the *New York Times Magazine* (Sidibé and Kokkino 2009a).

In this exposition, several of Sidibé's relatives, neighbors, friends, and models are pictured in the photographer's studio wearing the latest ready-to-wear fashions by haute couture designers. Accompanied by a dearth of contextualizing information and a provocative title, this project prompted a surge of responses from the African Studies community and raised a number of critical questions: What was the impetus for this commission? How was it conceived and negotiated? What does it communicate about

Figure 12.1 Title page, featuring Assitan Sidibé. Malick Sidibé and Andreas Kokkino in "Prints and the Revolution: From Milan to Mali, a Riot of Checks, Stripes, Patterns, and Polka Dots." *New York Times Magazine* (April 5, 2009), 40. Courtesy Magnin-A. © Malick Sidibé.

Africans, particularly those depicted? Given the context, what does it express concerning Western interpretations of fashion, culture, and people in Africa?

In an attempt to answer these queries, while shedding some light on the hidden processes and consequences of the photo shoot, this essay recounts its narrative and contextualizes it within the broader scope of Sidibé's work. Moreover, it identifies the role that he and other agents played in negotiating the collaborative undertaking. With emphasis on the politics of representation—both of self and other—this analysis focuses on the portrayal of individuals in these images, considering the ways in which the subjects have been dressed, staged, and framed according to acculturated, often imagined, constructs of modernity and anachronism. Finally, it looks at the effects of transculturation (Ortiz 1947: 97)—processes of multidirectional cultural exchange—on the creation, reception, and reinterpretation of Sidibé's images within Mali and in the global market.

To highlight the complex agency,[2] or the capacity of individuals to "act within a socially and historically constituted space of possibilities and constraints" (Bangstad 2006: 36), and critical practices of transculturation that have informed the production and interpretations of the *New York Times Magazine* fashion shoot, the project must first be contextualized within the larger sphere of Malick Sidibé's oeuvre, its eventual introduction into the global art market, and its ongoing relationship with international fashion.

PORTRAITURE IN MALI

The photographic archive for which Sidibé is internationally celebrated consists of black-and-white portraits taken in informal settings or inside his studio in Bamako, Mali's capital city, since the 1960s.[3] Originally commissioned by West African clientele, these prints were produced in small rectangular formats intended to be displayed in albums and picture frames as personal keepsakes. For these patrons, photography was foremost a venue in which to express themselves and to record their accomplishments, desires, and fluctuating trends in portraiture.

Sidibé's young clientele regularly sought self-representations that evoked affluence, success, and education, suggesting access to coveted socioeconomic opportunities. They achieved this in part by donning the latest "cosmopolitan fashions" (Eicher and Sumberg 1995: 296), which they obtained at used clothing markets and high-end boutiques in the capital as well as through the commission of locally crafted items or by traveling abroad. To complete these ensembles, clients posed with imported commodities from Europe and the United States, such as watches, records, and radios, that were either personal possessions or studio-provided props. Addressing the social potency of these materials, Sidibé opined, "The mere fact that [an item] came from the West gave the wearer a certain kind of power, a kind of power that kids are looking for" (Lamunière 2001: 55).

To reinforce this power in portraiture, young trendsetters often appear aloof to the camera or candidly engage it. Directed by Sidibé, they assume strong postures and cool expressions, usually partially obscured behind heavily tinted sunglasses. Accentuating this attitude, during the 1960s, Sidibé began experimenting with a new perspective in his portraits, which he has since termed *Vue de Dos* (Back View). To convey the contemporary urban style and independent comportment of young male patrons, Sidibé modeled the pose after the confident manner in which French and American actors exited a scene, for example with a jacket flung over one shoulder while glancing backward at the camera.

Inspired by Western cinema, young men and women would also emulate popular fictional characters in their portraits. These figures commonly embodied liberation and fortitude, displayed an identifiably unique style, and were thus respected for their stark individuality. Favorite examples included Brigitte Bardot in *And God Created Woman* (1956) and heroic protagonists in French spy films such as Lemmy Caution, played by American actor Eddie Constantine in the 1950s and 1960s (Sidibé and Laurent 2003: 214; Magnin 1998: 37). Sidibé's portraits from this era depict several young men—or *kamalenbaw* (playboys)—personified as the latter, adorned in fedora-style hats, casual suits or dress slacks, collared shirts, and loafers, often accompanied by a cigarette (Sidibé 2003).

Participating in an international youth revolution, as Manthia Diawara has argued, these individuals also rallied behind rock 'n' roll and rhythm and blues, actively pursuing social liberties and recent trends promoted by performers such as James Brown, who helped popularize "tight turtleneck shirts" and "above-the-ankle-bell-bottom pants" in Bamako (Diawara 2003: 14). Related so-called "hippie" fashions were made famous in Mali by The Beatles, French Yé-Yé musicians, and other celebrities of the epoch, as evident in Sidibé's portraits of youths sporting afro hairstyles, platform shoes, and miniskirts. Emphasizing local contemporaneous engagement with global movements of popular culture, Sidibé exclaimed, "Look at my photos of that time, and nobody could say we were behind the times!" (Magnin 1998: 169).

To underscore the emotive energy and kinetic dynamism of youth culture during that period, Sidibé often employed high-contrast, boldly patterned backdrops and flooring within his portraits. The most iconic of these are two vertically striped textiles, and checkered and polka-dot linoleum, used interchangeably over the course of his career. Juxtaposed against the printed fabrics of his clients' fashion ensembles, these material aids have enabled him to experiment with the visual intensity of his images. Layering patterned clothing, backdrops, and flooring, Sidibé effectively flattens the picture plane and frames the visage of his subjects, emphasizing their distinctive features, expressions, and individuality.[4]

In addition to these creative strategies, Sidibé has assayed a variety of postures and employed his sense of humor in the studio to intentionally convey a sense of intimacy, playfulness, and jubilancy in his images, stating, "I've always felt the need to bring some life into my photos... Above all I have wanted to show laughter [and] joy" (Sidibé 2004).

MULTIDIRECTIONAL AND FLUID PROCESSES OF TRANSCULTURATION

As youths in Mali reveled in imported couture from the West, fashion designers, fine artists, and patrons in Europe and the United States contemporaneously drew inspiration from Africa. Much like colonialist fantasies of the continent, however, the Westerners' creations typically perpetuated primitivist notions of an imagined Africa. For example, in 1967, with emphasis on rural, ethnic-based realities and an appreciation for African abstraction and graphic symbolism, Yves Saint Laurent introduced his "Bambara" dress, named after the French pronunciation of Mali's largest culture group (Bergé 2008: 111).[5] Title aside, the design does not directly relate to fashion in Mali but rather adheres to the longstanding practice of representing an exoticized continent.

By the 1980s, more direct influences of fashion from West Africa were expressed with similar attitudes in, for instance, the *boubou* dresses of Kenzo and the lines of French, Italian, and American designers such as Hermès, Jean Paul Gaultier, and Donna Karan (Loughran 2009: 243). The following decade, "ethnic"-inspired attire from the region continued, with particular reference to locally crafted textiles such as *bogolanfini* (mud-cloth from Mali). Tailored into collared shirts, sport coats, and dresses, African-inspired designs by John Galliano, Kenzo, Dolce & Gabanna, Paco Rabanne, Yves Saint Laurent, and Oscar de la Renta have graced the runway and appeared on the pages of fashion magazines since in the 1990s (Loughran 2009; Rovine 2009).

Thus, while youths in Mali appropriated Western fashion to express their modern, cosmopolitan sensibilities and membership within global youth movements, elements of African fashion were being reinterpreted by European and American urbanites in a manner that reinforces the idea of a timeless, alien continent. The latter practice has been justly criticized by scholars as primitivist due to the exoticizing treatment of "Africa as fashion" (Rovine 2009: 135) often through what Jean-Loup Amselle has called the recycling of African "kitsch" (Amselle 2005: 53). This practice was brought to the fore by Wendy Grossman in a recent exhibition that featured photographs Man Ray published in *Harper's Bazaar* in 1937. In these images, models don beaded hats from central Africa coupled with ivory bracelets, recontextualizing African objects as exotica and, by extension, symbols of high fashion (Grossman 2009: 144).

Complicating this critical perspective are African designers, such as Malian artist Chris Seydou, who have worked collaboratively on ready-to-wear and haute couture lines with colleagues in Europe and the United States. For instance, four years after Yves Saint Laurent introduced his Bambara dress, Seydou began working in the designer's Paris atelier where he remained until the opening of his own boutique in West Africa a decade later (Rovine 2004: 200–201). Renowned for using bogolanfini-inspired textiles to create suits, skirts, scarves, hats, and jackets, his work likely inspired that of his Western-based colleagues, as well as those in Africa. After Seydou, Malian designers, such as Lamine Kouyaté (Xuly Bët) and Alphadi (who has incorporated bogolanfini patterns in his creations), have become important in international fashion since the 1990s, with boutiques in Europe, Africa, and the United States.

Recently, African-inspired elements have been emphasized in composite fashions by designers from all regions of the world, including Max Osterweis, Junya Watanabe, and John Galliano. Among aesthetic components drawn from nearly every continent, popular trends inspired by Africa include colorful, multilayered patterns and exaggerated head wraps, as well as the incorporation of exotic animal prints. Since 2008, many of these have been evident in the exposé of new lines during international fashion weeks, on websites, and in fashion spreads, such as that created by Malick Sidibé and Andreas Kokkino for the *New York Times Magazine*.

FROM PERSONAL PORTRAITS TO FINE ART AND FASHION

Like many Westerners, Kokkino was introduced to Sidibé's oeuvre through the work of André Magnin, who has authored seminal monographs on Seydou Keïta and Malick Sidibé (Kokkino 2009). One of several French agents to bring West African portraiture to international audiences in the 1990s, Magnin traveled to Bamako and made the acquaintance of Sidibé and Keïta in 1992. Thanks to his relations with collectors, promoters of contemporary African art, and Parisian-based fashion designers, by 1994 the Cartier Foundation had hosted a solo exhibition of Keïta's work, agnès b. had displayed photographs by Sidibé at her Galerie du Jour, and the premier Rencontres de la Photographie Africain (African Photography Meetings) had featured prints by both artists at its Bamako biennale.

The recontextualization of commissioned portraiture from Mali by Westerners in fine art galleries, catalogs, and biennials around the globe has dramatically altered its appearance, function, meaning, and aesthetic quality. Through these transitions, like those of his compatriots, Sidibé's medium-format negatives from past decades have been repeatedly reprinted in greatly enlarged, uncropped, high-contrast images—often overseas by select individuals in France and the United States—and they have regularly been given titles, although it is not always clear by whom. Equally transformed are the identities of the people the images depict, who have become anonymous Africans representing an urban past. Such processes, therefore, have raised concerns about the creative property rights of photographers and their clients, and have incited questions regarding the authorship and ownership of these portraits, as Elizabeth Bigham has effectively pointed out concerning the work of Seydou Keïta (Bigham 1999).

Recently, Amselle has critiqued the position of West African portraiture in Western art contexts as an example of "neo-primitivism," akin to the exoticization and recycling of African "kitsch" by fashion designers throughout the twentieth century (Amselle 2005). For him, the current popularity of portraits taken in Bamako during the 1950s through 1980s results from Western nostalgia for fashions and popular culture of those eras—part of what Amselle refers to as Western discarded "trash" (Amselle 2005: 52)—which have been renewed by their use in African contexts. Conflating contemporary trends with urban African pasts, an anachronistic Africa is created as fuel for Western, and now global, imaginations. On this point, referencing the reproduced negatives of Sidibé's archive, Amselle reproachingly argued, "It is no longer in the jungles of the Amazon or New Guinea but in the jungles of African or European cities . . . [where] one can find the primordial Eden" (Amselle 2005: 87).

On the surface, Amselle's neo-primitivist critique could readily apply to the fashion shoot created in early 2009 by Sidibé and Kokkino for the *New York Times Magazine*. Containing eight images accompanied by a dearth of contextualizing information, the display generates an anachronistic space by presenting the latest European and American couture designs on African actors set within a striking, revamped 1960s–1980s visual stage. Several factors collaborate to convey this sense, including the title, "Prints and the Revolution: From Milan to Mali, a Riot of Checks, Stripes, Patterns and Polka Dots" (Figure 12.1), which doubles as a pun for the musical artist Prince and his band of the 1980s and as a reference to the emphasis on pattern and dynamic juxtapositions of bold prints in the series. Typed in a stylized font that harkens back to the 1970s, the retro theme is reinforced by the black-and-white quality of Malick Sidibé's photographs, which reveal today's fashions in an antiquated light.

Such culturally loaded symbols, coupled with minimal text, compel viewers to interpret the stunning, densely patterned imagery according to their own experience and imagination, which might call to the fore a degree of exoticism or "otherness." For instance, the extreme use of amalgamated prints and multilayered garments could reinforce stereotypical notions of unkempt Africans (Figures 12.1, 12.3). Or, the juxtaposition of tailored suits cut from loudly patterned cloth worn by black men in these images might recall popular imagery of the 1960s and 1970s African American "pimp," particularly when the suit is accompanied by a brimmed hat (Figure 12.2).

However one interprets the particulars, with such visual and material excess, the spread seems to highlight an imagined African or black urban style *as* fashion, rather than feature specific fashion items as one might expect in this venue. This sense is reinforced by the final and most compacted image in the series (Figure 12.4). Although all of the photographs occupy a position somewhere between portraiture, art, and

Figure 12.2 Second page, featuring, from left to right, Abdoulaye Diakité and Mamoutou Koné. Malick Sidibé and Andreas Kokkino, "Prints and the Revolution: From Milan to Mali, a Riot of Checks, Stripes, Patterns, and Polka Dots." *New York Times Magazine* (April 5, 2009), 41. Courtesy Magnin-A. © Malick Sidibé.

advertisement, this most ambiguous image features seven people, including three of the photographer's grandchildren, wearing a combination of couture designs, their own clothing, and locally crafted jewelry such that the fashion items themselves are largely or entirely hidden within the collective display. Thus, while they are individually indicated in a caption beneath the image, they are not the intended focus of the shoot—as explicated in the title. Therefore, this collection of images appears to present a partially fabricated African aesthetic style as high fashion.

Moreover, it does so in a manner that only an outsider could orchestrate. Anyone familiar with Bamako would recognize the staged ensembles as uncommon contemporary local dress: Plaid is not typically worn today in Mali, and belts and hats on women are rare, as are vests and cummerbunds on men (Figure 12.3). Nevertheless, most viewers would not be aware of these facts. Unfamiliar with Mali, some might not discern that the images were taken in Africa. On the first day of class, for example, my students assumed that the photographs depict African Americans in a neighborhood such as Harlem, likely taken in the 1970s or 1980s when stylized "ethnic ensembles" were popular. Kokkino himself admitted, "Some people didn't realize that we did [the shoot] in Mali" (Kokkino 2009).

More familiar audiences, unnerved by the socioeconomic juxtapositions in the images, might raise ethical queries concerning the implications of featuring elite fashions on people who reside in one of the poorest countries in the world.[6] For this reason, the magazine intentionally omitted the prices of pictured items from photo captions (Kokkino 2009). Other cynics might assume that a professional photographer and amateur models would receive a pittance in Mali for what peers would earn in the United States and, thus, be troubled by perceived economically driven, exploitative agendas behind locating the shoot in Africa.

While offering some compelling critiques, such neo-primitivist arguments remain largely formalist, essentializing, and speculative, based on hegemonic assumptions concerning dynamics of power. As such, they deny agency to Sidibé and the models in the collaborative project, while overlooking the impact the project has had on these individuals. At the same time, they misrepresent the intent of Kokkino and others at the *New York Times*. Therefore, to cultivate a more nuanced and informed perspective on the impetus and creative processes behind the project, this discussion turns to its inception in New York City.

TRANSCULTURATED DISPLAYS AND COMPLEX AGENCY: THE *NEW YORK TIMES* FASHION SHOOT

A few years ago, stylist Andreas Kokkino was inspired to do a photo shoot with Malick Sidibé for the "Style" section of the *New York Times Magazine*. However, it was not until December 2008 that his editor agreed, envisioning the project carried out in New York City with West African models (Kokkino 2009). Drawn to the pride Sidibé's subjects convey in having their picture taken, coupled with the photographer's repetitious use of the boldly patterned backdrops and flooring in his studio portraits, Kokkino insisted that the shoot take place in Bamako at Studio Malick with local models selected by the photographer. Kokkino was also adamant that the shoot be photographed in black and white, he said, "because that's what Malick Sidibé does" (Kokkino 2009). With the magazine's approval, Kokkino telephoned Sidibé in Mali and negotiated an agreement: Sidibé would be paid the industry-standard professional photographer rate and would gather a group of young men and women for the shoot, which would take place in February 2009 (Kokkino 2009; Sidibé 2009). In return, Kokkino was asked to bring the photographer several rolls of 120-speed medium-format film, which is not regularly available in Mali (Kokkino 2009). The final selection of the models and their payment would be determined in February 2009.

Excited by what Kokkino perceived as visual, stylistic synergy between the boldly juxtaposed patterns and "implication of color without color" in Sidibé's portraits with the new African-inspired, print-dominated, ready-to-wear lines by Junya Watanabe and John Galliano, the stylist began ordering various items and accessories, on loan, from more than forty designers (Kokkino 2009). While in New York City, he arranged in excess of twenty-five outfits, shoes, and extra accessories that he and his assistant, Stella Greenspan, would bring in two large duffle bags to Mali.

Meanwhile, in Bamako, Malick Sidibé began amassing a group of potential models among his relatives, neighbors, and friends who had worked for him during the past ten years. All of them were generally thrilled to participate in the upcoming project as several had benefitted from a similar commission for Pennyblack, a MaxMara Fashion Group line based in Milan, in 2008 (Malick, Dia, and Siné Sidibé 2009).

In February 2009, Kokkino and Greenspan arrived in Mali. On their second day, they were introduced to the prospective models: first women and, the following day, men. The stylists decided to work with all seventeen of them. To determine their individual wages, the group discussed their concerns amongst themselves. Leading the negotiations was Mariam Sidibé, a professional model in Bamako and distant relative of the Sidibé family (Kokkino 2009; Malick, Dia, and Siné Sidibé 2009). Finally, it was determined that each of the nine women would receive 50,000 CFA francs (approximately US$100) and each of the eight men would collect 25,000 CFA francs (roughly US$50), which was somewhat less than what models in New York City were paid (about US$125–$150) for an editorial shoot (Kokkino 2009).[7] Although these individuals belonged to middle- and upper-class populations of Bamako, with the average annual income in Mali at about US$350, these wages amounted to a substantial sum.

In this regard, Malick Sidibé used the opportunity to provide young women, who do not typically hold paying jobs, with a temporary source of income, opining, "That was good for the women. They should be happy with what they got"[8] (Sidibé 2009). As such, the commission enabled him to perpetuate one of his community service projects, which he had begun during the past decade working with neighborhood women on a series of *Vue de Dos* photographs. About this philanthropic practice, Sidibé stated,

"The first woman I asked to model for a *Vue de Dos* was Fatim...[and] I gave her some money afterward. Another [woman] I chose because she is an orphan, and I wanted to help her...It is a way to help women obtain some money" (Sidibé 2004).

Once Kokkino determined the number of models with whom he would work, and calculated the amount of pages he would have for the magazine spread, he was able to ascertain the number of individuals he could include in each picture. With Kokkino arranging people and fashion ensembles according to size, and a bit of trial and error, the shoot commenced with the men changing out in front of the studio while the women dressed inside (Kokkino 2009). Many of the outfits Kokkino arranged for the models referenced Sidibé's earlier work, fashioning men in suits and, in one case, a fedora-style hat—which recalled *kamlenbaw* portrayals of Lemmy Caution (Figure 12.2)—and adorning women in short, billowy skirts and dresses reminiscent of those inspired by Brigitte Bardot in the 1950s and 1960s. Some of the ladies sported hats and purses akin to those worn by predecessors pictured in earlier portraits by Malick Sidibé and Seydou Keïta, while other models donned dynamic prints, miniskirts, and sunglasses related to fashions that were popular in the 1960s and 1970s (Figures 12.3, 12.4).

The process was a lively affair as individuals took turns modeling their attire and accessories for those gathered around the studio. Most, like Malick Sidibé's son Dia, enjoyed dressing up. About his experience, Dia stated, "I liked the clothes. They made me feel like a big man, a *kamalenba* [playboy]" (Dia Sidibé 2009). The studio audience agreed, finding him the most attractive of the male models and determining that he would be the one man photographed solo. Malick Sidibé, on the other hand, found the clothing amusingly out of touch (Sidibé 2009). Kokkino relayed that when Sidibé saw Abdoulaye Diakité and Mamadou Koné dressed in their suits (Figure 12.2), the photographer asked, "Are these old clothes?," explaining that he hadn't "seen anyone dress that way since the 1970s!" (Kokkino 2009).

Although the general aesthetic of the fashion shoot references eras between the 1950s and 1980s, the particular items Kokkino selected presented something new: Most of the pants are tapered as opposed to bell-bottomed, platform shoes are absent, and rather than the tight turtlenecks and flowered shirts of Diawara's youth, the fabrics employed respond to the interior of Studio Malick. For example, the variety of stripes, checkerboards, and polka dots that Kokkino chose intentionally recall and complement Sidibé's signature backdrops and flooring (Figures 12.1, 12.3, 12.4).

While individuals in Mali were introduced to new dimensions of contemporary international fashion, Kokkino and Greenspan were educated about elements of African fashion that had inspired the clothing they brought with them to Bamako. Specifically, Kokkino learned that the African-inspired attire he had selected for the shoot appropriated aspects of fashions specific to certain regions of the continent. For example, when Fatoumata Cissé appeared wearing an ensemble by Junya Watanabe, to the stylist's surprise, the group identified the style as "South African" (Kokkino 2009).

Figure 12.3 Fifth page, featuring, from left to right, Habib Tounkara, Sekuba Sidibé, and Aichata Sylla. Malick Sidibé and Andreas Kokkino, "Prints and the Revolution: From Milan to Mali, a Riot of Checks, Stripes, Patterns, and Polka Dots." *New York Times Magazine* (April 5, 2009), 44. Courtesy Magnin-A. © Malick Sidibé.

During the shoot, which transpired over two-and-a-half hours on a single day, Sidibé asked Kokkino to present him with the models he wanted to use in a given photograph, and Sidibé arranged them into specific poses and configurations, selected the backdrop and flooring to complement their attire, and provided additional direction (Kokkino 2009; Sidibé 2009). Indicative of his creative style and his recognition of Kokkino's deliberate pattern selections, the photographer made regular use of his striped backdrops and checkered flooring. He also employed several *Vue de Dos* poses in the shoot, although only two of these sustained the final cut (Figure 12.1). Sidibé utilized other customary poses as well, such as his ovular composition, which depicts a centrally positioned individual flanked by two companions (often members of the opposite gender) who lean their heads inward to create a sense of camaraderie and intimacy (Figure 12.3). Finally, attesting to his aesthetic interests, Sidibé was able to capture some

Figure 12.4 Eighth page, featuring from left to right, back to front, Mouibatou Cissé, Lassine Sidibé, Saoudatu Traoré, Másara Magossouba, Koudé Sidibé, Sira Sidibé, and Matakari Dembélé. Malick Sidibé and Andreas Kokkino, "Prints and the Revolution: From Milan to Mali, a Riot of Checks, Stripes, Patterns, and Polka Dots." *New York Times Magazine* (April 5, 2009), 47. Courtesy Magnin-A. © Malick Sidibé.

of the liveliness, humor, and joy of the event in these photographs, as reflected in the facial expressions of several of the models (Figures 12.1, 12.3, 12.4).

A truly collaborative project, the photo shoot produced images that result from the—at times conflicting—ideas, opinions, and desires of its multiple parties. For example, although Kokkino had requested the addition of studio props and other material aids to augment the arrangements, recalling Sidibé's images from decades past, the photographer did not oblige (Kokkino 2009). He also did not indulge the stylist's desire to include several of his young grandchildren in the shoot (Kokkino 2009; Sidibé 2009). However, a compromise was made at the last moment, during the final shoot (Figure 12.4), when Kudé and Sira Sidibé arrived at the studio from school and, encouraged by Kokkino, were incorporated into a group photo (Kokkino 2009).

In another case, Dia Sidibé preferred to select his own poses, after viewing a collection of his father's portraits from previous eras, rather than be directed by the photographer in the studio (Dia Sidibé 2009).

Demonstrating his expertise, Sidibé took two to three photos for each composition using his Twin Lens Reflex camera, totaling no more than thirty-six exposures (Sidibé 2009). In the era of digital photography, when photographers often take hundreds of images per shoot, such photographic precision was remarkable for Kokkino. According to the stylist, in fact, it was the photographer's film-based technology that comprised the project's predominant cost-savings (Kokkino 2009). Like a number of critics in the United States, Sidibé assumed that the magazine had asked to take the photographs in his Bamako studio rather than in New York City because the model fees were much less costly and "the clothes look better on Africans" (Sidibé 2009). Although Kokkino concurs with the last portion of Sidibé's statement, he explained that "a typical shoot in New York City requires a studio fee, [plus] camera and equipment rental... With Malick Sidibé, there was no equipment to rent, no digital assistant, and he has his own studio... The difference in these costs amounts to about $10,000" (Kokkino 2009).

The technology also granted Sidibé a certain degree of control over the production and exhibition of his images. As with local commissions, the photographer retained all of the negatives from the shoot. A portion of these were printed in 24-by-30 centimeter format by his colleague Youssouf Sogodogo in Bamako at C.F.P. (Cadre de Promotion pour la Formation en Photographie) to be published in the *New York Times Magazine* (Sidibé 2009). Eight of those appeared in the April 5, 2009, issue. Later that year, the body of negatives was printed a second time for an exhibition Sidibé held at the National Museum in Bamako during the city's ninth rendition of the Rencontres de la Photographie Africain (African Photography Meetings) in November 2009 (Krifa and Serani 2009).

Five days after their arrival in Mali, Kokkino and Greenspan returned to New York with the clothing and accessories that they had borrowed for the assignment, while the prints were sent to the magazine a few weeks later by Sidibé's son Mody (Kokkino 2009). Some of the models were disappointed by the fact that they were not able to keep any of the items that they wore during the shoot, particularly Sidibé's son Siné (Figure 12.4), who had hoped to retain a pair of Raf Simons sunglasses (Siné Sidibé 2009). Others would have liked to have been paid more, comparing this project less favorably to the one undertaken with Macs Iotti for Pennyblack a few months earlier (Malick, Dia, and Siné Sidibé 2009). Nevertheless, generally, both Sidibé and his models were happy to have participated in the photo shoot, enjoying both their experiences in the studio and later viewing their images in print (the magazine sent a box of issues to the studio during the summer of 2009). Of those I interviewed in Bamako, however, none could comprehend the meaning of its title, though they did not find this particularly disconcerting (Malick, Dia, and Siné Sidibé 2009).

After much deliberation and some failed attempts, I was told, the title was finally authored by Kokkino's managing editor, satisfying the magazine's fondness of puns (Kokkino 2009). Overall, according to Kokkino, the *New York Times Magazine* and its audience found "Prints and the Revolution" an overwhelming success. He cited several responses that applauded the magazine's refreshing, "positive portrayal of Africans" as opposed to the "exoticizing representations" of the continent and its inhabitants still prevalent in *National Geographic* and other media in the United States (Kokkino 2009). Others appreciated the use of "real people" as welcomed alternatives to the emaciated, extraordinarily tall models typically employed in Western fashion shoots and advertisements. For the stylist's perspective, it surpassed his greatest expectations and remains his favorite editorial fashion shoot to date (Kokkino 2009).

One critic, however, assuming a neo-primitivist argument, disparaged the project by comparing it to the "exoticizing" ethnographic photographs by American portrait and fashion photographer Irving Penn (Kokkino 2009). His critique, alongside those of suspecting Africanists, is not entirely baseless, particularly in the context of elite fashion and its penchant for the shocking, provocative, and nostalgic. Case in point: Six months after the *New York Times Magazine* spread was published, *French Vogue* (2009) featured Dutch model Lara Stone with painted dark skin, which for many audiences felt pejorative, primitivising, and tactless due to associations with early-twentieth-century "blackface" performances and thriving racial tensions. Interestingly, however, the primary complaint aired by viewers was the absence of African or African American models in the *Vogue* issue, which had been dedicated to supermodels since the 1980s, arguing, "Why not simply hire a black model?"[9] To address the aesthetic and social implications of this line of inquiry would warrant another important discussion. However, this situation calls attention to the fact that, in the context of designer fashion, Andreas Kokkino and the *New York Times Magazine* specifically chose to hire African models.

Yet, neo-primitivist criticisms persist—resulting, in part, from the highly decontextualized presentation of the imagery, which, after all, is not unique to the project but remains characteristic of most editorial shoots. Thus, part of what this analysis seeks to illuminate is the discrepancies that exist between artistic intent and audience reception, and the treatment of individuals versus the ways in which relationships are publicly perceived. Unlike reproductions of Sidibé's negative archives, the *New York Times* project does not raise ethical concerns of authorship, ownership, or personal rights. The photographer was paid the industry standard wage, supplemented with additional materials, and has been credited for his work. His images appear as he intended, closely cropped and printed to local aesthetic standards, and his named subjects are willing and informed participants who have been able to depict themselves in images that evoke affluence and access to coveted socioeconomic opportunities, receiving their set price as compensation.

What this investigation draws to light, therefore, are deeply imbedded social retentions that culturally sensitive audiences bring to the reading of these images, underscoring the need to move beyond snap judgments and primitivist assumptions founded on presupposed hegemonic power dynamics. Without wholly discounting neo-primitivist criticisms, this discussion argues for more holistic investigations that acknowledge multivalency in fluid, ongoing processes of transcultural production. In this case, that entails recognizing the agency of Malick Sidibé as well as the models and Andreas Kokkino in this collaborative project, acknowledging each of their roles within the negotiation processes, and, ultimately, appreciating their collective contributions to contemporary aesthetics and global popular culture.

CONCLUSION

Malick Sidibe's photographs—particularly his most recent series, created initially for the *New York Times*—illustrate dynamic processes of transculturation, facilitated by the agency of multiple actors. As negotiated displays, they are products of cultural imagination and hybrid exchange, conflating Western appropriations of aesthetic and material culture from Africa with Malian articulations of "cosmopolitan fashions" and popular culture from Europe and the United States. Thus, they present an aesthetic that is at once fresh and familiar, local and global. Embellishing meticulously framed performances and urban symbolism with juxtaposed patterns and visual obscurity, Sidibé has introduced a new style—a new visual aesthetic. His photographs, which variously function as art, portraiture, advertisement, and popular culture, do not simply parrot Western trends or recycle Western "trash" but, as the creations of a vital contemporary artist, introduce new ways of viewing that have been publicly revered and emulated across the globe.

ACKNOWLEDGEMENTS

This essay is part of continuing research on the histories of photography in Mali with which I have been engaged since 2002, working most closely with Malick Sidibé. It has been written in response to the *New York Times Magazine* editorial fashion shoot created by Andreas Kokkino and Malick Sidibé in the spring of 2009 and the onslaught of inquiries I received after the issue was released on April 5th of that year. The information presented in this account derives from interviews I conducted with Malick Sidibé and members of the Sidibé family between 2002 and 2005 and during the summer of 2009, as well as in September 2009 via telephone and the Internet with stylist Andreas Kokkino and designer Max Osterweis. To each of these individuals I am forever indebted. *Alla kaw sara.*

NOTES

1. See, for example, Als 1997; Dosunmu and Sidibé 1999; Arakas and Elgort 2005; Hype Williams's film *Belly* (1998); and Janet Jackson's video "Got 'Til It's Gone" (1997).
2. For eminent discussions on complex agency, consult Bourdieu 1977; Giddens 1979; Jackson 1989, 1996; and Carrithers 1992.

3. I have previously written on the original contexts of Malick Sidibé's photographs (Keller 2008a and 2008b).
4. Lauri Firstenberg has made similar arguments with regard to the juxtapositions of printed textiles in portraits by Seydou Keïta (2001: 176).
5. Bamana (*Bambara* in French) comprise the largest culture group in Mali and originate from Ségu, just north of the capital Bamako.
6. The average annual family income in Mali is estimated between US$350 and US$600. The clothing and accessory items featured in the fashion shoot range from US$188 to US$1,445.
7. Malick Sidibé believed the women were paid 47,500 CFA francs (about US$100) and the men were given 42,500 CFA francs (around US$90) for the shoot. It is my understanding that Sidibé augmented the salaries to these amounts in order to offset potential discord among the group and to avoid insulting Kokkino (Sidibé 2009).
8. See viewer responses at: http://allday.msnbc.msn.com/archive/2009/10/14/2098358.aspx; and http://stylelist.com/2009/10/13/french-vogue-blackface-model-lara-stone.
9. See viewers remarks at: http://www.stylelist.com/2009/10/13/french-vogue-blackface-model-lara-stone/.

REFERENCES

Amselle, Jean-Loup. 2005. *L'Art de la Friche: essai sur l'art africain contemporain.* Paris: Éditions Flammerion.

Anderson, Benedict. 2006. *Imagined Communities: Reflections on the Origin and Spread of Nationalism.* London: Verso.

Arakas, Irini, and Arthur Elgort. 2005. "Bring It On Home." *Vogue* (January): 138–145.

b., agnès. 2009a. "AGNÈS B. Runway/Ready-to-Wear/Spring 2009." *Elle.* Available at: http://www.elle.com/Runway/Ready-to-Wear/Spring-2009-RTW/AGNES-B/AGNES-B/(imageIndex)/43.Accessed October 4, 2009.

b., agnès. 2009b. "Agnès b." *Black Rainbow Extraordinaire Magazine.* Available at: http://www.bkrw.com/whoswho/agnes-b.html. Accessed October 4, 2009.

Bangstad, Sindre. 2006. "Diasporic Consciousness as a Strategic Resource—a Case Study from a Cape Muslim Community." In Lief Manger and Munzoul A. M. Assal, eds., *Diasporas Within and Without Africa: Dynamism, Heterogeneity, Variation,* 32–36. Uppsala: Nordiska Afrikainstitutet.

Bergé, Pierre, ed. 2008. *Yves Saint Laurent: Style.* New York: Abrams.

Bigham, Elizabeth. 1999. "Issues of Authorship in the Portrait Photographs of Seydou Keïta." *African Arts* 32 (Spring): 56–67, 94–96.

Bourdieu, Pierre. 1977. *Outline of a Theory of Practice.* Cambridge: Cambridge University Press.

Carrithers, Michael. 1992. *Why Humans Have Cultures: Explaining Anthropology and Social Diversity.* Oxford: Oxford University Press.

Diawara, Manthia. 2003. "The Sixties in Bamako: Malick Sidibé and James Brown." In Hasselblad Center, *Malick Sidibé Photographs,* 8–22. Göttingen: Steidl.

Dosunmu, Andrew, and Malick Sidibé. 1999. "African Holiday." *Paper* (July): 64–77, 124.

Eicher, Joanne B., and Barbara Sumberg. 1995. "World Fashion, Ethnic, and National Dress." In Joanne B. Eicher, ed., *Dress and Ethnicity: Change Across Space and Time,* 295–306. Oxford: Berg.

Firstenberg, Lauri. 2001. "Postcoloniality, Performance, and Photographic Portraiture." In Okwui Enwezor, ed., *The Short Century: Independence and Liberation Movements in Africa 1945–1994,* 175–179. Munich: Prestel.

Giddens, Anthony. 1979. *Central Problems in Social Theory: Action, Structure, and Contradiction in Social Analysis.* Berkeley: University of California Press.

Grossman, Wendy A. 2009. *Man Ray, African Art, and the Modernist Lens.* Washington, D.C.: International Arts & Artists.

Hasselblad Center. 2003. *Malick Sidibé: Photographs.* Göttingen: Steidl.

Hastreiter, Kim. 2007. "Bravo, Malick Sidibe!" *Paper* (May 31). Available at: http://www.papermag.com/blogs/2007/05/bravo_malick_sidibe.php. Accessed October 4, 2009.

Jackson, Michael. 1989. *Paths Toward a Clearing: Radical Empiricism and Ethnographic Inquiry.* Bloomington: Indiana University Press.

Jackson, Michael. 1996. *Things as They Are: New Perspectives in Phenomenological Anthropology.* Bloomington: Indiana University Press.

Keller, Candace, M. 2008a. "Visual Griots: Social, Political, and Cultural Histories in Mali through the Photographer's Lens." PhD diss., Bloomington, Indiana University.

Keller, Candace, M. 2008b. "Regardez-Moi!: Photographs by Malick Sidibé." Exhibition brochure. San Diego State University.

Krifa, Michket, and Laura Serani. 2009. "Frontiers, Rencontres de Bamako 9: Biennale Africaine de la Photographie, 7 Novembre–7 Decembre." Unpublished program.

Lamunière, Michelle. 2001. *You Look Beautiful Like That: The Portrait Photographs of Seydou Keïta and Malick Sidibé.* New Haven: Yale University Press.

Le Nouëne, Patrick, ed. 2003. *Malick Sidibé: photographies de la vie bamakoise de 1960 aujourd'hui.* Angers: Musée Pincé.

Loughran, Kristyne. 2009. "The Idea of Africa in European High Fashion: Global Dialogues." *Fashion Theory* 13(2): 243–272.

MacSweeny, Eve. 1998. "Sunday Best." *Harper's Bazaar* (May): 172–179.

Magnin, André. 1997. *Seydou Keita.* Zurich: Scalo.

Magnin, André. 1998. *Malick Sidibe.* Zurich: Scalo.

Nimis, Érika. 1998. *Photographes de Bamako de 1935 à nos jours.* Paris: Éditions Revue Noire.

Njami, Simon, and Malick Sidibé. 2002. "The Movement of Life." In Gerald Matt, Thomas Miessgang, eds., *¡Flash Afrique!: Photography from West Africa,* 94–96. Göttingen: Steidl.

Ortiz, Fernando. 1947. *Cuban Counterpoint: Tobacco and Sugar.* New York: Alfred A. Knopf.

Paulicelli, Eugenia, and Hazel Clark, eds. 2009. *The Fabric of Cultures: Fashion, Identity, and Globalization.* New York: Routledge.

Revue Noire. 1991. "Photographes Noirs." 3 (December).

Revue Noire. 1995a. "Photographie Photographes: Abderramane Sakaly, Ahmed Makky Kanté, Seydou Keïta, Malick Sidibé, Harouna Racine Keïta, Alioune Bâ." 17(July–August): 20–24.

Revue Noire. 1995b. "Mode Fashion: Chris Seydou, Soumaïlia Traoré, Awa Cissé, Nassira Magassoura, Gogo Semega Maïga, Xuly Bët." 17 (July–August): 25–29.

Revue Noire. 1995c. "Mode Fashion: Alphadi le Magnifique." 17 (July–August): 68–71.

Roitfeld, Carine, and Steven Klein. 2009. "Spécial Top Models." *Vogue Paris* 901 (October).
Rovine, Victoria. 2004. "Fashionable Traditions: The Globalization of an African Textile." In Jean Marie Allman, ed., *Fashioning Africa: Power and the Politics of Dress,* 189–211. Bloomington: Indiana University Press.
Rovine, Victoria. 2009. "Viewing Africa through Fashion." *Fashion Theory* 13 (2): 133–140.
Saint Léon, Pascal Martin, and N'Goné Fall, eds. 1998. *Anthologie de la Photographie Africaine et de l'Océan Indien.* Paris: Èditions Revue Noire.
Sidibé, Malick, and Andreas Kokkino. 2009a. "Prints and the Revolution: From Milan to Mali, a Riot of Checks, Stripes, Patterns, and Polka Dots." *New York Times Magazine* (April 5): 40–47.
Sidibé, Malick, and Andreas Kokkino. 2009b. "The Backstory: Malick Sidibe." The Moment Blogs, *New York Times* online (April 3). Available at: http://themoment.blogs.nytimes.com/author/andreas-kokkino. Accessed September 9, 2009.
Sidibé, Malick, and Caroline Laurent. 2003. "Malick Sidibé, l'oeil African," *Elle* (March 24): 214.
Sokkelund, Karen Mohr. 2003. "Malick Sidibé: Photographs with a Touch of Humour." *Katalog: Journal of Photography and Video* 16(2): 2–11.
Steward, Sue. 2003. "The Magic of Malick." *Observer Magazine* (March 2): 40–46.

–13–

Spectacular Dress: Africanisms in the Fashions and Performances of Josephine Baker, 1925–1975

Bennetta Jules-Rosette

We must first study how colonization works to *decivilize* the colonizer.

—Césaire (1955: 11, author's translation)

Legendary Franco-American performer Josephine Baker made enduring contributions to the display and dissemination of African-inflected fashion on an international scale. Beginning with her 1925 performance of the now iconic *danse sauvage,* Baker capitalized on exotic imagery to capture the attention of a European audience. The notorious danse sauvage, however, is only the tip of the iceberg. A crucial issue concerns how images travel across cultural contexts and historical periods. Baker's strategies of layering and performative transformation converted her original images into a lasting template for diffusion around the world. Her images continue to be explored, exploited, imitated, and transformed into fashion styles, costuming, theatrical performances, and art.

The stage and film provide important keys to understanding these transformations. Baker's changing images are indicative of her growth on stage and off, as she mastered critical strategies of identity construction, often using fashion as her primary expressive vehicle. The friction between her public and private uses of fashion fueled the energy of her image-making process. Photographers such as *Vogue* photojournalist and editor George Hoyningen-Huene and independent German photographer Madame d'Ora further polished and immortalized Baker's sophisticated Black Venus image as she began to move away from her persona as the one-dimensional primal dancer by reinforcing the power and breadth of her early performances.

FASHIONING IDENTITY

Born Freda Josephine McDonald to an impoverished family in St. Louis, Missouri, on June 3, 1906, Josephine Baker came to France in the autumn of 1925 as a dancer with the black American vaudeville troupe La Revue nègre. The troupe's first show opened on October 2, 1925, for a short run at the Théâtre de Champs-Elysées in the fashion district of Paris. Baker entered France during the height of the colonial period at a point of rapid social and economic change between two world wars. She was an instant success with her danse sauvage, which she performed first in feathers and later in a banana belt. Within two years, she rose to fame in Paris and became the toast of the worlds of art and theater. Her growing visibility as an international star made her a dominant figure in black Paris. She stayed in France for the rest of her life, and in her later years, she became a humanitarian with a unique vision of Paris and the world.

Josephine Baker fashioned herself as an icon through performance and ultimately transformed her theatrical performances into social and political statements. Baker's early appeal was based on an exotic performative image that used a primitive non-Western other as a point of reference and a source of fantasy. Baker constantly reinvented herself to suit the purposes of her projects. Homi Bhabha has referred to this reinvention process, which he calls doubling, as a performance in which the self as subject becomes its own object. Bhabha elaborates:

> We are no longer confronted with an ontological problem of being but with the discursive strategy of the moment of interrogation, a moment in which the demand for identification becomes, primarily, a response to other questions of signification and desire, culture, and politics (Bhabha 1994: 49–50).

In other words, the personal construction of identity not only reflects but also restructures the subject's social world. Fashion mirrors and sustains identity transformations. As individuals adapt fashion to their own purposes, a fluid borrowing occurs across cultures and historical periods.

Pivotal transitions in Baker's life reveal the role of image construction and reinvention in the social and cultural production of identity discourses. As ways of speaking about one's perceived and desired location in the social world, identity discourses express virtual states of existence.[1] These discourses are performative affirmations, rather than statements of fact, that link individuals to larger collective identities. Baker used these discourses in her work in the French music hall while developing practices that would make her unique. In complicity with her promoters and audiences, Baker employed five performative strategies of image and identity construction: (1) exoticizing race and gender; (2) reversing racial and cultural codes and meanings; (3) displaying difference through nudity, cross-dressing, song, and dance; (4) exploiting the images of difference; and (5) universalizing the outcomes to allow the performative messages to reach a larger audience. These strategies emerged gradually and with varying degrees of sophistication.

Early in her career, Baker's role in her own image construction was orchestrated by her managers and promoters, but later it became more forceful and autonomous. This image-making process may be traced through the evolution of the famous banana skirt—at first an idea concocted by Jean Cocteau and Paul Colin, who drew on Miguel

Covarrubias's caricatures for his sketches of Baker. The skirt's modifications reflect the evolution of artistic agency within a framework of social control. The original skirt was a collection of realistic-looking bananas. The early designs were used as templates of advertisements for Bakerfix pomade and on postcards. A 1925 version of Baker's primitivist banana skirt is depicted in Figure 13.1. By 1927, the bananas had become pointed spikes—a parody of the original skirt and a humorous design innovation in which Baker took part.

In just one year, Baker began to take control of and modify her primal image through costuming. For the 1936 Ziegfeld Follies in New York, Baker's bananas were transformed into a series of horizontal spikes and a pointed headdress created by renowned set designer and filmmaker Vincente Minnelli, making a visual allusion to the original costume without any bananas at all. During the course of Baker's later life, younger female and male dancers played her part in banana skirts in theatrical retrospectives, some of which were choreographed by Baker herself. The skirt's evolution and its place in Baker's narratives and performances reveal the changing character and extent of her agency.

Figure 13.1 Josephine Baker Wearing the Original Banana Skirt, 1925. © Getty Images

DISROBING PRIMITIVISM

The evolution of Baker's fashions parallels her rise to stardom in the French music hall and in film. This process cannot be separated from larger cultural and historical forces that shaped images of black women and exoticism in Europe. However, these influences operated in a specific way within the world of fashion by linking theatrical costuming to quotidian images and attire. This sartorial system is one in which elements of a myth, or a mystique, are transferred from one system of signification to another. According to Joanne Eicher, dress functions as "a coded sensory system of nonverbal communication" (1995: 1).[2] These nonverbal codes also build upon existing cultural narratives and stereotypes, several of which may coexist and clash with each other in a particular social context. In Baker's early performances and costumes, Africa emerges as part of an ambiguous cultural imaginary. If we consider African dress to consist of clothing fabricated on the African continent or in relationship to its specific cultural settings, Baker's performances are elusive. They refer instead to an illusion of an imagined Africa derived form the colonial archive. When Africanisms are examined as integral parts of colonialist ideologies and discourses, Baker's performances offer new ways of constructing links between the West and a self-fashioned cultural other.

Two important cultural influences shaped the danse sauvage and assured its popularity and success. The first originated not in the world of fashion aficionados, but instead in the natural history museum. The tragic case of naturalist Georges Cuvier's anthropological and biological experiments with the Khoikhoi (Hottentot) Venus, Sartjee Baartman, reinforced the power of the primitive stereotype. In 1810, twenty-two-year-old Baartman was transported from Cape Colony to London, where she was placed on display as a curiosity exhibit. Four years later, Baartman was taken to Paris, where scientists and entrepreneurs exhibited her as a curiosity (the Hottentot Venus) and also examined her as a laboratory specimen (Strother 1999: 32–33). As an object of what Bernth Lindfors has termed "ethnological show business," Baartman was placed on display at expositions and in private salons (1999: vii–xi). Cuvier measured her, recorded her reflexes, and arranged to have her painted and diagrammed. In this pre-photographic era, paintings and drawings exaggerated the features of cultural stereotypes. Plays and stories were written about Baartman, who provided a dramatic link between show business and science in the early nineteenth century. Along with literary fantasies and artistic caricatures, Baartman's presence casts an ominous shadow over images of the black female body in France.

A second myth, still well-known at the time of Baker's arrival in France, was epitomized by Pierre Loti's popular 1881 novel, *Le Roman d'un spahi,* in which a French explorer in Africa becomes infatuated with a savage jungle girl, Fatou-gaye. In fact, Baker enacts the character of Fatou-gaye in her danse sauvage. This exotic imagery parallels the development of rapid industrialization in France after World War I and the arrival in the city of rural immigrants (not necessarily foreign) whose backgrounds and behaviors challenged the haute bourgeoisie with alternative sensory codes of dress and conduct.

Baker initially fit into the cultural stereotypes of both the exotic other and the untutored immigrant in her public performance persona and in her private life.

In her autobiography with Jo Bouillon, Baker describes her dress when arriving in Paris as consisting of a red-and-yellow checkered outfit made in Harlem (Baker and Bouillon 1977: 5). She later referred to this outfit as awkward, gaudy, and out of place. Colin immediately suggested that Josephine visit the couturier Paul Poiret, who quickly removed the homemade Harlem outfit and clothed her in a silver satin gown. For several years, Poiret, known as the father of the 1920s flapper movement, remained one of Baker's primary dress designers along with Vionnet, Schiaparelli, and other leading designers for *Bon Ton* and *Vogue* (Vreeland 1977: 17).[3] Baker's new image for high society contrasted radically with her staged primitive look. As her public persona evolved, so did a clash in her on- and off-stage fashions. Sociologist Fred Davis emphasizes that the ambiguity of fashion permits "contradictory and oscillating" subjectivities to emerge (1992: 21). In Baker's case, these contradictions were not merely a matter of whim or fancy. The seminudity of the banana skirt costume became a uniform that she used to play a predetermined role associated with primal and exotic stereotypes. It also became an essential part of Baker's trademark.

From the perspectives of Colin, Cocteau, Poiret, and Baker's other early costume designers, nudity for the primal savage dancer and the Black Venus represented freedom of action and liberation from guilt. Clothing was the terrain on which much of the battle of "civilization" was waged in Africa. An unclad figure represented an "uncivilized" spirit. But in Europe, an unclad figure also reflected the secret desires of the audience. Historian Tyler Stovall succinctly explains the mixed audience response to Baker's early images: "Jazz triumphed in France at roughly the same time as Hollywood. Consequently, during the 1920s French listeners embraced jazz (and black Americans) as a symbol of both primitivism and hypermodernity, of both Africa and America" (2006: 57–58).

Paul Colin designed the stage sets for the 1925 debut of La Revue nègre in collaboration with Covarrubias, who had come from Mexico to Paris. Colin's lithographs, inspired by Baker, further reinforced the primal image. For his 1927 publication, *Le Tumulte noir,* Colin presented forty-five lithographs that incorporated Baker's image into cubist renditions and cartoon-like caricatures. Among the images in the volume was the publicity poster for La Revue nègre that used a minstrel-like caricature with large red lips, dark skin, and black-and-white clothing. Colin introduced color to signify racial difference, using red, white, and black on his most obvious caricatures. He also depicted a transsexual figure, resembling Baker, in a tuxedo similar to the one that she wore on stage as a bandleader in *La Joie de Paris* a few years later, in 1932.

Some of Colin's most controversial lithographs used dancing monkeys to depict the savage and earthy rhythms of the jazz age. These images were imitated by other artists, including cartoonist Georges Goursat, who drew a caricature of Baker with a monkey's tail. The primal iconography of savagery fascinated the French public of the 1920s and was echoed in the racialized images by artists of the era. In this instance, costuming, performance, and art merged together in the cultural construction of Josephine Baker as a primitivist icon in a modern society.

Baker played upon and manipulated the controversial images that were designed for her in both her performances and her everyday life. Many of Baker's early followers belonged to the bohemian and pansexual world of the Parisian demimonde. Baker, and her close friend Colette, used transgender imagery in much more than a symbolic manner. Among Baker's fans in the 1920s and 1930s were young, tuxedo-clad women who followed her from performance to performance in complete admiration. Baker's audiences were so attached to her primal images and performances that they were outraged when she wore a blonde wig and bleached her skin with lemon juice for her ironic 1932 rendition of "Si j'étais blanche" (If I Were White) for *La Joie de Paris* in which she parodied her music-hall archrival Mistinguett. In public, Baker played out the roles of the sexualized savage, the male-female, and the saint-like Madonna with equal passion and perfection.

The iconography of Baker's fashion images was based on stereotypes and objectification—that is, on her transformation into an object for the audience's gaze. A detailed deconstruction of Baker's public and private images, however, cautions against reducing her to essentialist projections without reviewing the historical and cultural contexts of image production. Baker's own actions suggest that she was less concerned with the constraints placed on her image by racial and gender stereotypes than she was with the freedom achieved by appearing on the French stage and screen as a rising musical and film star. When Baker left Paris on her European tour in 1928, she carried with her 15 steamer trunks, 137 dresses and costumes, 196 pairs of shoes, and 64 kilos of stage powder, a powerful combination of props for a primitive dancer (Hammond and O'Connor 1988: 79).[4]

DRESSING UP FOR THE MOVIES

The contrast that Baker established between primitivism and high fashion on stage and in her private life became a thematic thread of her most popular films. Two of these films—*La Sirène des tropiques,* directed by Henri Etiévant and Mario Nalpas (1927), and *Princesse Tam-Tam,* directed by Edmond T. Gréville (1935)—deploy Africanisms, or allusions to Africa and the African diaspora, as narrative resources and inspirations for costuming (Jules-Rosette 2007: 76).[5] The plots of both films involve a rags-to-riches trajectory with a contrast of "primitive" and "civilized" worlds and identities. *Sirène* entails unconditional sacrifice on the part of Baker as an exotic heroine, while *Princesse* is a Pygmalion story. Both films allow Baker to make costume changes from a scantily clad primal subject to a glamorous star.

In *Sirène,* a silent film, Papitou, a young Antillian, lives a carefree island life with her French father. When André Berval, a French explorer and engineer arrives on the island from Paris, Papitou befriends him. Together, Papitou and Berval uncover the nefarious schemes of the overbearing landlord and overseer, Alvarez, whose plots to kill Berval are intercepted by Papitou. Smitten with Berval, Papitou decides to follow him when he returns to France. In France, Papitou rises to music-hall stardom and reconnects with

Berval. After saving Berval's life once again, she ultimately has to forgo him. The film concludes with the biblical message that "sacrifice is the purest form of joy on earth." Privately, Baker complained to the film's producers about this ending, wondering why her character always had to pay the price for assimilation through sacrifice.

With regard to fashion, the film provides Baker with ample opportunities to make significant costume changes. As the island waif, Papitou wears a printed sarong, a long head-kerchief, and hoop earrings. Barefooted, she performs a frenetic savage dance at an island celebration. When Papitou departs for France as a stowaway on a luxury liner, she changes into a long Victorian dress complete with a bustle and a matching hat. Shipboard, she falls into a bin of coal, turning her black, and a bin of flour that changes her complexion and wardrobe to white, while making an ironic commentary on race. To wash off the color changes, she ends up in the captain's bathtub completely nude. Baker disliked dressing up for this portion of the film because it required her to do numerous retakes of comic stunts, with heavy costumes, in sweltering tropical heat.

Once in Paris, Papitou becomes a nanny, wearing convent nurse's clothes until a nightclub entrepreneur, played by her real-life partner and manager, Giuseppe "Pepito" Abatino, discovers her. For the nightclub sequences, she is scantily clad in a sequined outfit and then reappears in a sumptuous evening dress. Viewed from the perspective of fashion, *Sirène* allows Baker to display a gamut of contemporary outfits, ranging from exotic island attire to haute couture. Using costuming as a vehicle, the savage/civilized opposition is played out to the fullest extent. Fashion underscores Papitou's character changes and highlights the uneasy tensions and ambivalence of the French *mission civilatrice.*

Princesse Tam-Tam, shot on location in Tunisia, is the third, and arguably best-known, of Baker's films. It was her largest box office success. While the sequences of costume changes are similar to those in *Sirène,* the manipulation of attire is more sophisticated in accordance with the complexities of the plot. Dance and song sequences punctuate the costume changes as Aouina (or Alwina), whose name we are told means a *petite source,* or small stream, is transformed from a Berber shepherdess and street urchin into the elegant Princess of Parador (in the model of the Black Venus, or African Aphrodite).

Pepito Abatino served as the artistic director of *Princesse,* a film produced by his brother-in-law, Arys Nissotti. The film's credits list wardrobe by Philippe and Gaston and stage costumes by Zanel, who also did the costuming for Baker's second feature film, *Zouzou.* Zanel was adept at moving between exotic dress stereotypes and high fashion, both of which, as already emphasized, were integral to Baker's trademark. *Princesse* is based on a multiframed and entangled narrative in which the Berber shepherdess-turned-Indian-princess, Aouina, is revealed to be the fictive creation of novelist Max de Mirecourt in a phantom version of North Africa. The Orientalism of the Tunisian landscape and décor is combined with the Africanisms of sensual dance and seductive music used to suggest the exotic origins of this mysterious dream princess.

Aouina is contrasted with Max's wife, Lucie, a frail blonde beauty played by Germaine Aussy. The exoticism of Aouina is highlighted in three lengthy dance sequences in the film. The first sequence briefly precedes Aouina's encounter with Max and a group of tourists at the Ruins of Dougga, an ancient Roman temple just outside of Tunis. Aouina runs up the steps of the ruins, followed by a gang of local street urchins. In front of the Romanesque pillars, she performs a bizarre exotic dance that combines modern ballet, an Oriental belly dance, the Cakewalk, and an imitation of a chicken. Lasting just over three minutes, the chicken strut foreshadows the other two savage dances that Baker does later in the film. Baker performs the chicken strut draped in a Berber peasant dress held together at the shoulders by two crescent-shaped, handcrafted silver brooches, which appear somewhat incongruous on a peasant girl turned street urchin. This sequence establishes Aouina's freedom and sense of abandon. After her meeting with de Mirecourt at the ruins, Aouina follows him home, and he entices her to become his protégé in preparation for a trip to Paris, where she will be passed off as a princess.

Two circumstances, represented through dress, jeopardize Aouina's feral freedom from civilization. They both involve the removal of her traditional North African garb. In the first instance, immediately following her arrival at Max's home, Aouina is intercepted by Tahar (Dar), Max's servant, who threatens to beat her as a trespasser and tear off her clothes. Max intervenes to save Aouina from this fate. In the second case, Aouina is offered new evening clothes and accessories, both in Tunisia and in Paris. Aouina classifies these objects as "false things," which, again, would require the removal of her peasant clothes. Being without traditional clothing would be tantamount to losing her authentic cultural identity.

As she learns to walk in high heels, eat with a knife and fork, and improve her French under Max's tutelage, Aouina's costumes and makeup become more refined. Although she expresses displeasure with her new status by throwing off her shoes and eating with her hands, Aouina's transformation appears almost complete and proceeds rapidly. Uncertain of the depth of these changes, Max engages his assistant, Coton, to watch over Aouina and report on her every move.

Lodged in a luxurious apartment in Paris, Aouina manages to escape surveillance for a night alone on the town. She ends up at a sailor's bar where she performs yet another savage dance, a frenetic version of the Charleston. Slumming at the bar, Lucie and her friends witness the exhibition of Aouina's "true" identity. At the sailor's bar, Aouina wears a simple shirtwaist dress with a large white collar, a black patent leather belt, and matching patent leather high-heel pumps, allowing her to blend in with the rest of the clientele, including a "mirror-image" prostitute in blackface.

Lucie persuades the Maharajah of Daetane, an expatriate Indian nobleman in Paris, to organize a sumptuous soirée to impress Aouina. The maharajah's Orientalist costuming, complete with a jeweled turban, is also noteworthy. No one appears to doubt his pedigree. Escorted by Coton, Aouina arrives at the party bedecked with jewels in a stunning evening gown. The maharajah entertains the guests with a full music-hall show consisting of elaborate dance numbers, Chinese plate twirlers, an African drummer, and hypnotic animation. These scenes are filmed in extravagant Busby Berkley Hollywood musical style.

Emboldened by several drinks, Aouina agrees to dance to "Ahé Conga," throwing off the glamorous gown of a princess to reveal an upscale, sequined version of the Berber peasant dress. She dances the Conga (later recorded in Baker's 1936 release of *Conga Blicoti* with Columbia records) with improvised abandon to the shock and delight of the Parisian audience. This musical scene sutures the climactic moment of the film, in which Baker appears in several full-body shots with the camera lingering on her in front of an anonymous audience.[6] Baker, once again, becomes an emblem and an icon for the sensualized primitive object. Dress, and its transformation through layering, play key roles in creating the powerful impact of this scene. At the close of the film, Aouina returns to Tunisia as the domesticated wife of Tahar, and Max receives accolades for his award-winning book on civilization. The characters dutifully resume their original social and cultural positions with little change as the nested narrative closes. This exotic adventure reworks the colonialist fantasies through which Baker achieved her early stardom.

ECHOES OF BAKER'S FASHION IMAGES

During World War II and the years immediately following, Baker reviewed and modified her fashion images. Although she retired her banana skirt, primal imagery continued to influence Baker's performative strategies and legacy. As a special agent and French Air Force sublieutenant during the war, Baker expanded her international political commitments. Her military uniform entered the picture not only as an article of clothing, but also as a symbol of her commitment to the fight for freedom. She wore her military uniform, along with the numerous medals that she had been awarded, for state visits and many public speeches. Much like some African political leaders, she used the uniform to signify her status and authority as the leader of a humanitarian social and political cause. During the 1950s, Baker worked with new fashion designers and stylists, such as Lucien Bertaux and Jean Clément. She also adopted twelve Rainbow Children of different nationalities and ethnicities and installed them in her utopian community at the Château des Milandes in southwestern France. The children further enhanced her image as a mother, or the Madonna and Marian motifs, which had begun to emerge in the writings and performances of her early career. Baker used these maternal images in conjunction with her earlier primal images—the savage dancer and the Black Venus—to secure publicity for her humanitarian work until her death in 1975.

Echoes of Josephine Baker's life and images reverberate across the successive generations that have come into contact with her. Although each image originates within a specific narrative frame and worldview, Baker's multifaceted persona transcends cultural settings and historical epochs. Baker's legacy may be seen not only in terms of her direct influence on artists, performers, and her audiences, but also with respect to the structures of communication that she engendered. These structures involve a combination of visual images, fashions, and discourse that creates new frameworks of representation. In this context, the term "image" refers to visual, verbal, and sensory symbols, and the concept of "representation" encompasses a collection of images. Through its strategies of juxtaposition and appropriation, postmodernism returns us to Baker's primal image. While Baker separated the primitivist and the Marian images during her lifetime, postmodernism relies on their kaleidoscopic combination and juxtaposition.

From Madonna and Grace Jones to the late Michael Jackson and his sister La Toya, many contemporary performers have drawn directly on Baker's primal image and her identity-doubling persona. These performers use Baker and her legacy as an inspiration and are not merely her clones. To varying degrees, they are concerned with both image construction and changing the world. When Baker gave three taxi-loads of her designer gowns to female impersonator Lynne Carter in 1970, she repositioned her own image in a new cultural frame (Rose 1989: 252–253; Silva 2009: 73–74). Baker's gift helped to launch Carter's career at the Jewel Box Revue. In addition to promoting Baker's camp and retro images, Carter also impersonated Marilyn Monroe, Bette Davis, Marlene Dietrich, and Pearl Bailey, taking his show as far as Carnegie Hall. Parisian transsexual cabaret performer Michou also used Baker's image as a savage dancer by donning his own version of the 1920s banana skirt in 1975. Films, posters, postcards, and book releases inaugurated further representations that incorporated Baker's primal and her glamour images as a "referential illusion" (Barthes 1975: 237).

Baker was fascinated by her own reflection and by performers who were her copies and clones. Each of Baker's images spawned a new one, resulting in an echo effect within shifting narrative frames. In the simulation of Baker's images—whether primal, glamour, or Marian—the signifier is reproduced in a cycle of expression, display, commodification, and exchange. Nevertheless, the core primal image constitutes the backdrop and foundation for each new simulacrum. Baker artfully referred to this process as "doing Joséphine."

Manthia Diawara's description of the African and the African-American "homeboy cosmopolitan" provides a productive framework for reconfiguring part of Baker's contemporary legacy (1998: 246–248). The homeboy cosmopolitan is a composite image linking the streetwise rude boy and the sophisticated fashion trendsetter. In contrast, the homegirl cosmopolitan, derived from Baker's imagery, is not a simple binary opposite. The homegirl makes the homeboy's actions and fashion statements possible by providing an audience and an arena for his symbolic displays. Baker's homegirl cosmopolitan also dominates the scene by setting new trends of her own and exchanging social positions with the homeboy. Her identity transformations provide a powerful recoding of male-centered images and narratives. Among others, three prominent performers come to mind as inheritors of Baker's popular cultural and fashion legacies: Grace Jones, Madonna, and La Toya Jackson.

In different ways, all three figures have used Paris as a staging ground for building some aspect of their careers. Their images use sensuality and sexuality as a source of appeal while challenging what E. Ann Kaplan terms the "patriarchal feminine," or traditional male-centered roles for women, by introducing androgyny and the image of the tough woman and single survivor into some feature of their role representation

(1987: 122). This condensation is achieved by the surface presentation of a simulated role (i.e., Madonna's "virgin" or Jones's "vampire"), underneath which a contradictory role and set of messages appear through a process of continual layering and unveiling that may be imitated or reproduced by others. The allure of power and control, combining public success with materiality, is also critical to the appeal of these divas. Jackson admits to patterning some of her strategies on Baker's images, while Jones and Madonna sample Baker in undeniable and obvious ways that have attracted the attention of cultural critics. In addition to adopting children and writing books dedicated to them, Madonna also posed in a series of 2009 advertisements for Louis Vuitton dedicated to the revival of Baker's fashions in the Paris-based Baker Remix.

Similarities among the three performative figures and Baker, building on the primal image, range from superficial allusions to more profound ideals. The Parisian music and art scenes influenced all three celebrities. Jones and Jackson use performative mimesis, while Madonna combines artifice with more complex appropriations of Baker's images and fashions. Of the three personalities, Jackson copies Baker's music-hall career directly without the identity-doubling mystique. Baker's legacy as a chameleon, changing characters to suit her narratives and using simple props to transform her identity, is readily adapted to the postmodern structures of communication reflected by Jones and Madonna. The androgynous aspects of Baker's performances also have parallels in the images constructed by male pop icons such as David Bowie and Michael Jackson and in the works of cross-gender performers such as Lynne Carter and Michou, who have deliberately imitated or impersonated Baker. Baker's mantle has now settled on male personalities and not exclusively on the women who have used her as a role model. Through her own self-impersonations, Baker created a template for these performances. The three key postmodern personalities—Grace Jones, Madonna, and La Toya Jackson—demonstrate how Baker's pattern of cultural coding has influenced artists' entire careers, as well as public perceptions of their fashion statements and performances. In these performances, Baker's images have been sampled, simulated, and reworked for a new generation across cultures via film, video, and the Internet.

CONCLUSIONS

Baker recycled her primitivist, performative, and fashion images as a source of cultural capital. Through the performance of politics in her later life, she combined old images and new models to make a social statement. The debates emerging from the image-politics strategy raise questions about the appearance of authenticity and authority among artistic performers in the public domain. By transforming herself into an icon during her lifetime, Baker attempted to preserve her memory. She blended primal and Marian imagery and made sure that everything was displayed in lights. She even thought that the cows at her chateau's experimental farm would produce more milk with their names in neon lights. These self-styled efforts at publicity were not, however, the source of the survival of Baker's image, which has outlived them and changed beyond the fads of future generations. Instead, she was able to appropriate archetypal gender images (the primal dancer and the Black Venus) nested in a series of narratives that could be reworked over time, giving the impression of timelessness. The meanings of colonialist primal imagery and costuming in the 1920s and the uses to which Baker put them as an artifact of memory in the 1970s were very different. The reinvention of these images by postmodern pop divas decades later relied on yet another type of mediated memory work. Across all of these processes of rediscovery and symbolic change, Baker's primal image has remained intact, and she still influences the presentation and interpretation of exoticism in fashion and performance on the global scene.

NOTES

1. In his literary criticism of the works of Cameroonian poet Paul Dakeyo, Yves Dakou (1988: 41–42) develops a theory of virtual identity discourse based on the poet's affirmations of belonging to France as well as Africa and his wish for a more egalitarian society. Identity construction is an integral part of the shaping of concepts of self through the communicative messages of dress and clothing.
2. Karen Tranberg Hansen elaborates on this point when she argues that clothing places sensory cultural symbols of the body in a social and institutional context (Hansen 2004: 167).
3. Turbaned, corpulent, and bearded, Poiret often dressed in an Orientalist style himself. He is famous for introducing the flapper look in Paris as well as ethnic designs and loose-fitting apparel for women. His interactions with Baker were ultimately fraught with tension (Jules-Rosette 2007: 142–143).
4. Bryan Hammond and Patrick O'Connor enumerate the contents of Baker's luggage when she left for her 1928 European tour (1988: 76–79). In order to play the role of a "primitive," Baker required the use of a great deal of modern paraphernalia.
5. Luis Buñel brought a surrealist perspective to the film, but he quickly parted company from Henri Etiévant and Mario Nalpas over creative differences (Jules-Rosette 2007: 76).
6. Both Ezra (2000) and Sharpley-Whiting (1999: 116–117) agree on the importance of the dance sequence finale in establishing the African connections in the film. The African drummer, who appears briefly only twice, provides a concrete image of Africa, which, otherwise, in many respects is left an unstated topic of the film. Ezra argues that the Africanisms in *Princesse Tam-Tam* are ideologically salient for the plot, although they are less prevalent than the film's Orientalist imagery (2000: 125–126).

REFERENCES

Baker, Josephine, and Jo Bouillon. 1977. *Josephine*. New York: Harper and Row.

Barthes, Roland. 1975. "An Introduction to the Structural Analysis of Narrative." *New Literary History* 6(2): 237–272.

Bhabha, Homi K. 1994. *The Location of Culture*. New York: Routlege.

Césaire, Aimé. 1955. *Discours sur le colonialisme.* Paris: Présence Africaine.

Colin, Paul. 1927. *Le Tumulte noir.* Paris: Éditions Success.

Dakou, Yves. 1988. "La Quête identitaire, dans 'j'appartiens au grand jour' de Paul Dakeyo: Approche sémiolinguistique." PhD diss. Université de Toulouse, Le Mirail.

Davis, Fred. 1992. *Fashion, Culture, and Identity.* Chicago: University of Chicago Press.

Diawara, Manthia. 1998. *In Search of Africa.* Cambridge, MA: Harvard University Press.

Eicher, Joanne B. 1995. "Introduction: Dress as an Expression of Ethnic Identity." In Joanne B. Eicher, ed., *Dress and Ethnicity,* 1–5. Oxford: Berg.

Etiévant, Henri, and Mario Nalpas, directors. 1927. *La Sirène des tropiques* (film). Script by Maurice Dekobra. Paris: Centrale Cinématographique.

Ezra, Elizabeth. 2000. *The Colonial Unconscious: Race and Culture in Interwar France.* Ithaca, NY: Cornell University Press.

Gréville, Edmond T., director. 1935. *Princesse Tam-Tam* (film). Script by Pepito Abatino and Yves Mirande. Paris: Arys Nissotti and Arys Productions.

Hammond, Bryan, and Patrick O'Connor. 1988. *Josephine Baker.* London: Jonathan Cape.

Hansen, Karen Tranberg. 2004. "Dressing Dangerously: Miniskirts, Gender Relations, and Sexuality in Zambia." In Jean Allman, ed., *Fashioning Africa: Power and the Politics of Dress,* 166–185. Bloomington: Indiana University Press.

Jules-Rosette, Bennetta. 2007. *Josephine Baker in Art and Life: The Icon and the Image.* Urbana: University of Illinois Press.

Kaplan, E. Ann. 1987. *Rocking Around the Clock: Music Television, Postmodernism, and Consumer Culture.* New York, London: Methuen.

Lindfors, Bernth. 1999. "Introduction." In Bernth Lindfors, ed., *Africans on Stage: Studies in Ethnological Show Business,* vii–xiii. Bloomington: Indiana University Press.

Loti, Pierre. 1881. *Le Roman d'un spahi.* Paris: Éditions Calmann-Lévy.

Rose, Phyllis. 1989. *Jazz Cleopatra: Josephine Baker in Her Time.* New York: Vintage Books.

Sharpley-Whiting, T. Denean. 1999. *Black Venus: Sexualized Savages, Primal Fears, and Primitive Narratives in French.* Durham, NC: Duke University Press.

Silva, Horacio. 2009. "Temptress Josephine: A Fashion Perennial." *The New York Times Style Magazine* (spring): 73–74.

Stovall, Tyler. 2006. "Freedom, Community, and the Paris Jazz Age: Josephine Baker and the World of Black Montmartre." In Olivia Lahs-Gonzales, ed., *Josephine Baker: Image and Icon,* 55–68. St. Louis: Reedy Press.

Strother, Zoe S. 1999. "Display of the Body Hottentot." In Berndt Lindfors, ed., *Africans on Stage: Studies in Ethnological Show Business,* 1–61. Bloomington: Indiana University Press.

Vreeland, Diana. 1977. "Introduction." In Irving Penn, ed., *Inventive Paris Clothes, 1909–1939: A Photographic Essay,* 8–13. New York: Viking.

–14–

Dressing Out-of-Place: From Ghana to Obama Commemorative Cloth on the USAmerican Red Carpet

D. Soyini Madison

> Like words, clothing images become significant only when they are used in a specific social context.
>
> —Ruth P. Rubinstein (1995)

This chapter examines the firestorm of controversy that arose when the African American actress Victoria Rowell walked the red carpet at the 2009 Emmy Awards, in New York city, dressed in an evening gown made of Barak Obama commemorative cloth from Ghana. Focusing on the charged reactions against the Obama cloth as well as Rowell's own response to the controversy, I will discuss the dressed body as both a provocative sign and a critical performative when what we wear is transformed into a symbol that is "out of place" or outside its normative context and usual purposes. This essay will then take a turn to argue that the appropriation of African aesthetics and reclamations of African identities—by Americans wearing Africa dress might consider the hidden abode and political economies of how African textiles are imagined, produced, distributed, and consumed.

The dressed body is always worn somewhere. It enters a social space with others and where other dressed bodies entered before it arrived. If we believe Rubinstein (1995; see introductory quote), that the dressed body is "like words" and it is "significant" only within a particular "social context" then it follows that the dressed body becomes either more adored or more contentious in some surroundings and under certain conditions than it does in others; like words, dress is a communicative sign that is understood or misunderstood, valued or devalued and felt to be pleasing or displeasing depending on the location and the other social actors present. When we equate dress as a sign, conjoined by communication and context, it opens up larger questions of meaning and value as well as the social and political effects of the dressed body, particularly when it is worn "out-of-place." Jean Allman states: "And it is precisely because of this strategic positioning that dress functions as a salient and powerful political language—one comparable in eloquence and potency to the spoken words of the most skilled orator or the written words of the most compelling propagandist" (2004a: 1–10).

If we think of dress as a communication system—a "language" or a sign constituted by particular geographies, communities, social customs, and desires—what happens to the expectations and assumptions about the clothes we choose to wear when we travel across unfamiliar terrain, when we enter different domains of meaning, or when we willfully (dis)place what we wear from its expected social context to an unexpected, perhaps, contentious one? This examination of dress that serves as a kind of "matter-out-of-place" invokes prior conceptualizations of dress as a sign as it also extends our understanding of dress to theories of the *performative.* The question I explore is, What is performatively affected/effected when dress, as sign, is worn out-of-place?

Because dress as a sign has a specific purpose, function, or role within a particular context, it does something and therefore creates certain effects. According to Rubinstein, dress as sign is "task-oriented or instrumental; having one primary meaning; being generally recognized as a sign by those who wear it." She goes on to state, "Clothing signs make visible the structure and organization of interactions within a specific social context" (1995: 7). Categories of clothing as a sign represent or become codes for authority, gender, politics, class, geography, sexuality, power, ethnicity, ideology, and so forth. The question becomes, what is revealed when we move from dress as a sign to dress as a *performative*? In employing the term performative, I draw from J. L. Austin as well as contemporary theories of performance in conceptualizing the performative not as an utterance that refers to an extralinguistic reality but as a heightened or symbolic act that makes something happen, disturbs, reinvents, or creates—large or small—a consequence. In other words, a performative serves as a distinct moment, punctum, or rupture from the ordinary and familiar that results in a specific causal effect (Austin 1975; Conquergood 1991, 2002; Diamond 1996; Hamera 2007; Johnson 2003; Madison 2010, 2012; Rivera-Servera 2011). I use the performative to illuminate how the dressed body, in certain instances, becomes a spectacular act that yields new meanings and possibilities and that yields a distinct action that creates, imagines, or disturbs a particular social phenomena.[1] This chapter examines dressing out-of-place as a cross-current of identities and belongings when Ghanaian commemorative cloth literally crossed the Atlantic at the 2009 Emmy Awards: a West African textile depicting an East African-descended USAmerican[2] president and worn by an African American actress that sparked antipathies over politics, taste, and race.

THE OBAMA CLOTH ON THE RED CARPET

When Victoria Rowell walked along the glamour and glitter of the red carpet—where celebrity dress is elaborately staged and where fame and fashion are high drama—her "Obama dress" set off strong responses. The celebrity and fashion blogosphere had much to say:

> *The Young and the Restless* actress Victoria Rowell made quite an impression on the red carpet at the 61st Annual Primetime Emmy Awards 2009... She was wearing a blue strapless

dress with oval photos of Barack Obama adorning the tablecloth-like fabric. The bizarre fashion has likely earned her the distinction of topping the 2009 Emmys Worst Dressed list.[3]

There is nothing remotely glamorous about that Obama dress. The print looks sort of like a tablecloth fabric, only no one with any taste would put something like that on their table.[4]

It's great to have beliefs. And it's sometimes good to wear something a little bit different, especially when everyone else at the Emmys is sticking to the same old script. But there's really never a good time to wear someone else's face on your torso. Or your legs. Or...well, all over your body.[5]

Wow! That's a statement.[6]

The dressed body as a social-political act was unleashed as responses to the Obama cloth on the blogs surged—other comments were more pointed in reflecting racial bigotry, cultural taste, and partisan politics—and, therefore, reminded us of the implications of dress as "social skin."[7] The sampling below represents a series of postings (from September 20 to 22 of 2009) geared to a primarily black readership. *The Hinterland Gazette,*[8] the site of these postings, describes itself as a source for a "daily dose of community and social and political breaking news for African American centrists." The postings read as follows:

What was she thinking?

Victoria's dress is cute but Obama's face is messing up it. I'll never wear something with someone's face on it!

I'm VERY, VERY upset that Victoria had the nerve to wear that dress! I mean I'm just as happy as the next person that Obama is in office as our Prez, but does she have to be so tacky and extreme with it??!!

The fabric Victoria's wearing is extremely popular in West Africa. In addition to Obama's picture, it's decorated with Ghanaian adinkra symbols. It's so easy to not be ignorant people...Google it and learn something!

I can appreciate the African fabric but maybe not for an Emmys dress. Yeah I actually dig the dress. I thought it was a clever choice and I got it. African style dress with an African on it and adinkra symbols on it. I think what would have elevated the dress more to couture level is if it had some sort of organza or toule (sp?) fabric underneath and ruffles and more sculpture to it, but I can appreciate the black conscious effort statement nonetheless.

The next series of postings (September 20–21) represent a more general USAmerican readership from three blogs: TMZ.com, moejackson.com, and examiner.com.[9]

Typical. Hey, I'm black, Obama is black, let me prove a point by being a stupid black attention whore. What's the point? That black people actually did something. Wow.

If the president was white and she voted for him, I am sure his picture would not be on her dress...The only reason he is on her dress is to promote that he is black.

> I agree that the dress is (a) ugly and (b) cult-like, but there's no cause to bring her race into this.
>
> Why is she wearing a table-cloth to the Emmy's?
>
> She needs a goofy donkey hat to complete the outfit.
>
> There is nothing remotely glamorous about that Obama dress. The print looks sort of like a tablecloth fabric, only no one with any taste would put something like that on their table.

The controversy over the Obama dress was not purely grounded in racial bigotry and anti-Obama sentiment. It was also a matter of "taste" and the social and cultural implications of how taste is formed. In the mix of all the heat was the taste factor and the belief that this "tablecloth" fabric was out of place among the more proper and elegant attire where "screen gems cloaked in dazzling gowns to marquee hunks donning tuxes" looked their dressed-up and cosmopolitan best (Byrd 2009).

One of the more balanced and informative responses to the dress was on the *Essence Magazine* website:

> Victoria Rowell marched to the beat of her own hem, so to speak, when she arrived on the red carpet in the boldest of fashion statements—a strapless dress emblazoned with President Barack Obama's face. Rowell admits that her favorite designers off stage include b. michael, Jane Wilson Marquis and Carolina Herrera and onstage Colleen Atwood and Ann Roth. But last night's ceremony wasn't about high-end labels she might have been sporting. When media inquiries on the CBS Primetime Emmy red carpet begged the question of her designer of choice, she proudly replied, "A statement" (Byrd 2009).

The "statement" Rowell was referring to was President Obama's controversial health care reform initiative which was hotly debated across the country at the time. Rowell's participation in the red carpet spectacle of fun, fashion, and fame—a showcase intended for posh, not politics—transgressed the expected dress code of high fashion formal wear for the rich and famous. Her dressing for the purpose of dissent to make a "statement" was roundly considered out of place. For many, the dress spoke the wrong language—it was a distasteful and misstated language; it served less as a "statement" and more of a misstatement in support of the public option for Obama's health plan. Dress as a sign is always a layered and complex "language" about identity, context, and communication. Yet, what is most significant in the Rowell case is not only how she staged her dressed body as a performative act of dissent, as a sign out-of-place, but also her rhetorical response to the question when asked about the designer of the dress. Calling it a "statement" was on one hand courageous, but on the other hand deeply problematic. In naming this performative act "a statement" she ironically, and, I would argue, innocently and unintentionally, became complicit in *not* stating a particular kind of U.S. hegemony. The irony here is that the "language" of the dress, and its potential to make a more effective intervention, was silenced by Rowell's word "statement."

COMMUNICATION AND DRESS AS A (NON)STATEMENT

Karen Tranberg Hansen describes the "efficacy of surfaces" in noting that the dressed body "materializes as a surface that constitutes meanings and relations and states of being" (2004a: 372). In Rowell's later elaboration of the dress as a "statement" for health-care reform, she commented: "Yesterday, the opportunity presented itself. Lights, camera, and *no* health care *action*?" (quoted in Byrd 2009). She went on to add: "Setting the ruffles and caviar dreams aside is but a meager gesture to echo the herculean efforts of a health care reform package long overdue and one which President Obama is introducing for all Americans" (quoted in Byrd 2009). In her role as an advocate for children, particularly under the foster care system, Rowell eloquently expressed a personal thought: "I spent 18 years in foster care, enduring inadequate health and dental care and unforgivably turned away more than once at a doctor's office. Nationally, 25,000 foster youth annually emancipate from foster care without health coverage" (quoted in Byrd 2009). She went on to attest to her own survival: "I emerged from Washington, D.C. Health and Human Services as a proud American citizen—an advocate not a victim" (quoted in Byrd 2009). When attacked, at that time, by the right-wing radio host and Fox News commentator Glenn Beck, Rowell's intelligence and poise was further demonstrated, in sharp contrast to the fear mongering, hate speech, and race baiting for which Beck is known. When Beck stated that all of President Obama's policies are about "one idea" based on "conspiratorial ulterior motives" to transform America so that black people get "reparations," he perpetuated racial division and anti-Obama sentiment by suggesting that white Americans will lose everything, including their country to "a new America, a new model, a model that will settle old racial scores" (quoted in Byrd 2009). Rowell, taking the high ground and further substantiating her dressed body as a "statement" responded to Beck:

> This has nothing to do with reparations, Mr. Beck, and everything to do with all things American . . . Health care shouldn't be divided or thought of as *the young* and *some of us*. I have witnessed Black and White foster mothers struggle to raise children, choosing food over medical needs. That does something to a child. At least it affected me most profoundly. And if a frock [on the Emmys red carpet] donned with the President's face sparks dialogue about health care, a life-and-death issue, so be it. I was taught, "If you don't stand for something you'll lie down for anything." (quoted in Byrd 2009)

Rowell's dressed body certainly made a statement on several levels. At one level, wearing a gown adorned with Ghanian cultural symbols of *Gye Nyame* (adinkra) and Asante stools with President Obama's face superimposed upon red, white, and blue West African fabric not only served to communicate support for the first African American president and his health care bill, but also the choice of the red, white, and blue fabric was in keeping with Rowell's own expression of patriotism in voicing "all things American" and being "a proud American citizen." It was also a performative symbol illuminating the efficacy of surfaces against assertions of being "true" and "real" by those who denigrate the patriotism of citizens (like Rowell) who were on the other side of the health care issue. The cloth, boldly set against a red, white, and blue background, was a conscious choice by Ghanaian designers to honor the colors of the United States—making it a distinctly USAmerican iconic feature. The draped cloth wrapped around the body of this African American woman voicing her citizenship and American pride, in her own terms, became a counterclaim to right-wing, anti-American name calling. The second level at which Rowell's choice of dress made a statement is related to her advocacy agenda. Rowell is known to be an outspoken and socially conscious actor. She does not shy away from issues of social justice, as evidenced in her *New York Times* bestselling book, *The Women Who Raised Me: A Memoir.* Because Rowell is no neophyte to pursuing just causes, wearing the "Obama dress" to make a statement about health care, particularly as it relates to the disenfranchised within the foster care system, is not inconsistent with her advocacy agenda. Rowell's dressed body was layered with qualities of performative spectacle: It was charged by public dissent; it traversed from one context to another as matter out-of-place; it was a sign transformed into a symbol inciting race, taste, and rumblings of a left-against-right divide—all for a just cause.

However, one question arises from this dressed body as a performative of dissent: Can an analysis of the Obama cloth be contained by reactions to the mere appearance of a dress? The major criticism and opposition to the cloth was clearly about race, culture, and anti-Obama sentiment, for racial bigotry and cultural tensions are part of the USAmerican landscape, and anti-Obama sentiment was becoming a growing presence. It is clear that much of the firestorm was about the sociality and politics of taste, race, and difference, particularly as it relates to Africa and, I would argue, resonances of abject blackness. If the same dress design replaced the Obama cloth for a shiny, shear, and shimmering one, the dress would be speaking the appropriate language in its proper social context of glamour and fame. The design or lines of the dress—strapless with a low-cut, fitted bodice and flowing skirt with train—are familiar on the red carpet. When Rowell was asked about the designer, the question was more about the anomaly of the fabric that was superimposed upon a classic style. The numerous comparisons to a tablecloth, the aversions to the "strange" cotton print, and the disdain for wearing a "face" are criticisms of the cloth, specifically. So, the question regarding Rowell's designer of choice was more a question about the fabric and its origins (see Figure 14.1): "Where did it come from?" "How or who conceived of it?" "What does it mean?"

By responding that her choice of dress was a "statement" was to claim an advocacy position, which many considered noble and brave, but in doing so, Rowell also dismissed a history, economy, and geopolitics of West African fabric that is just as complex, contentious, and deeply relevant as health care is in the United States. In that particular and strategic moment, by not stating who the designer was, by not indicating the dress's origins, and by not recognizing the fabric as a "sign" within a particular history and location, her "frock" was open to more insults as some kind of ambiguous, "tacky," up-in-your face, strange black costume than might otherwise have been the

Figure 14.1 Barak Obama commemorative cloth from Ghana. Photo by D. Soyini Madison.

case if its cultural relevance were named and claimed as commemorative cloth from Ghana. Or, perhaps the criticisms might have been even more robust if explicitly linked to Africa and explicitly made more black and more foreign. The point is that the lack of awareness toward the Obama cloth—its origin and production—was upheld and became a missed opportunity to actually make a statement about the fraught geopolitics and imperial machinations relative to African textiles and the "designer of choice."

Perhaps it is asking too much of Rowell to make a statement that gestures toward a political economy of African textiles. Why should it matter that this smart, beautiful, talented, and committed advocate for social equity did not address the question of the fabric's origin? It matters because there are significant implications for wearing African textiles in the United States that beg questions of exploitation. It matters because there is a timeworn history in the political economy of fabric and fashion in Africa that separates its producers from its consumers (White and White 1998; Boateng 2004; Hansen 1994; Holsey 2008; Madison 2005a; Nielsen 1979; Picton 1995; Rabine 2002; Rovine 2009; Skoggard 1998). It matters because there is an American and African American legacy of appropriating and adorning African material culture that lacks an awareness of the uneven and contradictory factors of production, trade, labor, and capitalist expansion (Boateng 2004). When Rowell wore the Obama dress, it certainly unleashed a firestorm about the appropriateness of the fabric that was fueled by class, race, partisan politics, the foreign, and cultural taste. The debate about *where and how the fabric came to be produced* went unstated, albeit for noble reasons. What I want to now enumerate is an alternative firestorm that could (or should) have also been unleashed that day when the Ghanaian commemorative cloth was worn but *unstated.*

TRAVELING CLOTH AND DIASPORIC CONSUMPTION

Contemporary African commemorative cloth is part of the larger category of printed textiles. Since the nineteenth century, it has represented a visual communication that conveys and records a special event, individual, institution, or location that is meant to be commemorated (Bickford et al. 2007; Owusu-Ansah 1990; Madison 2005; Picton and Mack 1979; Rovine 2004; Spencer 1982). Since commemorative cloth is worn for specific reasons at a specific time, it follows that the efficacy of its surface is most graphically illustrated through the printed photographic images. Anne M. Spencer describes an observation by a British manufacturer in the early days of independence who stated, "In the absence of television and with the high level of illiteracy, a portrait on cloth enabled many more Africans to see the leader who had led their country to independence. It was good publicity" (Spencer 1982: 7).

Various forms of commemorative cloth are worn across the continent. One popular example is the rectangular shape kanga cloth of East Africa, with its decorative borders that frame elaborate designs and colors that inscribe greetings, well wishes, and congratulations, as well as political affiliations, development projects, and public health campaigns. "When words are difficult to articulate with a mouth, inscribe them on kanga and wait for a response" (Zawawi 2005). Just as the Obama cloth was proudly worn during Obama's visit to Ghana, Obama proudly wore the kanga while in his father's home county. With few exceptions, both the Obama commemorative cloth from Ghana and the kanga cloth from Kenya are primarily designed in bright red, white, and blue to celebrate the new American president, who has been described as the "illustrious son of Africa."[10] Rowell's cloth was specifically produced in Accra, Ghana, at Akosombo Textiles to commemorate the inauguration of the forty-fourth president of the United States and his visit to Ghana in July 2009.

The Obama cloth embodied a polyvocal layering within African, African American, and black diasporic relations. When draped around Rowell's African American female body, the cloth became a visual marker for "black Atlantic" diasporic pathways of belonging. By "black Atlantic," I refer here to J. Lorand Matory's conception of "Afro-Atlantic dialogues," which "highlight the ways in which the mutual gaze between Africans and African Americans, multidirectional travel, and migration between two hemispheres"—as manifest in "the movement of publications, commerce and so forth"—have consequently "shaped African and African-American cultures in tandem, over time and at the same time" (quoted in Holsey 2008: 162). This "multidirectional travel" that constitutes Afro-Atlantic dialogues is described by Bayo Holsey in terms of a "back and forth traffic between Africa and the diaspora" (2008: 152). What I want to examine are the tensions of reciprocity and the hidden consequences that result in this back-and-forth traffic or these Afro-Atlantic dialogues—for example, culture, products, ideas, behaviors, discourses, economies, and so forth that are in circulation between Africans on the continent and African Americans in the United States (Matory 1999). What are the consequences for continental Africans when this "multidirectional travel" is mostly a one-way affair? What happens when the back-and-forth traffic becomes an uneven exchange? How encompassing is African American belonging for the "motherland" in the face of capitalist expansion?

This Afro-Atlantic dialogue became another instance of an Afro-Atlantic performative, rich and complicated in its black diasporic layering: an Afro-American woman, wearing the language of West African adinkra symbols, superimposed over a red, white, and blue Ghanian textile of USAmerican colors, framed the image of a black North American president. This triad of African, North American, and African American diasporic presences were made possible on the red carpet that September afternoon because the Obama cloth, in the words of Leslie Rabine, was a "traveling text." It was a traveling text that Rabine describes as intertextual in its "web of intersecting semiotic symbolic elements" (2002: 176). I will now turn to how these intersecting semiotics of diasporic layers must necessarily include an added materialist layering of economic exchange and value.

When we consume African artifacts in USAmerica and proudly wear African fabrics, the question that arises is whether or not the economic exchange is as informed and ideologically considered as the cultural exchange. When the desire to possess African artifacts is usurped by the demand for fair trade, how are we participants in unequal power relations? In examining the "symbolic links established through the use of textiles by Diasporic Africans to create an African identity," Boatema Boateng states that these connections are not only about symbols of culture, "but are also mediated and affected by globalization in its current form of accelerated capitalist expansion" (2004: 212). When asked who the designer was and the response was "a statement," Rowell was reflecting (or stating by her ironic nonstatement) the prevailing silence that does not "account for conflicts between symbolic economies and political economies," particularly as it involves African textiles (Rabine 2002: 195). The argument against separating the product from its processes of production, or the production of meaning from the production of its object, is not new. This argument is classic and timeworn, yet it is also ironically new and compellingly urgent as capitalist expansion has taken different forms through the ages and as each of its iterations is differently and uniquely manifest in the social world, whether it regards the food we eat, the machinery we depend on, the water we drink, the oil that allows for transportation, or the clothes we wear.

Rowell may or may not have known that day when asked about her designer of choice that the Obama cloth she was wearing was designed at Aksombo Textiles Limited (ATL) and that it was the only major textile manufacturing company still operating in the country at that time. Ghana Textiles Printing (GTP) and Ghana Textiles Manufacturing Company (GTMC) shut down their spinning and weaving departments because of cheaper imports from abroad, particularly China.[11] According to an editorial in the highly respected and award-winning Ghanaian newspaper *The Public Agenda,* "These defunct sectors were employing a chunk of the labour force in the industrial economy." The editorial goes on to state, "Total local production of textiles which peaked at 130 million metres per annum in the 1970s has dropped to below 39 million metres per annum currently and the labour force in the industry has consequently reduced from 25,000 workers in the 1970s to less than 3,000 as of now" (Public Agenda, October 9, 2009, editorial). The problems in the Ghanaian textile industry are certainly indicative of problems throughout Africa and the global South; the popular Ghanaian scholar and journalist Kwame Osei, states: "The reason why Ghana has to go cap in hand to the IMF/World Bank is quite simple—this is because Ghana as a country does not earn enough from its exports in order to invest in schools, roads, transport, local government, healthcare and so forth."[12]

Boatema Boateng, in her book *The Copyright Thing Doesn't Work Here: Adinkra and Kente Cloth and Intellectual Property in Ghana,* calls for a "consumer consciousness" particularly on the part of "African Americans in their use of African products" (2011: 182). This is a call for attention to the issue of trade and exports and, moreover, for African Americans to support and lobby for Ghana's copyright laws of 1985 and 2000 which were revised and amended to include folklore. The law stipulates that folklore extends beyond oral narratives and music to include material culture, specifically textiles. The revision of the copyright law was established in great part because imitations of local, handmade adinkra and kente textiles were being mass-produced by East Asian textile factories without the payment of royalties to Ghana or local producers (Boateng 2004: 212). Boateng states, "Informed and activist African American consumer organizations acting in concert with African textile producers could join indigenous peoples in lobbying for broader definitions of intellectual property." She goes on to state, "A pan-Africanist consumer lobby could also hold individual African nations accountable to the artisans who make the products that constitute their national heritage" (2004: 225). Boateng asserts that this "activism" already exists for those African Americans who want to "ensure that the African products they procure and sell are made by African Artisans who benefit from their sale." She adds, "Such a lobby could play a crucial role in moving Africa beyond its current status as a market and source of cheap labor in the global economy" (2004: 226).

When the Obama cloth, as a traveling text (literally and figuratively), landed on the red carpet creating a controversy, some of it rooted in shades of bigotry and some of it rooted in affinities of taste and appropriateness, the language of the cloth spoke to an embedded tension that was less bout the responses Rowell encountered and more about the questions she left unanswered: Who is the designer? Where do these fabrics come from? The point is that where these fabrics come from carries with them a political economy of the Global South too often hidden and unspoken. The Obama cloth controversy opened larger and more urgent issues as it travelled between hemispheres: indigenous People are required to work longer, harder, and faster for less—often beyond human capacity—because transnational corporations compete for mass-produced cheap products; factories close down and hundreds of thousands (Boateng 2011;

Amankwah 2009; Kopytoff 1986; Rabine 2002) of workers lose their jobs under free-trade policies; local weavers and artisans suffer because local people can buy cheaper cloth dumped from abroad. If we believe that "clothing matters and dress is political" (Martin 2004: 227), then the controversy emanating from the symbolic economy of the Obama cloth is inseparable from the question of capitalist expansion which was literally left unstated. That the dressed body was that of an African America woman on USAmerican soil further complicates this instance of dressing for performative dissent because it reflects the legacy of African Americans adorning African artifacts while, most often, being unaware and uniformed of processes of production of those artifacts and the consequences of this production for local Africans.

The social statement Rowell made by wearing the Obama commemorative cloth was an admirable and courageous performative act of dissent, against the rising voices castigating public health care. Her dressing for dissent spoke to one of the most important issues of our time within the USAmerican political landscape, yet it left silent one of the most important issues on the shores of the African continent.

CONCLUSION

Dress is a communication system and, like language, may be constituted as a sign. Dress as a sign is always already situated within particular associations or contexts. This chapter discusses what happens when the sign moves or is strategically displaced from its specific association for the purpose of dissent. Dressing for dissent becomes an effective performative when the dressed body is out of place. The Obama commemorative cloth demonstrated that dressing out-of-place is certainly provocative and draws attention, but its production and where it "belonged" reinscribed the classic disconnect between wearing African dress and the political economy of its production. To what ceremony in Ghana or to what occasion does the Obama cloth belong? Rowell's dress was considered out of place, but where was its place? When the question was posed, the response that it was a "statement" ironically became a nonstatement relative to meaning, context, history, and the economies of African products and producers. We might trouble the question, Would the cloth, as a traveling text and as a spectacle of dressing-for-dissent, have been an effective "statement" and performative tactic if the West African origins of adinkra and commemorative cloth been familiar or understood? The Obama cloth complicates this question because some people did appreciate it within the context of a West African aesthetic, and others for its rhetorical and symbolic support of the president. For many others it was disparaged for those very reasons, while for most, the negative reactions stemmed from issues of cultural taste and appropriateness and were not necessarily influenced by an aversion to Obama or an African aesthetic. What did happen was that there was a missed opportunity to make an explicit statement about why "clothing matters and dress is political" (Allman 2004b); in this instance, it affects political economies and material intertextualities of African cloth that travel across the Atlantic. What is certain is that dressing out-of-place and African dress understood as traveling texts open the possibilities for other and more iterations of performative dissent.

NOTES

1. The "performative," unlike performativity, extends beyond (performativity's) repetitions that stabilize, fix, or naturalize identity. The definition of performativity as the stylized repetition of acts—not a singular act but "always a reiteration of a norm or set of norms"—does not include the interventionist potential of the performative, which punctures and disrupts the expectation or naturalized behaviors. This is what I want to emphasize relative to the dressed body (see Diamond 1996: 1–2).
2. I write USAmerican instead of the more common usage of "American" in referring to the United States to recognize and honor other nations, histories, and populations that occupy the North American continent. I prefer the term USAmerican instead of United States or United States of America to avoid length, redundancy, and cumbersomeness and to more pointedly demarcate (and decolonize) the term America and American.
3. "Victoria Rowell Obama Dress Photos, Worst Dressed Emmys 2009," Bitten & Bound, http://www.bittenandbound.com/2009/09/21/victoria-rowell-obama-dress-photos-worst-dressed-emmys-2009/
4. "Victoria Rowell: Obama Dress—Emmys," Freedom Eden, http://freedomeden.blogspot.com/2009/09/victoria-rowell-obama-dress-emmys.html
5. "Victoria Rowell Wears Barack Obama Dress to the 2009 Emmys," The Fashion Police.net, September 21, 2009, http://www.thefashionpolice.net/2009/09/victoria-rowell-wears-barack-obama-dress-to-the-2009-emmys
6. CakeGrrl, "Wow! That's a statement," Democratic Underground.com, September 20, 2009, http://betterment.democraticunderground.com/discuss/duboard.php?az=view_all&address=132x8664076#8664087
7. I am referring her to Karen Tranberg Hansen's elaboration of social skin (Hansen 2004a: 369–392).
8. Janet Shan, "Actress Victoria Rowell Wears Obama Dress to 2009 Emmy Awards Ceremony," Hinterland Gazette, http://hinterlandgazette.com/2009/09/actress-victoria-rowell-wears-obama.html Janet Shan
9. Emmy Awards 2009 – No Effort Required," TMZ.com, September 20, 2009, http://www.tmz.com/2009/09/20/emmy-awards-2009-no-effort-required/; "Victoria Rowell vs Sarah Silverman: Ugly Dress @ The Daytime Emmys Matchup," moejackson.com, September 21, 2009, http://moejackson.com/2009/09/21/2009-victoria-rowell-vs-sarah-silverman-ugly-dress-the-daytime-emmys-matchup-0921/; Ronda Racha Penrice, "We love Obama too, but what was Victoria Rowell wearing at the Emmys?" Examiner.com, September 21, 2009, http://www.examiner.com/article/we-love-obama-too-but-what-was-victoria-rowell-wearing-at-the-emmys
10. See *The Public Agenda,* July 2009. This is an award-winning and progressive weekly newspaper published in Accra. Available at www.ghanaweb.com/publicagenda.

11. Ama Chaiaa (2009). "Smuggled Textiles Still Killing Industry." *The Public Agenda* (October 9). Available at: allafrica.com/stories/200910090709.html.
12. Kwame Osei (2009). "Ghana and Africa Trapped by IMF/World Bank." *Public Agenda* (August 28). Available at: allafrica.com/stories/200910090709.html.

REFERENCES

Allman, Jean. 2004a. "Fashioning Africa: Power and the Politics of Dress." In Jean Allman, ed., *Fashioning Africa: Power and the Politics of Dress*, 1–10. Bloomington: Indiana University Press.

Allman, Jean. 2004b. "'Let Your Fashion Be in Line with Our Ghanaian Costume': Nation, Gender, and the Politics of Cloth-ing in Nkrumah's Ghana." In Jean Allman, ed., *Fashioning Africa: Power and the Politics of Dress*, 144–165. Bloomington: Indiana University Press.

Austin, J. L. 1975. *How to Do Things with Words*. Cambridge: Harvard University Press.

Bickford Barbara, Randall E. Peter, and Tim Gaudreau. 2007. *An African Portrait Revisited*. New York: Randall Publishers

Boateng, Boatema. 2004. "African Textiles and the Politics of Diasporic Identity-Making." In Jean Allman, ed., *Fashioning Africa: Power and the Politics of Dress*, 212–226. Bloomington: Indiana University Press.

Boateng, Boatema. 2011. *The Copyright Thing Doesn't Work Here: Adinkra and Kente Cloth and Intellectual Property in Ghana*. Minneapolis: University of Minnesota Press.

Byrd, Kenya N. 2009. "Victoria Rowell Makes Bold Statement with Obama Dress." *Essence* [online]. http://www.essence.com/2009/09/21/victoria-rowell-makes-bold-statement-wit/

Conquergood, Dwight. 1991. "Rethinking Ethnography: Cultural Politics and Rhetorical Strategies." *Communication Monographs* 58: 179–194.

Conquergood, Dwight. 2002. "Performance Studies: Interventions and Radical Research." *The Drama Review* 46: 145–156.

Diamond, Elin. 1996. "Introduction." In Elin Diamond, ed., *Performance and Cultural Politics*, 1–2. New York: Routledge.

Hamera, Judith. 2007. *Dancing Communities: Performance, Difference, and Dancing in a Global City*. New York: Palgrave.

Hansen, Karen Tranberg. 1994. "Dealing with Used Clothing: Salaula and the Construction of Identity in Zambia's Third Republic." *Public Culture* 6: 503–523.

Hansen, Karen Tranberg. 2004a. "Dressing Dangerously: Miniskirts, Gender Relations, and Sexuality in Zambia." In Jean Allman, ed., *Fashioning Africa: Power and the Politics of Dress*, 166–185. Bloomington: Indiana University Press.

Hansen, Karen Tranberg. 2004b. "The World In Dress: Anthropological Perspectives on Clothing, Fashion, and Culture." *Annual Review of Anthropology* 33: 369–392.

Holsey, Bayo. 2008. *Routes of Remembrance: Refashioning the Slave Trade in Ghana*. Chicago: University of Chicago.

Johnson, E. Patrick. 2003. *Appropriating Blackness: Performance and the Politics of Authenticity*. Durham: Duke University Press.

Kopytoff, Igor. 1986. "The Cultural Biography of Things: Commoditization as Process." In Arjun Appadurai, ed., *The Social Life of Things: Commodities in Cultural Perspective*, 64–92. Cambridge: Cambridge University Press.

Madison, D. Soyini. 2005. "My Desire is for the Poor to Speak Well of Me." In Della Pollock, ed., *Remembering: Performance and Oral History,* 143–166. New York: St. Martin's.

Madison, D. Soyini. 2012. *Critical Ethnography: Method, Performance, and Ethics.* Thousand Oaks, CA: Sage Publications.

Madison, D. Soyini. 2010. *Acts of Activism: Human Rights as Radical Performance.* Cambridge: Cambridge University Press.

Martin, Phyllis M. 2004. "Afterword." In Jean Allman, ed., *Fashioning Africa: Power and the Politics of Dress,* 227–230. Bloomington: Indiana University Press.

Matory, J. Lorand. 1999. "The English Professors of Brazil: On the Diasporic Roots of the Yorùbá Nation." *Comparative Studies in Society and History* 41: 72–103.

McCracken, Grant. 1988. *Culture and Consumption: New Approaches to the Symbolic Character of Consumer Goods and Activities.* Bloomington: Indiana University Press.

Nielsen, Ruth. 1979. "The History and Development of Wax-Printed Textiles Intended for West Africa and Zaire." In Justine M. Cordwell and Ronald A. Schwarz, eds., *The Fabrics of Culture: The Anthropology of Clothing and Adornment,* 467–498. New York: Mouton.

Owusu-Ansah, Nana J. V. 1990. *The Traditional Ways of Putting on Cloth for Men and Women.* K'si: Degraft Graphics.

Picton, John, and John Mack. 1979. *African Textiles: Looms, Weaving and Design.* London: British Museum Publications for the Trustees of the British Museum.

Picton, John, and John Mack. 1995. *The Art of African Textiles: Technology, Tradition, and Lurex.* London: Lund Humphries Publishers.

Rabine, Leslie W. 2002. *The Global Circulation of African Fashion. Dress, Body, Culture.* Oxford: Berg.

Rivera-Servera, Ramon. 2011. "Dancing Reggaetón in Cowboy Boots." In Alejandro L. Madrid, ed., *Transnational Encounters: Music and Performance at the U.S.-Mexico Border,* 373–392. Madrid: Oxford University Press,.

Rovine, Victoria L. 2004. "Fashionable Traditions: The Globalization of an African Textile." In Jean Allman, ed., *Fashioning Africa: Power and the Politics of Dress,* 189–211. Bloomington: Indiana University Press.

Rovine, Victoria L., ed. 2009. "African Fashion/African Style Special Issue." *Fashion Theory: The Journal of Dress, Body, and Culture* 13(2).

Rubinstein, Ruth P. 1995. *Dress Codes: Meanings and Messages in American Culture.* Boulder: Westview Press.

Skoggard, Ian. 1998. "Transnational Commodity Flows and the Global Phenomenon of the Brand." In Anne Brydon and Sandra Niessen, eds., *Consuming Fashion: Adorning the Transnational Body,* 57–70. Oxford: Berg.

Spencer, Anne M. 1982. *In Praise of Heroes: Contemporary African Commemorative Cloth: An Exhibition at the Newark Museum, September 14, 1982-February 27, 1983.* Newark: Newark Museum.

White, Shane, and Graham White. 1998. *Stylin': African American Expressive Culture from Its Beginnings to the Zoot Suit.* Ithaca: Cornell University Press.

Zawawi, Sharifa. 2005. *Kanga: The Cloth That Speaks.* New York: Azaniya Hills Press.

Index

Lightning Source UK Ltd.
Milton Keynes UK
UKOW04f0657130916

282866UK00008B/166/P

9 780857 853813